School Social Work

Skills and Interventions for Effective Practice

David R. Dupper

LEARNING
RESOURCES
CENTRE

JOHN WILEY & SONS, INC.

Library of Congress Cataloging-in-Publication Data:

Dupper, David R.
    School social work : skills and interventions for effective practice / by David R. Dupper.
        p.   cm.
    Includes bibliographical references and index.
    ISBN 0-471-39571-4 (cloth : alk. paper)
        1. School social work—United States.   I. Title.
    LB3013.4 .D86   2002
    371.4'6—dc21
                                                            2002069128

Printed in the United States of America.

10 9 8 7 6 5 4

In memory of Maryanna Contole,
who was a constant source of
encouragement and support.

David R. Dupper, PhD, is an associate professor and the associate dean of the Knoxville Campus at the University of Tennessee College of Social Work. He received his MSW and PhD degrees from Florida State University. Prior to his academic career, Dr. Dupper was a school social worker in the Positive Alternatives to Student Suspensions Program (PASS) in Pinellas County, Florida, for eight years. Following that, he was the coordinator of the Model School Adjustment Program (MSAP), a pilot dropout prevention program for at-risk middle school students. Later, he served for two years as a school social worker in Leon County, Florida.

Authoring numerous journal articles that focus on enhancing the school success of at-risk students, Dr. Dupper's particular research interest is the development and evaluation of alternatives to punitive school disciplinary policies and practices. He has served on the editorial boards of *Social Work in Education* and the *School Social Work Journal*. He currently serves as a consulting editor for *Children and Schools* (formerly *Social Work in Education*). Prior to his tenure at the University of Tennessee, Dr. Dupper was a faculty member and chair of the school social work specialization program at the School of Social Work at the University of Illinois at Urbana-Champaign.

Dr. Dupper lives in Knoxville, Tennessee, with his wife, Ann, and their three daughters, Amy, Christine, and Laura.

I wrote this book for a number of reasons. School social workers are broadly trained but often used too narrowly in the schools they serve. This book defines the enlarged roles and tasks of school social workers, advances the integration of practice-based research, and attempts to "bridge the chasm" between research and school social work practice. While recent research has provided a wealth of information regarding empirically supported interventions in school settings, most of this literature has been written from the perspective of psychologists or educators. Although a small body of literature on effective interventions has been produced for social workers, this literature has not been compiled nor have its implications been examined for school social work students or practitioners. In other words, although the knowledge base of "what works" in addressing the wide range of problems found in school settings has increased significantly over the past several decades, this knowledge has yet to be presented in a format specifically intended for school social work students or school social work practitioners. The primary purpose of this book is to fulfill that need—to provide school social work students and practitioners with a compendium of proven and promising, developmentally appropriate interventions that address a wide variety of problems encountered in schools.

In addition to providing comprehensive information about student-focused interventions, this book informs school social work students and practitioners about proven and promising programs that target classrooms, schools, families, neighborhoods, and communities for change. An entire chapter is devoted to the knowledge and skills necessary to function effectively in the unique organizational setting and political environment of the school. There are chapters on the emerging and essential role of the school social worker as consultant as well as the role of the school social worker in establishing and maintaining school-community collaborations designed to enhance the school success of at-risk students. To address the increasing concern over violence in schools, this book contains descriptions of exemplary student-focused and comprehensive violence prevention programs.

The increasing emphasis on accountability mandates that school social workers be able to evaluate their own practices. Therefore, this book includes chapters that discuss currently available assessment instruments that can be used to evaluate the effectiveness of interventions. Of particular note, Chapter 12 is devoted to recently developed standardized measures designed to assess changes at the classroom, school, family, neighborhood, and community levels and concludes with a discussion of guidelines for successfully planning, implementing, and evaluating new programs based on comprehensive quality programming (CQP) strategies. To keep the reader informed of the latest research and developments on a number of issues, this book includes Internet resources, as well as other references, at the end of each chapter. Case vignettes and questions for discussion are included to deepen the reader's understanding and application of the material.

DAVID R. DUPPER

I want to express my deep appreciation to a number of people who have assisted me in countless ways while writing this book. Catherine Dulmus and John Wodarski originally approached me and encouraged me to take on this project. I am also very grateful to Karen Sowers for her belief in me and her consistent encouragement throughout this project. I want to acknowledge John Kackley as the original author of the "School Survival Group" (see Appendix).

I also want to thank Nancy Meyer-Adams for her hard work and willingness to assist me with a number of different tasks throughout the course of this project and to Kathy Davis for "hitting the ground running" and helping me with a number of important tasks during the final stages of this project. I also want to acknowledge the contribution of Gary Shaffer, Vaughn Morrison, and Catherine Dulmus for their constructive feedback and suggestions for improvements. My thanks to Sylvia Nash for her excellent editing skills, to LeeAnn Killion for her assistance in preparing the tables, and to Natalie Crippen for her help with figures and typing. Gina Cox fixed several computer glitches along the way. Kristi Brookshire wrote the majority of the case vignettes that appear at the beginning of each chapter and Marcus Adams used his artistic skills (see Figure 11.1). I also want to acknowledge my assistant, Linda Broyles, who keeps my work life organized and whose support was invaluable throughout this project. In addition, I want to extend my appreciation to my editor at Wiley, Tracey Belmont, for her feedback and enthusiastic support over the course of this project. Most of all, I want to thank my wife, Ann, and my three daughters, Amy, Christine, and Laura, for their unwavering support and patience throughout all the months it took me to write this book; I love you!

D. R. D.

Chapter 4

Internalizing Behavior Problems 67

Chapter 5

Social Problems 87

Chapter 8

Chapter 9

Chapter 10

Section Four
Evaluating School Social Work Practice   207

Chapter 11
Evaluating Student-Focused Interventions   209

Chapter 12
Evaluating System-Focused Interventions   225

Appendix
"School Survival Group" Curriculum

241

FOUNDATIONS

This section provides a foundation and context for the remainder of the book. Chapter 1 provides both an historical and a theoretical context for school social work practice by discussing the ecological perspective as an organizing framework for school social work practice, roles, and tasks of school social workers, and a brief history of school social work including major educational legislation and court cases that have and continue to impact school social work practice. In addition to understanding how history, legislation, court cases, and theory have shaped and continue to influence school social work practice, it is also essential to understand the unique organizational setting in which school social workers must function. Chapter 2 discusses the distinctive organizational structure and processes of the school and their impact on the delivery of social work services. This chapter also discusses the political environment of the school, the development of political "savvy," and the 20-60-20 theory of school change.

School Social Workers: History, Roles, and Functions

In this chapter, we discuss:

- *The ecological perspective as an organizing framework for school social work practice.*

- *Ethical dimensions of school social work practice.*

- *Roles and tasks of school social workers and other professional support staff.*

- *A brief history of school social work including major educational legislation and court cases.*

Susan, the school social worker at Anderson High School, received a referral on a 16-year-old student, Becky, whose excessive absenteeism and fighting resulted in a series of out-of-school suspensions. During several sessions with Becky, Susan learned that Becky had been diagnosed with depression, lived with an alcoholic out-of-control mother, and was sexually abused by her father, who was currently serving time in prison for the offense. Becky identified her mother as her only support system and often stayed home from school to catch up on sleep after transporting and caring for her intoxicated mother the night before. Becky's deep sense of distrust in others had alienated her from peers at school. This distrust also led to frequent fighting when provoked.

As Becky's advocate, Susan adopted several roles in the next few weeks to increase Becky's support system and improve her school attendance. With Becky's and her mother's consent, Susan initiated several meetings with both Becky and her mother to improve basic communication skills. Susan also provided the mother with literature and phone numbers of area treatment centers and AA meetings. In addition, Susan worked individually with Becky once a week on anger management

1

Chapter

3

skills and began investigating local Al-Anon and Ala-Teen chapters. When Susan discovered that there were no Ala-Teen meetings available in the county, she called Al-Anon's World Service Office to inquire about starting a meeting in Becky's high school.

Agrowing number of social workers provide direct services in schools. There are over 9,000 social workers serving students across the country. (Torres, 1996)

Introduction

As illustrated in this case vignette, Susan fulfilled numerous roles in the process of helping her client. At different times, she assumed the role of broker, networker, advocate, counselor, educator, and community organizer. All of these varied roles and accompanying skills are part of an effective school social worker's tool kit. Using the ecological perspective as an organizing framework, we discuss the various roles that social workers assume in addressing the wide range of problems found in school settings. We also discuss several ethical dimensions of school social work practice and compare and contrast the similarities and differences among the roles and functions of school social workers, guidance counselors, and school psychologists. This chapter concludes with a brief history of school social work and an overview of major federal educational legislation and court orders that have influenced and continue to impact school social work practice.

Ecological Perspective as an Organizing Framework for School Social Work Practice

School social workers must be equipped with an intervention framework that does not view student misbehavior or learning problems in isolation. The ecological perspective uniquely focuses on the reciprocal interactions of students with environmental factors. Within an ecological perspective, each child is viewed as an inseparable part of the various social systems (e.g., school, home, neighborhood, peer group) within which he or she must function (Apter & Propper, 1986). This perspective enables school social workers to broaden their conceptualization of students' problems and enlarges potential targets of intervention. Rather than viewing problems as disturbances located within the child, problems are viewed as a lack of "goodness of fit" between the child and his or her surrounding environments. This view assumes that the academic and social tasks of the school environment present formidable challenges for children and youths with behavior and learning problems. That is, within the school setting, problems experienced by children and youth are viewed as a discrepancy between the academic and social tasks of the school environment and the academic or behavioral competencies of children and youth (Schinke & Gilchrist, 1984). To address this discrepancy, school social workers must be *dually focused* in their interventions. That is, they must address specific environmental stressors as well as enhance the coping skills of students. Germain (1999) described this dual function of social work as strengthening students' coping patterns and growth potential on the one hand, and improving the quality of the impinging environment on the other. This dual focus, as illustrated in the case vignette at the beginning of this chapter, provides the student with a better chance of achieving positive outcomes (Whittaker, Shinke, & Gilchrist, 1986). The ecological perspective, with its dual focus, enables school social workers to carry out their unique mission in schools—assisting students as well as targeting detrimental conditions in schools, families, neighborhoods, and communities, especially those conditions that are harmful to vulnerable students.

The goal of *student-focused* interventions is to enhance the social competence of at-risk students through the teaching of specific skills as well as increasing environmental supports.

Section Two of this book focuses on proven and promising student-focused interventions that can be implemented by school social workers. The goal of *system-focused* interventions is to make the school, family, neighborhood, and community more responsive to the needs of students during their development as well as to minimize the detrimental impact of risk factors that may provoke or exacerbate problematic student behavior. Section Three of this book focuses on effective system-focused interventions that can be implemented by school social workers in collaboration with other school professionals.

The ecological perspective is congruent with a strengths-based and empowerment approach to practice. School social workers identify and build on strengths rather than focusing on deficits. Interventions based on strengths are an innovative approach to practice that are easily integrated into the school setting (Sessions, Fanolis, Corwin, & Miller, 2001). In addition, the ecological perspective allows school social workers to be preventive *and* proactive in designing their interventions. For example, it is possible to identify at-risk students and implement interventions long before their learning and behavior problems become entrenched and serious. However, it is difficult to implement interventions based on the ecological perspective in schools. School social workers feel a tremendous "pull" to view all problems as disturbances within the child and it is much easier, as well as expected, to help students adjust to dysfunctional school conditions, rather than targeting these detrimental conditions for change. Strategies for bringing about systemic-change will be discussed in Section Three (Chapters 7 through 10) and in Chapter 12 of this book.

Ethical Dimensions of School Social Work Practice

School social workers will inevitably confront a number of ethical dilemmas where obligations to the client conflict with obligations to the school, where professional ethics conflict with a particular law, or where what ought to be done conflicts with his or her personal values. In providing services to students in the school setting, school social workers must strike a balance between their legal and ethical responsibilities. To do so, school social workers must be conversant with the National Association of Social Workers (NASW) Code of Ethics; federal, state, and local laws; as well as policies and procedures established by the local school board. Loewenberg, Dolgoff, and Harrington's (2000) book focusus on ethical dilemmas confronting social workers in a number of practice settings. The following are examples of ethical dilemmas applicable to school social work practice:

- A 14-year-old girl who is 10 weeks pregnant wants to carry the baby to full term but doesn't want the school social worker to let her parents know that she is pregnant.
- A student obtains a low score within the "normal" range on an intelligence test but needs the extra help afforded by special education; but to receive this help, this student will be given a label that will follow him for the rest of his life.
- A sexually active student asks the school social worker, who has been assigned to the school health clinic, for a condom in a school system that has recently adopted a policy that condoms can be distributed only with written parental permission.
- A school social worker who personally believes that pharmaceutical control of a student's behavior interferes with the child's welfare and freedom is asked to meet with parents who want to prescribe drugs for their child, whose behavior is disruptive.

A fundamental principle of all school social work practice is confidentiality. However, the school setting is one of the most problematic settings for social workers to maintain client confidentiality (Kopels, 1993). School social workers are frequently faced with having to decide what information needs to be shared and with whom this information should be shared. This is further complicated by the fact that laws and policies that pertain to other school personnel such as school psychologists, school counselors, and school nurses may differ from those governing school social workers. To assist school social workers in evaluating the need to share confidential information involving students and their families, the NASW (2001) and the School Social Work Association of America (SSWAA, 2001) have provided several guidelines, including:

- School social workers must become familiar with specific state laws and regulations as well as school district policies governing confidentiality and minors, since these vary from state to state. For example, they should be aware of state statutes that protect the confidentiality of minor students seeking treatment for sexually transmitted diseases, information about and access to birth control, and pregnancy-related health care and counseling.

- In obtaining informed consent, school social workers must tell students and families, at the onset of services, that absolute confidentiality cannot be guaranteed and openly discuss the limits of confidentiality. For example, all states mandate that school social workers must report suspicions of child abuse and neglect to the local child protection agency or to police, even when this information is shared in confidence. Additionally, if students indicate intent or plans to harm themselves or others, school social workers must disclose this information.

- Disclose information obtained from students or parents with other school personnel only on a "need-to-know" basis and only for compelling professional reasons.

- Parents have the right to inspect and review their child's education records; however, personal notes kept for use by school social workers are not considered education records and are, therefore, confidential.

- Confidential reports should be sent via fax only when necessary. In such cases, the cover letter should note that the material is confidential and is intended for professional use only by the designated recipient.

- School social workers should maintain written documentation indicating with whom confidential information has been shared.

- School social workers must become familiar with the limits of confidentiality and "information sharing" as they pertain to the Individuals with Disabilities Education Act (IDEA).

- In instances where there are no clear-cut policies or laws, in deciding whether to share confidential information, the school social worker must consider his or her responsibility to the student and weigh this against responsibility to the family and the school community. Specifically, the school social worker should ask why it is important that this information be shared and how the student and the student's family will benefit by a decision to share information. Before sharing any confidential information, school social workers should involve the student and student's family in decisions involving a breach of confidentiality.

- School social workers must always weigh the consequences of sharing any information and assume responsibility for sharing this information. However, it is important to remember that any action of a professional social worker is judged by a *reasonable standard of care,* that is, what a reasonable person in a similar situation would do.

Roles and Tasks of School Social Workers and Other Professional Support Staff

In discussing the roles and tasks of the school social worker, it is important to consider that school social workers do not practice in isolation but are members of a multidisciplinary team of school professionals. Unfortunately, being a team member can sometimes result in role confusion and "turf battles." For example, school social workers and school counselors may both provide individual and small group counseling, or school social workers and school psychologists may both provide consultation to teachers. However, there are distinctions in the roles and tasks among professional groups that comprise a school's multidisciplinary team. The following is a very brief description of these distinct roles and tasks:

School psychologists are primarily responsible for administering academic and psychological tests with students having learning or behavioral problems, interpreting these test results, and, as a member of the multidisciplinary team, determine eligibility for special education services. School psychologists also frequently provide consultation to classroom teachers, and some also provide individual and group counseling to students and work with parents.

School counselors in elementary schools may provide individual and small group counseling to students. They may also conduct activities with entire classrooms of students. In some instances, they may function as disciplinarians or as a linkage between home and school. In secondary schools, school counselors are focused primarily on assisting students with their class schedules and monitoring their academic progress as well as assisting students with college and career choices.

School nurses provide vision and hearing testing in an effort to determine possible obstacles to learning and sometimes monitor youngsters who have health problems. School nurses are also increasingly involved in developing health education curriculums.

School social workers draw on a number of diverse roles and tasks to meet the unique needs of each school and the priorities of each building principal. Using the ecological framework as an organizing principle, these tasks include advocating for at-risk students and their families; empowering families to share their concerns with school officials; maintaining open lines of communication between home and school; helping families understand their children's educational needs; consulting with teachers about students' living situations and neighborhood conditions; making referrals to community agencies; tracking students involved with multiple agencies; and working with the larger community to identify and develop resources to better serve the needs of at-risk students and their families. As members of a school's multidisciplinary team, school social workers are involved in a number of activities including: participating in conferences related to students' behavior and academic progress; collaborating with teachers and other school professionals to assess student needs and developing strategies to meet their needs; being a member of a schoolwide crisis response team; preparing a comprehensive developmental assessment and social history as part of the required multidisciplinary evaluation; and preventing inappropriate labeling of students by assessing adaptive behavior, cultural background, and socioeconomic factors that may interfere with a child's learning or impact a child's behavior in school. School social workers also provide individual and group counseling to students; conduct classroom activities; and design, implement, and evaluate school-based prevention programs.

Many of these roles and tasks will be explored in detail in subsequent chapters of this book. To understand how these roles and tasks of school social workers have evolved, it is important to consider the major federal educational legislation and court orders that have impacted school social work practice since its inception at the turn of the twentieth century.

A Brief History of School Social Work Including Major Educational Legislation and Court Cases

For the past 90 years, school social workers have been influenced by conditions and events in the educational system where they practice, as well as by larger societal conditions (Hare & Rome, 1999). Table 1.1 contains a listing of major

Table 1.1   **Major Events in the History of School Social Work**

1906–1907	School social work services begin independently in New York City, Boston, and Hartford.
1913	Rochester, NY becomes the first school system to finance school social work services.
1921	National Association of Visiting Teachers is established.
1923	Commonwealth Fund of New York increases the visibility of school social workers by providing financial support for a program to prevent juvenile delinquency that includes the hiring of 30 school social workers in 20 rural and urban communities across the United States.
1945	The U.S. Office of Education recommends that a professional school social work certificate be a master's degree in social work (MSW).
1955	NASW by-laws provide for the establishment of school social work specialty.
1959	Specialist position in school social work is established in the U.S. Office of Education.
1969	"Social Change and School Social Work" is the national workshop held at the University of Pennsylvania and its proceedings resulted in the publication of the book entitled *The School in the Community* (1972).
1973	NASW Council on Social Work in Schools meets for the first time.
1975	Costin's school-community-pupil relations model of school social work practice is published.
1976	The first set of standards for school social work services are developed by NASW. These standards emphasize prevention as an important theme.
1985	NASW National School Social Work Conference "Educational Excellence in Transitional Times" is held in New Orleans, Louisiana, and results in the publication of *Achieving Educational Excellence for Children At Risk,* which contains papers from this conference.
1992	The school social work credentialing exam, developed by NASW, the Educational Testing Service, and Allen-Meares is administered for the first time.
1992	Standards for social work services in schools are revised by the NASW Education Commission Task Force.
1994	NASW launches school social work as its first practice section.
1994	The School Social Work Association of America (SSWAA) is formed, independent of NASW.

Source: Adapted from Allen-Meares, Washington, and Welsh, 2000; "School Social Work Overview," by E. M. Freeman, 1995, in R. L. Edwards (Ed.), *Encyclopedia of Social Work*, Washington, DC: NASW Press; "Securing Equal Education Opportunity," by S. Kopels, 2000, in P. Allen Meares, R. O. Washington, and B. L. Welsh (Eds.), *Social Work Services in Schools*, Needham Heights, MA: Allyn & Bacon; *Digest of Education Statistics, 1999*, by H. N. Snyder and C. Hoffman, 2000. Retrieved October, 28, 2000, from nces.ed.gov/pubsearch/pubsinfo.

events that have shaped school social work practice throughout its history. In addition to these historical events, school social work practice has been influenced by major federal legislation and Supreme Court decisions. The following is a brief discussion of events, legislation, and court decisions that have shaped school social work practice over the past century.

In the early 1900s, compulsory school attendance laws were introduced state by state. The requirements of a free, compulsory public education compelled school social workers to focus on those factors that contributed to truancy and poor school performance. One of the principle activities of the school social worker at this time was helping teachers understand how particular neighborhood and social conditions such as poverty, poor health, and exploitation of children through child labor impacted school attendance. This emphasis continued until the 1920s when the mental hygiene movement impelled school social workers to turn their focus away from societal factors and toward therapeutic casework with children who were viewed as having emotional and behavioral disturbances (Germain, 1999).

The Great Depression of the 1930s returned the focus of school social work toward adverse social conditions and the physical needs of students. During the 1940s and 1950s, the number of school social workers grew and, once again, their focus shifted from adverse social conditions back to clinical practice (Freeman, 1995). This shift can be partially explained by the increased prestige associated with clinical practice compared to the stigma attached to the role of "truant officer" (Radin, 1989).

A number of social forces during the 1950s, 1960s, and 1970s continued to shape school social work practice. The 1954 *Brown v. Board of Education of Topeka, KS* decision concluded that separate educational facilities on the basis of race are inherently unequal and unconstitutional. As a result, schools were faced with the daunting task of desegregating classrooms and educating increasing numbers of students "whose lifestyles and languages differed from the middle-class orientation of the school"

(Germain, 1999, p. 34). At the same time, a flurry of federal educational legislation during the 1960s and 1970s significantly increased the federal government's role in public education. For example, the:

- *Civil Rights Act of 1964,* prohibited discrimination in federally assisted programs based on race, color, or national origin, assisted school staff in dealing with problems caused by desegregation.

- *Elementary and Secondary Education Act of 1965 (ESEA),* through Title I, authorized grants for compensatory education in elementary and secondary schools for children of low-income families.

- *1972 Education Amendment* (Title IX) was the first comprehensive federal law to prohibit sex discrimination in the admission and treatment of students by educational institutions receiving federal assistance. Title IX also prohibited schools that were receiving federal funds from discriminating against pregnant teens and teen mothers.

- *Vocational Rehabilitation Act of 1973* (Section 504) covered students who have a disability and may need special accommodations but not "special education and related services" as specified in the Individuals with Disabilities Education Act (IDEA). Children with attention deficit disorder with hyperactivity (ADHD) and students infected with the AIDS virus are often served under a 504 Plan.

- *Child Abuse Prevention and Treatment Act,* enacted in 1974, provided federal financial assistance to states that had implemented programs for the identification, prevention, and treatment of child abuse and neglect. A component of this act was the creation of the National Center of Child Abuse and Neglect.

- *Juvenile Justice and Delinquency Prevention Act of 1974* provided resources to develop and implement programs to keep elementary and secondary students in school.

- *Family Education Rights and Privacy Act of 1974* (FERPA), also known informally as the Buckley Amendment, responded to concerns that schools were "encroaching upon the basic rights of parents regarding access to and control of their children's educational records" (Allen-Meares, Washington, & Welsh, 2000, p. 132). While schools can disclose some information without parental consent, this law specified that any educational institution receiving federal funds would lose those funds unless it provides parents with full access to their child's full educational records as well as the right to change inaccurate or misleading records.

- *Education for All Handicapped Children Act* (Pub. L. No. 94-142), passed in 1975, brought about a major shift in responsibility for educating children with disabilities by establishing the right of all children with disabilities to a free and appropriate public education (FAPE) in the least restrictive environment. *This Act* also provided, for the first time, legislative recognition to social workers for their contribution to the educational process. In 1990, Congress reauthorized Pub. L. No. 94-142, renaming it as the Individuals with Disabilities Education Act (Pub. L. No. 101-476), more commonly known as IDEA. Pub. L. No. 101-476 was amended again in 1997 and named the Individuals with Disabilities Education Act Amendments of 1997 (Pub. L. No. 105-17).

In addition to this legislative activity, a number of court decisions during the 1960s and 1970s focused on balancing the interests of the school against the rights of students in matters related to student discipline. One example is the legal doctrine of *in loco parentis* ("in place of the parents") that was established early in U.S. history. This doctrine gives power to school officials to exercise the "same control over students at school that parents exercise at home including control over students' clothing, speech, and even students' behavior away from school"

(Allen-Meares et al., 2000, p. 112). A number of court rulings have centered on balancing the legal doctrine of *in loco parentis* with the constitutional rights of students. For example, in 1969, the landmark decision in *Tinker v. Des Moines School Board* established that students do not abandon their constitutional rights at the schoolhouse door and that their constitutional rights include freedom of expression. On the other hand, in 1977, the Supreme Court, in *Ingraham v. Wright*, refused to extend the Eighth Amendment's prohibition of "cruel and unusual punishment" to prohibit use of corporal punishment in the schools. This balance between the doctrine of *in loco parentis* and the constitutional rights of students shifted again in *Goss v. Lopez* (1975) when the Supreme Court ruled that, for short suspensions, a student must be given an informal notice and hearing (including a statement of the charges and evidence against him or her), as well as an opportunity to tell his or her side of the story. The 1975 decision, *Wood v. Strickland*, expanded on the *Goss* ruling by stating that school officials may be sued for monetary damages if they know or reasonably should have known that their disciplinary actions would violate the constitutional rights of students. However, in *Baker v. Owen* (1975), the balance shifted again when the Supreme Court affirmed the right of the state to use corporal punishment to maintain order in the classroom. In this case, the Supreme Court specifically ruled that schools could use "reasonable" physical punishment on a child if the child was forewarned, if less drastic measures had been tried first, if a second staff member was present to witness the punishment, and if the spanking was reported to parents who wished to be informed. Another important issue involving the interests of the school versus the constitutional rights of students is the right to search and seizure. For example, the Supreme Court in *New Jersey v. T.L.O.* (1985) held that Fourth Amendment protections against unreasonable search and seizures also apply to school settings.

In response to these changing social conditions and the flurry of legislative and judicial activity during the 1960s and 1970s, the literature on school social work practice renewed its focus on school social work's responsibility to help modify school conditions and policies that had a detrimental impact on students by incorporating general systems theory and the ecological perspective as frameworks for social work practice (Costin, 1978). It was also during this time that group work methods were incorporated into school social work practice. However, despite this renewed emphasis on school and community conditions as targets of intervention, the vast majority of school social workers continued to focus on traditional casework models (Costin, 1978).

During the 1980s and 1990s, schools faced the challenge of educating growing numbers of students with learning and behavioral problems. In addition, schools were faced with educating an increasingly diverse student population. To further compound the challenges facing schools, legislation was passed to ensure that all vulnerable groups of children receive an education. For example, in 1987, the *Stewart B. McKinney Homeless Assistance Act* provided funds to ensure that homeless children and youth receive a public education; and three years later, the *Stewart B. McKinney Homeless Assistance Amendments Act of 1990* increased the capacity of public schools to provide the services that homeless children and youth need to be successful in school. The *Hawkins-Stafford Elementary and Secondary School Improvement Amendments of 1988* reauthorized a number of major elementary and secondary education programs including Title I programs for disadvantaged students (ESEA legislation has used the terms "Chapter 1" and "Title 1" at different times over the years). This Act expanded school social work services in the area of preventive interventions to high-risk children and youth. The *Improving America's Schools Act,* passed in 1994, reauthorized and revamped the *Elementary and Secondary Education Act* (Pub. L. No. 103-382) and included Title 1, the largest existing federal education program and extended services to teen parents and neglected or delinquent youth in state institutions and community day programs. This Act also specified that school social workers be included in a wide variety of programs including drug and violence prevention programs, and programs that address the needs of children with limited English proficiency, Native American children, and homeless children (Hare & Rome, 1999).

Several important pieces of legislation, that expanded services for children with disabilities, were passed during the late 1980s and 1990s. In 1990, the *Individuals with Disabilities Education Act (IDEA)*, formerly known as the *Education of All Handicapped Children Act*, extended services to infants, toddlers, and preschoolers. This legislation identified social workers as qualified providers of early intervention services including home visits, psychosocial assessments, counseling, and coordination of community resources. Also "in 1990, 'social work services in schools' was officially added to the list of 'related services' required to assist children with disabilities" (Hare & Rome, 1999, p. 107). The *Individuals with Disabilities Education Act Amendments of 1997* brought about additional changes when it established the Individualized Education Program (IEP) as the major tool in a student's involvement and progress in the general curriculum and mandated that students with disabilities be included in general state and districtwide assessment programs. It also emphasized positive behavioral interventions in addressing classroom management, school climate, social skills, and violence prevention. This Act also authorizes schools to remove a student up to 10 school days for minor disciplinary infractions and for up to 45 days for dangerous behavior involving weapons or drugs.

In addition to the legislation that was passed to expand services for children with disabilities in the 1980s and 1990s, Hare and Rome (1999) discussed a number of changes in the health care system that have impacted and will impact the delivery of school social work services. For example, Medicaid funding is being used in many school districts to "finance the social work services that are part of the targeted case management provisions of the Medicaid law or the early and periodic screening, diagnosis, and treatment provisions" (Hare & Rome, 1999, p. 117). These changes may result in the need for school social workers to obtain "clinical credentials so that they may be recognized as providers of Medicaid-funded services" (Hare

& Rome, 1999, p. 117). In addition, Congress enacted the *State Children's Health Insurance Program (S-CHIP)* in 1997 which made $20 billion over five years available to states to target previously uninsured low-income children whose family incomes do not exceed 200 percent of the federal poverty level. These expanded services "have implications for social workers in terms of identifying eligible children in school and providing increased funding for services to newly covered children" (Hare & Rome, 1999, p. 118).

During the 1990s, school violence grabbed the headlines and became a major focus of federal and state legislation. The 1994 federal *Gun-Free Schools Act* directed states to adopt zero-tolerance (i.e., no discretion) policies on weapons at school or risk losing federal funding. As a result, there has been a dramatic increase in the number of students expelled from U.S. public schools. The *Safe Schools Act of 1994* authorized the award of competitive grants to local educational agencies with serious crime problems to implement violence prevention activities and provided additional opportunities for school social workers in the area of conflict resolution and peer mediation. The *Goals 2000: Educate America Act,* also passed in 1994, formulated national educational goals that focused on improving high school graduation rates, setting high standards of student academic achievement, increasing parental involvement, and creating safe, disciplined and drug-free schools. School social workers are specifically mentioned in this legislation under "related services personnel" (Hare & Rome, 1999).

The 1990s also saw a movement emerge in a number of states to make schools "hubs" for the delivery of comprehensive, integrated services to at-risk students and their families. These "full-service" schools offer a range of services including medical, dental, and mental health services, recreational activities, teen programs, and parent education programs. They *require* concentrated efforts from school officials *and* heavy involvement from parents and community to integrate these services with the school (Dryfoos, 1996). See Chapter 10 for a detailed description of several exemplary "full-service" school models and how these and other school-community collaborations will inevitably reshape and expand the role of school social workers in the years to come.

Summary

To address the wide range of problems found in school settings, school social workers must be able to assume a number of roles including broker, networker, researcher, advocate, counselor, educator, public speaker, and community organizer. The ecological perspective enables school social workers to broaden their conceptualization of students' problems and enlarges potential targets of intervention. An ecological perspective demands that school social workers be dually focused in their interventions. This dual function of social work strengthens people's coping patterns and growth potential on the one hand, and improves the quality of the impinging environment on the other. The ecological perspective also allows the school social worker to identify and build on strengths rather than focusing on deficits. Interventions based on strengths are the most innovative approaches to practice as well as the most easily integrated into the school context. Since school social workers are not solo practitioners but members of a school's multidisciplinary team of professionals, they must understand the similarities and differences among school social workers, guidance counselors, and school psychologists with respect to roles and functions. School social workers must also have knowledge of those historical events, major federal legislation, and major court cases that have impacted and continue to impact school social work practice.

Questions for Discussion

1. Within an ecological framework, what dual roles are required of social workers?

2. What barriers need to be overcome before school social workers can implement an ecological approach in school settings?

3. This chapter discusses four examples of ethical dilemmas confronting school social workers (see page 7). How would you, as the school social worker, resolve each of these dilemmas? What ethical principles are involved in making decisions about possible courses of action?

4. How have the roles of school social workers evolved and changed over time? What major events have shaped the roles of school social workers over time?

5. Colorado, as well as some other states, has introduced state legislation to eliminate compulsory school attendance. Are compulsory attendance laws still needed today? Why or why not?

Refer to the case study at the beginning of this chapter:

1. What roles did Susan assume in this case? How did these roles reflect an ecological approach to school social work practice? Why were each of these roles important in helping Becky?

2. If Becky's mother was not cooperative, how could Susan best help Becky?

Additional Resources

The following professional journals focus specifically on school social work practice:

- *Children & Schools* (formerly *Social Work in Education*)
- *School Social Work Journal*

The following journal carries articles containing research findings on social work interventions carried out in a number of settings including school settings:

- *Research on Social Work Practice*

The following professional organizations focus on issues related to school social work practice:

- The National Association of Social Workers
  750 First Street, NE
  Washington, DC 20002-4241
  www.socialworkers.org
- NASW School Social Work Web site
  www.socialworkers.org/sections/ssw
- The School Social Work Association of America
  P.O. Box 2072
  Northlake, IL 60164
  www.sswaa.org

The following Web sites are recommended for school social workers:

- NASW Code of Ethics
  www.naswdc.org/pubs/code/default.htm
- NASW Standards for School Social Work Services
  www.naswdc.org/pubs/standards/school.htm
- U.S. Department of Education
  www.ed.gov
- World Wide Web Resources for Social Workers
  www.nyu.edu/socialwork/wwwrsw
- National Network of Regional Educational Laboratories
  www.nwrel.org/national/index.html
- Education Week on the Web (American Education's On line Newspaper of Record)
  www.edweek.org
- Center for the Future of Children
  www.futureofchildren.org
- Safe and Drug-Free Schools Program
  www.ed.gov/offices/OESE/SDFS
- Office of Special Education Programs
  www.offices/OSERS/OSEP
- Office of Juvenile Justice and Delinquency Prevention
  www.ojjdp.ncjrs.org

The Social Organization and Political Environment of the School

2

Chapter

In this chapter, we discuss:

■ *The organizational structure and processes of the school.*

■ *The culture and climate of the school.*

■ *The political environment of the school.*

■ *20-60-20 theory of school change.*

John has been the school social worker at Jefferson Middle School for the past three years. Over that time, he has observed boys making very offensive sexual comments to girls and witnessed boys who inappropriately touched, grabbed, and pinched girls while walking the hallways. He has also been made aware of the fact that students have been spreading sexual rumors about each other. John feels compelled to do something about this problem. Before he approaches school administrators and school staff to share his concerns and to explore possible solutions, John realizes that he needs to take some time to think through how he should approach this problem.

If school social workers are naive about the importance of power and politics in the schools they serve or discount their importance, they become frustrated, burned out, ineffective, or irrelevant. Conversely, if school social workers understand the political processes within a school, their actions will be purposeful and effective. (Lee, 1983)

Introduction

Over 35 years ago, Vinter and Sarri (1965) directed school social workers to focus their efforts on school conditions that contribute to student malperformance and not limit their efforts to
individual and small group contacts with students. These authors stated that "attempts to help malperforming pupils by
treating them in isolation or as though abstracted from the context of school circumstances must be viewed with extreme
skepticism" (p. 12). Their warning is even more important
today. This chapter provides some of the knowledge and skills
needed to broaden school social work practice to include consideration of the organizational and political dimensions of the
school setting and how the school itself can be a potential target
of intervention. We begin with a discussion of key organizational concepts that can be applied to social work practice in
schools. We then discuss the highly politicized environment of
schools and several concrete steps that school social workers can
take to develop "political savvy." We conclude with a discussion
of the 20-60-20 theory of school change and how to apply the
20-60-20 theory of school change to confront the problem of
peer sexual harassment, discussed in the case vignette at the
beginning of this chapter.

The Organizational Structure and Processes of the School

To practice effectively in the school setting, social workers must
understand the organizational context of the school and how
this unique organizational context influences the development
and delivery of social work interventions in schools. Just as we
cannot understand human behavior in isolation, we cannot understand what happens in schools without examining the forces
that influence a school from within and from without. All that
occurs in schools must be understood in relation to a school's
relationship with its environment.

A number of general systems theory concepts are useful in
understanding these complex relationships. The first of these

concepts is *open systems*. By their very nature, schools are open systems that are impacted by their immediate environment. To understand why things happen the way they do in schools, school social workers must understand the forces that are at work in the larger society because schools reflect and transmit the dominant norms and values of the larger society (Pawlak & Cousins, 1999). For example, school policies and procedures often reflect the racism, classism, sexism, and homophobia of the larger society. Punitive school discipline policies, by disproportionately targeting African American males for suspension and expulsion, reflect the institutional racism of the larger society. The verbal and emotional abuse directed at gays and lesbians in the larger society is also reflected in schools. Community violence also infects the school environment.

Another useful general systems theory concept in understanding the complex relationship between the school and its environment is the concept of *boundaries*. Even though schools are open systems, they do possess boundaries, or regions, that separate them from their environment (Barker, 1987). One example of a boundary that often separates a school and its environment are the norms and expectations that govern children's behavior. For some students, the norms that govern behavior in a school are in direct conflict with norms that govern behavior in their home and neighborhood. For instance, students who are encouraged by their parents to defend themselves by fighting back if they are struck by another person find that this behavior is not tolerated within the school environment and results in a suspension or even an expulsion from school. Where behavioral norms and expectations at home are congruent with those of the school, students have an easier time navigating through both environments. School social workers must understand the implications of this incongruity and reach out to those students and parents who have a difficult time understanding and, hence, following these norms and expectations.

Pawlak and Cousins (1999, p. 151) have offered a series of questions to assist the school social worker in assessing the norms that govern behavior, policies, and procedures in a school. These include:

- What are the rules and procedures used by school officials and faculty in their transactions with students?
- Are these rules and procedures applied equitably among students who, for example, face suspension and expulsion?
- Do students with particular characteristics experience different and less favorable career paths (e.g., low-income versus upper-income students, girls versus boys, White students versus minority students)?
- Do students with particular attributes have equal access to school curricula, programs, and activities?
- Are some groups of students often inappropriately classified?
- Which teachers or staff members are working with which students?

Other organizational concepts that help to increase school social workers' understanding of the social organization and processes of schools are *formalization, standardization, and centralization.* According to Pawlak and Cousins (1999), *formalization* refers to the degree to which rules, policies, and procedures that govern behavior in the organization are set forth in writing and codified. The degree of formalization in a school is reflected in a school's discipline handbook for students. For example, are there rules and consequences for every possible situation?

Standardization is a type of formalization in which organizations have uniform ways of dealing with uniform situations. For example, to what extent can school administrators exercise discretion in disciplining students?

Centralization refers to the concentration of power, authority, and decision making at the central office while *decentralization* refers to site-based management where building principals have the authority to make important decisions at the building level and where teachers have a "say" in decision making in their school.

These concepts are important because they impact the types of services that school social workers are able to offer in schools. For example, Chavkin (1993) found that school social workers employed by more formalized and centralized school districts were more likely limited to traditional microlevel interventions and less likely to implement macrolevel interventions.

Another organizational concept that is useful to school social work practice is the concept of *subsystems*. A subsystem "is a part of a system that itself comprises interacting and reciprocally influencing elements" (Barker, 1987, p. 160). Wassenich (1972) identified five subsystems in schools in which school social workers can intervene:

1. In the school, the classroom is the main part of the *production subsystem* where students are educated and socialized. School social workers are involved in the production subsystem when they conduct classroom activities.

2. The *maintenance subsystem* is concerned with "tying people into their functional roles" (p. 207). School social workers work within the maintenance subsystem when they serve as consultants in helping define the functional roles of teachers, principals, and students in the school.

3. The *supportive subsystem* is "concerned with exporting the finished product into the environment . . . and maintaining a favorable environment for the operation of the system" (p. 207). The school social worker works within the supportive subsystem by intervening with community agencies that link the school and the community and by aiding in the transition of students into the environment when they leave school.

4. The *adaptive subsystem* ensures "organizational survival in a changing environment" (p. 207). Since school social workers are often in a position to know students' and the community's criticisms of the school and what student needs are going unmet, they provide an important feedback function as a part of the adaptive subsystem.

5. The *managerial subsystem* consists of all the managers in the school system including principals, the superintendent, and

the school board. School social workers may "work with other managers toward establishing system goals and the responsibility for carrying them out" (p. 209).

A more detailed discussion of these various subsystems as they relate to school social work practice may be found in Wassenich's article.

The Culture and Climate of the School

Perhaps the most important organizational concepts for school social workers to be knowledgeable about are *culture* and *climate*. A school's culture and climate significantly impact and influence students' behavior and learning (Dupper & Meyer-Adams, 2002; Wang, Haertel, & Walberg, 1997). A school's *culture* has been defined as the beliefs and expectations apparent in a school's daily routine, including how colleagues interact with one another, and the norms or beliefs shared by students, teachers, administrators, and other workers in a school. Culture is the socially shared and transmitted knowledge of what is and what ought to be (Hamilton & Richardson, 1995). Closely related to culture is the concept of *climate*. A school's *climate* "is the heart and soul of a school. It is about that essence of a school that leads a child, a teacher, an administrator, a staff member to love the school and to look forward to being at their school each day" (Freiberg & Stein, 1999, p. 11).

A major challenge facing school leaders and school social workers today is to change the culture and climate of a school when it impedes progress. A number of factors are involved in determining the culture and climate of any given school. A list of school risk factors identified in the literature can be found in Table 2.1.

As seen in Table 2.1, discipline and attendance policies and practices, school size, teacher's expectations, curriculum, and influences outside the school have a negative impact on a school's culture and climate. Other risk factors include hostile

Table 2.1 **School Risk Factors**

- Suspension and corporal punishment (DeRidder, 1990; Hyman, 1990).
- Punitive or inadequate attendance policies (First, Kellog, Almeida, & Gray, 1991).
- Tracking and differential grading procedures (Wheelock & Dorman, 1988).
- Grade retention (Bracey, 1992; Hammack, 1986).
- Teacher expectations and attitudes (Gandara, 1989; Olsen & Moore, 1984; Pollard, 1989).
- Large school size (Bryk & Thum, 1989; Walberg, 1991; Wehlage & Rutter, 1986).
- Absence of a stimulating and innovative curriculum (Hahn, 1987; Wehlage & Rutter, 1986).
- Numerous grade-level transitions (Merritt, 1983).
- Climate of low academic expectations (Bryk & Thum, 1989; Wehlage & Rutter, 1986).
- Crime and violence (Menacker, Weldon, & Hurwitz, 1990).
- Gang-related activities in or around school (Reyes & Jason, 1993).

and suspicious relationships between administrators and school staff or between school staff and students (Corbin, 2001). An important role of the school social worker is to use his or her considerable mediation and group work skills to change these destructive patterns.

At the same time, a number of protective factors, if present in a school, can buffer these risk factors and result in a more positive school culture and climate. As seen in Table 2.2, positive relationships, bonding, and engagement, and an appropriate degree of structure and control are positively correlated with a school culture and climate that is humane and invitational for staff, students, and parents.

Given the risk and protective factors that are present in schools and the culture and climate they create, school social workers should focus their interventions on changing or modifying the culture and climate of a school so that schools become safe havens for all children and youth—places where teachers, students, administrators, parents, and support staff all feel invited to participate and welcome and share a psychological

Table 2.2   **School Protective Factors**

- Educational engagement, school membership or bonding (Wehlage, Lipman, & Smith, 1989).
- Attachment relationships with emotionally significant adults (Garbarino, Dubrow, Kostelny, & Pardo, 1992).
- Appropriate degree of environmental structure and control (Garbarino, Dubrow, Kostelny, & Pardo, 1992).
- A developmental approach to curriculum that supports coping and self-esteem (Garbarino, Dubrow, Kostelny, & Pardo, 1992).
- The acquisition of coping skills (Garbarino, Dubrow, Kostelny, & Pardo, 1992).

sense of community. A renewed understanding of the role of the school as a protective factor and caregiving environment in children's lives is critical (Garbarino, Dubrow, Kostelny, & Pardo, 1992). Fortunately, some schools are already leading the way in transforming their school culture to include positive approaches to discipline, opportunities for teachers and students to bond, and training for teachers in classroom management techniques (Civil Rights Project, 2000). See Chapter 7 for a discussion of several innovative programs designed to change a school's culture and climate.

The Political Environment of the School

School social workers practice in a "host" setting where the focus is education rather than social work. Unlike mental health centers or child welfare agencies, school personnel frequently do not understand or appreciate social work services. Consequently, school social workers are vulnerable; they may occupy a position of relatively low status within the schools they serve and are often under scrutiny.

To carry out their unique mission in schools—facilitating systemic change on behalf of vulnerable groups of students—school social workers must discover how to acquire more informal power and become more politically savvy. Rather than avoiding the political process, school social workers must become engaged in it, guided by personal and professional values and ethics. In an important and provocative article, Lee (1983) provided a very informative and detailed explanation of the many political processes that impact school social work services and provide guidance on how school social workers can acquire more informal power. For example, Lee stated that decisions made in schools result from "battles between competing interest groups" rather than a rational decision-making process. In other words, decisions are largely based on which group or persons wield the most power and influence in a school. Therefore, if school social workers want to influence decision-making processes in a school, they must discover which behaviors are rewarded or punished within a school, who has the ear of the school principal, who holds the most power on the school board, and how much authority the school superintendent wields. Much of this political knowledge can be acquired through direct observation, by finding a confidante in the school who can inform the school social worker about what is going on within the school, by reading newspapers or scanning the Internet for school-related news, by attending school board meetings (or watching them on cable TV), or a combination of these.

In addition to gaining this knowledge of the political processes within a school, school social workers must also learn how to become more politically savvy. Table 2.3 discusses a series of concrete steps that school social workers can take to become more politically savvy.

As shown in Table 2.3, school social workers need to learn how to market themselves by "blowing their own horn," offering compelling arguments about why they are needed in the schools, and why they are indispensable.

20-60-20 Theory of School Change

Another important "tool" for facilitating systemic change on behalf of vulnerable groups of students in schools is the 20-60-20

Table 2.3 Developing Political Savvy

- Rather than quietly doing their good work, school social workers must constantly "sell" themselves and "blow their own horn" since no one else will do this for them.
- School social workers must offer compelling arguments about why they are needed by schools, what specific contributions they make to the system, why no one else can do their job, and why more of them need to be hired.
- Having information means having power. For example, social workers should market their knowledge of community resources that can be used in support of education.
- Since conflicts are inevitable and unavoidable in schools, school social workers should develop and "market" their expertise in conflict mediation and problem-solving skills (e.g., take a leadership role in mediating conflicts or beginning a peer mediator program).
- School social workers can make themselves indispensable to the school by identifying needs and gaps in services and offering their expertise in addressing these needs and gaps.
- Identify and establish relationships with powerful individuals both within and outside of school (e.g., influential business people in a community, school board members, local and state representatives) and call on these individuals for assistance when needed.
- School social workers must choose their battles carefully. They should go for easy victories initially to build up their credibility in a school before tackling larger and more important issues later.
- School social workers should be prepared to cite statistics and research findings that support or refute an educational issue.
- School social workers must constantly show that their interventions result in improved educational outcomes (i.e., improvement in grades, attendance, behavior) for students.

Source: Adapted from "The Social Worker in the Political Environment of a School System," by L. J. Lee, 1983, *Social Work, 28*, pp. 302–307; and "Survival Strategies for School Social Workers," by J. G. McCullagh, 1982, *Social Work in Education, 4*, pp. 5–15.

theory of school change. This theory is illustrated in the case vignette at the beginning of this chapter. According to this theory, each school staff breaks down roughly into three groups. Members of the first group, comprising about 20 percent of the school staff, may be referred to as the "obstructers." This group will actively attempt to undermine any attempts to make changes in school policy, programs, or procedures and will try to discredit anyone who attempts to make any change, including school social workers. While this group is relatively small percentagewise, its members can be very vocal and they can be a destructive political force in the school. School social workers should not waste their time or energy trying to influence the obstructers. Instead, they should agree to disagree with them and focus all their efforts on the other two groups.

Members of the second group could be referred to as the "fence sitters." This group comprises the largest number of school staff, about 60 percent. Fence sitters often assume a "wait-and-see" attitude about any proposed school change. They remain neutral about any change until it is proven to them that a change is beneficial. Because of the size of this group and because this group can be won over, it is critical for school social workers to focus on this group to win support for any school change effort.

Members of the third group could be referred to as the "change agents." While this group comprises only about 20 percent of the entire school staff, members of this group can be counted on to be very enthusiastic about attempts to change school policies, programs, or procedures that benefit the students. The change agents will be *the* school social worker's primary support group in bringing about systemic change in a school. For example, change agents can be used to win over the fence sitters and to neutralize the destructive efforts of the obstructers.

The following is an illustration of how John, the school social worker in the case vignette at the beginning of this chapter, might go about applying the 20-60-20 theory of school change to address the problem of peer sexual harassment at Jefferson Middle School. John would first meet with the school principal to gain his support for addressing the problem. Once he has obtained at least minimal support from the principal, John next meets with those teachers and staff that he has identified as the change agents. John has identified a number of them during the three years he has been at the school by observing which teachers and staff are most enthusiastic about their jobs and love working with children. In his initial meeting with the change agents, John shares his concerns about the escalating number of very offensive sexual comments; spreading of sexual rumors; and the inappropriate touching, grabbing, and pinching that goes on in the school hallways. John shares that there will be a small but vocal group of teachers and faculty at the school who will deny that there is a problem or attempt to minimize the problem. They may say things like, "What's the big deal, boys will be boys!" or "Here comes the politically correct police, again!" John states that these comments should be ignored and that instead, members of the change agents group should focus all their energies on the fence sitters. To do this, John asks that each teacher and staff person in this group help him identify the teachers and staff who may not be aware or concerned at this time about the problem but who could be won over if persuaded that sexual harassment is a serious problem; that is, it is having a devastating impact on the learning environment of the school. He asks each member of the change agents group to identify between three to five teachers and staff who they believe are currently fence sitters but who can be won over to address this problem. Their next step will be for two members from the change agents group to meet with 6 to 10 members of the fence sitters group to discuss the problem and to develop a schoolwide plan of action to address this problem. They also decide to meet again with the principal as well as the president of the PTA to enlist their strong support and to further neutralize and alienate the obstructers. For further information on how to plan and implement change strategies in schools, see Chapter 12.

Summary

School social workers must understand the organizational and political dimensions of the school setting and how the school itself can become a potential target of intervention. A number of organizational concepts (e.g., open systems, subsystems, formalization, standardization, centralization, and culture and climate) are useful. To bring about systemic change in the schools they serve, it is also important that school social workers acquire extensive knowledge about the political environment of schools including how to obtain more informal power and how to develop political savvy. The 20-60-20 theory is an important tool for facilitating systemic change on behalf of vulnerable groups of students in schools.

Questions for Discussion

1. What is meant by the terms *culture* and *climate*?
2. Define an open system. Why are schools considered to be open systems?
3. What concrete steps can school social workers take to develop "political savvy"? Why is this important?
4. Becoming politically savvy often requires a very different set of skills from those for clinical practice. Referring to Table 2.3, which of these steps would be easy to undertake? Which steps would be more difficult? Why?
5. Describe the 20-60-20 theory of school change.

Refer to the case study at the beginning of this chapter:

1. How might John use "political savvy" to reduce the incidence of peer sexual harassment at Jefferson Middle School?
2. What political factors should John take into account in his efforts to reduce the incidence of peer sexual harassment at Jefferson Middle School?

Additional Resources

Organizational Change

Kohn, A. (1999). *The schools our children deserve: Moving beyond traditional classrooms and "tougher standards."* Boston: Houghton Mifflin Company.

Sarason, S. B. (1996). *Revisiting the culture of the school and the problem of change.* New York: Teachers College Press.

Sergiovanni, T. J. (1994). *Building community in schools.* San Francisco, CA: Jossey-Bass.

Deal, T. E. & Peterson, K. D. (1999). *Shaping school culture: The heart of leadership.* San Francisco, CA: Jossey-Bass.

Political Social Work

Haynes, K. S. & Mickelson, J. S. (2000). *Affecting change: Social workers in the political arena* (4th ed.). Needham Heights, MA: Allyn & Bacon.

STUDENT-FOCUSED INTERVENTIONS

This unit focuses exclusively on interventions targeting students individually, in small group settings, or in classroom settings. Chapters 3 and 4 are categorized according to the discrete patterns of behavior suggested by Achenbach (1982). Achenbach refers to aggressive, disruptive, and acting out behaviors as *externalizing behaviors,* and various forms of these behaviors that come to the attention of school social workers are discussed in Chapter 3. Achenbach refers to withdrawn, anxious, and depressed behaviors as internalizing behaviors; various forms of these behaviors commonly found in schools today are discussed in Chapter 4. Chapter 5 focuses on students suffering from one or more of a wide range of social problems including homelessness and abuse. Chapter 6 discusses the mandates of the Individuals with Disabilities Education Act Amendments (IDEA '97) and several categories of disabilities. All chapters highlight proven or promising student-focused interventions and programs available to school social workers to address the problems discussed.

Before implementing student-focused interventions, with the exception of crises, it is essential that school social workers conduct systematic and thorough assessments with students suspected of having behavioral, emotional, mental, and/or learning problems or disorders. A thorough assessment, often completed by an interdisciplinary team of school professionals, allows the school social worker to rule in and rule out the various intrapersonal, interpersonal, and environmental factors that may be contributing to school difficulties. Jay McTighe has referred to good assessment as a "photo album rather than a snapshot because we should use different pictures and different lenses to get at different aspects of student development and functioning." In general, assessments are composed of formal as well as informal procedures and include data on the individual student, data about the student's family, the student's relationship with peers, and data related to environmental factors that may impact on the student's functioning in school.

In conducting assessments, school social workers should identify students' individual strengths and social supports so that they have "something to build on" in designing and implementing their interventions. Shroeder and Gordon (1991) have developed a comprehensive assessment-to-intervention system (CAIS) for child behavioral problems. Their CAIS system is an excellent step-by-step guide for conducting thorough, systematic, ecologically based assessments in school social work practice. Hodges (1993), discusses how to use a structured interview in assessing children. Shapiro and Kratochwill (2000) have written a guide to help school social workers and other school professionals conduct assessments for a wide range of emotional and behavioral difficulties.

Assessment data are collected from various sources in a variety of ways. They include:

- Direct observations of the student across settings (e.g., classroom, playground, cafeteria, home) at different times of the day and days of the week.

- A review of the student's school records (i.e., cumulative folder).
- One or more interviews with the parent or guardian.
- Administration of one or more standardized child behavior rating scales and/or adaptive behavior scales.

Some of the most widely used standardized child behavior rating scales include the Child Behavior Checklist (Achenbach & Edelbrock, 1981), the Conners Parent Rating Scale (Goyette, Conners, & Ulrich, 1978), and the Eyberg Child Behavior Inventory (Eyberg & Ross, 1978). The Behavioral and Emotional Rating Scale (BERS) was developed to provide professionals with a standardized, reliable, and valid instrument to measure children's emotional and behavioral strengths in five primary areas: interpersonal strength, family involvement, intrapersonal strength, school functioning, and affective strengths (Epstein, 1999). The National Institute of Mental Health (NIMH) also has available an excellent online resource of publications related to child and adolescent mental health. These resources can be found at http://www.nimh.nih.gov/publicat/childmenu.cfm.

Externalizing Behavior Problems

In this chapter, we discuss:

- *The nature and extent of classroom behavior problems.*
- *The nature and extent of bullying behaviors in schools.*
- *The nature and extent of peer sexual harassment in schools.*
- *Guidelines for assessing potentially violent students.*
- *Proven student-focused interventions/programs that focus on externalizing behavior problems.*
- *Alternatives to out-of-school suspension and expulsion.*

3

Chapter

Mrs. Jones, Sam's mother, calls the school and requests a meeting with Mrs. Rhodes, the school social worker. Mrs. Jones is obviously anxious and very concerned as she explains that her son, Sam, refused to ride the school bus to school today and stated, "I will never ride that bus again." When asked about this, Sam stated that other students were constantly pushing him, calling him names, and saying mean things about his family, and that he can't take it anymore. Mrs. Jones goes on to explain to Mrs. Rhodes that she has been receiving calls from school stating that Sam is beginning to exhibit behavior problems in his third-grade classroom. Mrs. Rhodes thanks Mrs. Jones for sharing this information with her and tells Mrs. Jones that she will check into the problem about the bus.

In her meeting with the principal, Mrs. Rhodes shares her concerns about Sam and the constant bullying on the bus. The principal indicates that he is aware of the "bus situation" but that the bus driver is not able to adequately supervise the children while driving, and the budget does not allow for a bus aide. The principal appears frustrated and says that he is open to suggestions.

S ometimes problem behavior occurs because students simply don't know how to act appropriately. (Gaustad, 1992, p. 2)

Introduction

Although school shootings have grabbed the headlines and at-tracted public attention to violence associated with schools, other forms of acting out or externalizing behaviors also demand the attention of educators and school social workers. These externalizing behaviors include classroom behavior problems, bullying, and peer sexual harassment. This chapter begins with an overview of each of these forms of externalizing behaviors, which are commonly found in schools today. It then presents a series of guidelines for assessing potentially violent students and several cautions in using these types of assessments. The chapter concludes with a discussion of proven or promising *student-focused* interventions shown to prevent or minimize externalizing behaviors, including alternatives to out-of-school suspension and expulsion. While this chapter concentrates on student-focused interventions, a number of prevention programs that target systems, as well as students, have been developed and shown to be effective in preventing or minimizing violent and disruptive behaviors. These school-based prevention programs are discussed in Chapter 7.

The Nature and Extent of Classroom Behavior Problems

Classroom behavior problems include students leaving their seats, calling out, being loud or disorderly, failing to comply with teacher directions, and cheating. Needless to say, classroom behavior problems are frequent concerns of teachers, as well as students. According to a 1994 survey, 46 percent of all secondary school teachers reported that classroom misbehavior interfered with their teaching, and 17 percent of tenth graders reported that misbehavior by other students interfered with their learning at least six times a week (National Education Goals Panel, 1997). Classroom behavior problems can result from a number of circumstances alone or in combination. For example, a student may assume the role of the "class clown" or "troublemaker" because taking on these roles in a classroom is much less stigmatizing than being the "stupid kid" who can't do his or her schoolwork. Far too often, students' classroom behavior problems are provoked or exacerbated by their interactions with peers. For example, in the case vignette at the beginning of this chapter, Sam was being constantly bullied and taunted by other students on the school bus, and this bullying and taunting resulted in misbehavior in the classroom. A number of other situations may cause or contribute to classroom behavior problems. These include being the recipients of teachers' sarcastic and demeaning comments or low academic expectations or being so emotionally upset by difficulties or tensions at home that it is nearly impossible to concentrate on schoolwork.

The Nature and Extent of Bullying in Schools

In addition to classroom behavior problems, bullying is another example of externalizing behavior that demands the attention of educators and school social workers. In the United States, bullying has traditionally been viewed as a normal part of growing up. This attitude is perhaps best exemplified by the slogan "Kids will be kids!" However, bullying should be recognized for what it is—peer child abuse (Arnette & Walsleben, 1998). Bullying refers to unprovoked physical or psychological abuse of an individual by one student or a group of students over time to create an ongoing pattern of harassment and abuse

(Batsche & Knoff, 1994; Hoover, Oliver, & Thomson, 1993; Olweus, 1991). Bullying includes direct behaviors such as teasing, taunting, threatening, hitting, and stealing, as well as indirect behaviors such as causing a student to be socially isolated by spreading rumors about that student (Smith & Sharp, 1994). Boys are reported to be victims of bullying at a higher rate than girls (Furlong, Chung, Bates, & Morrison, 1995), and bullying appears to peak in the middle school/junior high years (Batsche & Knoff, 1994). Students are bullied at school for a variety of reasons. Girls who are viewed by their peers as physically unattractive or who do not dress stylishly are often victims of bullying. Girls who are physically well-developed or do not "fit in" in some other way are also more likely to be bullied. Boys are often victimized if they do not fit a stereotypic macho male image. Students who have a different religion, who wear unique and unusual clothing, or who exhibit physical weaknesses and differences in appearance are also more likely to be bullied in school (Furlong et al., 1995; Shakeshift et al., 1995).

The act of bullying has both short- and long-term implications for both victims and perpetrators. Victims of chronic bullying have poorer grades and increased rates of truancy and dropping out. They may experience a loss of self-esteem and feelings of isolation that can last into adulthood (Hazler, 1994). Moreover, victims of chronic bullying may push students into starting fights or bringing weapons to school "to exact vengeance on their tormentors" (p. 39). The detrimental impact of bullying extends even beyond its victims. For example, students who witness bullying are often intimidated and fearful that it will eventually happen to them, particularly if school personnel do not act on the bullying. Witnesses to bullying may also perform poorly in the classroom because their attention is focused on how they can avoid being harmed in school rather than on their school work (Chandler, Nolin, & Davies, 1995). Bullies themselves are at increased risk for negative outcomes. For example, bullies are five times more likely than their classmates to wind up in juvenile court, to be convicted of crimes, and, when they become adults, to have children with aggression problems

(Hazler, 1994). Olweus (1993) found that 60 percent of students characterized as bullies in grades six to nine had at least one criminal conviction by age 24.

Since bullying involves harassment by powerful children against children who are less powerful, rather than a conflict between peers of relatively equal status, conflict resolution strategies such as mediation may not be effective (Limber & Nation, 1998). First, school social workers must make every effort, and encourage other school personnel to make similar efforts, to protect the victim from harassment. The primary response in dealing with bullies and their parents is to talk with bullies individually and tell them in absolute terms that bullying will not be tolerated and that it will end. In working with victims of bullying and their parents, it is important to remember that the typical victim has been threatened with more bullying if he or she "tattles." Fear from such threats causes many victims to decide to suffer quietly, and they ask their parents *not* to contact the school (Olweus, 1993). Effective interventions that are available to school social workers to minimize bullying, as well as other externalizing behaviors, are discussed later in this chapter.

The Nature and Extent of Peer Sexual Harassment in Schools

Peer sexual harassment is another serious concern facing educators and school social workers. A major study of peer sexual harassment reported that 85 percent of girls and 76 percent of boys have experienced some form of sexual harassment in school and that 25 percent have been targeted "often" (American Association of University Women [AAUW], 1993). The types of peer sexual harassment in this AAUW study ranged from nonphysical forms such as making sexual comments, spreading sexual rumors, and flashing, to physical forms such as touching, grabbing, and pinching. The most common form of harassment, reported by 65 percent of girls and 42 percent of boys, was being the target of sexual comments, jokes, gestures, or looks. The second most common form of harassment, reported by 65 percent of girls and 42 percent of boys, was being touched, grabbed, or pinched in a sexual way. The AAUW study found that a child's first experience of sexual harassment is most likely to occur in middle/junior high school and that girls suffer more negative effects as a result of peer sexual harassment than boys. For example, girls reported "not wanting to go to school" (33 percent), "not wanting to talk as much in class" (32 percent), and "finding it hard to pay attention in school" (28 percent) as outcomes of being sexually harassed at school. Sixty-four percent of girls reported experiencing "embarrassment," 52 percent reported feeling "self-conscious," and 43 percent of girls reported feeling less confident of themselves as a result of sexual harassment.

The AAUW also reported a number of troubling findings related to the attitudes of perpetrators and school personnel. The majority of these perpetrators responded that their behaviors were "just part of school life," that "a lot of people do it," and that "it's no big deal" (AAUW, 1993). This indifferent attitude extends to adults in schools since teachers and other school staff rarely, if ever, intervene to stop peer sexual harassment in schools (Batsche & Knoff, 1994; Hoover, Oliver, & Hazler, 1992; Shakeshift et al., 1995; Stein, 1995). For example, in a study conducted by Shakeshift et al., a female respondent stated, "In science class, the boys snap our bras. The [male] teacher doesn't really care. He doesn't say anything . . . the boys just laugh" (p. 42).

What are school officials currently doing to minimize peer sexual harassment? While the threat of litigation has resulted in a growing number of school districts enacting polices against peer sexual harassment, the use of lawsuits as a primary intervention strategy for addressing this problem is inadequate. Rather than focusing on lawsuits, Kopels and Dupper (1999) argued that interventions should be proactive and comprehensive and should "focus on the elimination of factors that contribute to a hostile school environment" (p. 454). These interventions should include the development of clear policies against peer sexual harassment; grievance procedures; appropriate assistance to victims; and sensitivity training for students, parents, and teachers.

Guidelines for Assessing Potentially Violent Students

Given the increase in episodes of school violence in recent years, it is becoming increasingly important for school officials to be able to identify potentially violent students. Table 3.1 provides guidelines for assessing these students. However, school social workers are obligated to make sure school officials know that any assessment tool designed to identify students who may be at risk of violence can be misused and even abused. It is important to remember that any one risk factor will not identify every violent student and that each of these risk factors taken individually has a high probability of misidentifying students as potentially violent. Instead, school social workers and other school staff should focus on students exhibiting multiple high-risk factors (Juhnke et al., 1999). On the other hand, some individual risk factors warrant immediate attention even if other risk factors are not present and the student is not perceived as violent. For example, any student experiencing symptoms resulting from substance abuse or dependence should be treated immediately, or students making violent threats toward others should be required to undergo a comprehensive assessment and parental conferencing (Juhnke et al., 1999).

Proven Student-Focused Interventions/Programs That Focus on Externalizing Behavior Problems

Cognitive-behavioral (C-B) interventions have been shown to be particularly effective in minimizing externalizing behavior problems in school settings. Elliott (1998) concluded that cognitive-behavioral approaches are generally effective while supportive or insight-oriented programs like psychotherapy and

Table 3.1   Guidelines for Assessing Potentially Violent Students

Violent Drawings or Writings. Violent students often indicate their intentions before acting violently via drawings or writings. Counselors learning of such violent drawings or writings should not easily dismiss such violent expressions. Violent poems, letters to friends, or letters to the intended victim are clear indications of violent potential. Hence, further assessment is warranted whenever a student uses age inappropriate violent drawings or writings.

Threats of Violence toward Others. Any threat of violence toward others should be immediately assessed and appropriate intervention actions should be taken to insure safety. Direct threats such as, "I'm going to kill him" as well as veiled threats such as, "Something big is going to happen to you after school" clearly are inappropriate and warrant immediate assessment and intervention. Threats should be assessed for: (a) lethality, (b) the degree to which a violent plan exists, and (c) the student's ability to secure the indicated weapon or harm instrument (e.g., poison, automobile). Any threat indicated by a student which is realistic, well planned, and highly lethal should be considered viable.

Past Violent Behaviors or Aggressive History. Students who have been violent in the past or have demonstrated aggressive behaviors toward others are at greater risk of repeating such behaviors. Thus, these students are noted as being at greater risk for future violent behaviors.

Recent Relationship Break. Students who have recently experienced a relationship break (e.g., being jilted by a girlfriend or best friend) have an increased likelihood of being violent.

Isolation. The vast majority of students who isolate themselves from peers or who appear friendless typically are not violent. However, one high-risk factor which has been strongly correlated with violent behaviors toward school peers is isolation. For this reason, students isolating themselves or reporting feelings of being isolated from others should be considered at greater risk.

Teased or Perceptions of Being Teased, Harassed, or "Picked On." Violent students often have a hypersensitivity toward criticism. These students report perceptions of being teased, harassed or being picked on by those they were violent toward. Therefore, students indicating feelings that they are being teased, harassed, or "picked on" should be assessed to determine whether or not they either intend to harm or fantasize about harming others.

Animal Torturing. There exists a high correlation between students who torture animals and violence. Students who regularly torture animals or intentionally inflict harm upon animals should be assessed for violent ideation toward others.

(continued)

Table 3.1 *(Continued)*

Substance Abuse. Although substance abuse does not cause students to be violent, students under the influence of psychoactive substances often fail to think logically and experience increased impulsivity. Thus, there exists a strong correlation between substance abuse and violent behaviors.

Familial Stressors. Familial stressors can engender feelings of frustration, anger, and hopelessness among students as well as adults.

Low School Interest. The genesis of this risk factor could come from any of a multitude of reasons which by themselves may not evoke violent behaviors. However, in combination with other possible violence related risk factors noted within this scale, students presenting with low school interest may have an inability to perform as well as they desire to and may feel frustrated by such inability. Additionally, these students may perceive themselves as belittled by those performing more favorably. Thus, when challenged to increase performance or when feeling harassed by those performing at higher levels, these students may become violent. For these reasons, this factor has been included.

Social Withdrawal. Withdrawal from peers and familial supports can indicate the student is experiencing any of a number of concerns (e.g., depression, helplessness) which warrant assessment and intervention. When combined with other risk factors, social withdrawal may signal potential violence toward others.

Inappropriate Use or Access to Firearms. Students who inappropriately use firearms by shooting at people, homes, or vehicles or have improper, unsupervised firearm access have a clear potential to harm others and act violently. No student should be allowed to posses a gun or weapon on school property or at school-related functions (e.g., dances, sporting events). Given the general impulsiveness of students and the dangers of immediate access to lethal weapons, this factor is one of the most important which should be assessed.

Noted by Peers as Being "Different." On many occasions after student violence, peers and others will note that the perpetrating student was labeled as being "different" from peers or being associated with some group. Hence, students frequently labeled by peers as being "weird," "strange," "geeky," and so on may be at increased risk for violent behaviors.

Source: From *Assessing Potentially Violent Students*, by G. A. Juhnke, W. B. Charkow, J. Jordan, R. C. Curtis, R. G. Liles, B. M. Gmutza, et al., 1999, Greensboro, NC: ERIC Document Reproduction Service No. ED435894. This document is in the public domain.

intensive casework approaches are generally ineffective. C-B interventions:

1. Address the sequence of interactions as well as the role of cognitive distortions that result in the misbehavior (Henggeler, Schoenwald, Borduin, Rowland, & Cunningham, 1998).
2. Focus on the development of social competence, such as the ability to get along with others and cope with problems in an empathic and considerate manner (Cornell, 1999).

C-B interventions focus on the relationship between an individual's beliefs, expectancies, perceptions, and attributions about himself or herself, as well as on that individual's feelings and behavior. These interventions consider the influence of others in the environment on the individual's thoughts, feelings, and behaviors (Henggeler et al., 1998) and are, therefore, congruent with the ecological perspective. They also involve the implementation of a wide variety of techniques. Several of the more widely used C-B techniques, as well as descriptions of each technique, can be found in Table 3.2.

Hoagwood and Erwin (1997), in their 10-year review of the literature on school-based mental health services for children, found that only 16 out of 228 studies met their rigorous criteria of randomized assignment, inclusion of a control group, and use of standardized outcome measures. These authors cited the "school survival" group treatment program (Dupper & Krishef, 1993) as one of the 16 studies that met these three criteria. (See a detailed description in the School Survival Group box on pages 52–53; the complete School Survival Group curriculum can be found in the Appendix.)

The programs described in the following section were included because they have been formally evaluated (e.g., a comparison group design was used) and found to be effective with school-age children in school settings. Some focus on prevention while others are more remedial in nature. Several

Table 3.2   Cognitive-Behavioral Strategies

Modeling	The social worker verbalizes his or her appraisal of the situation and offers various solutions and consequences of each solution to the problem.
Role-play exercises	Students are provided with an opportunity to practice interpersonal social-cognitive skills as well as increase their skills in perspective taking.
Behavioral contingencies	Students are given rewards to modify the frequency and standards of self-evaluation.
Self-monitoring and self-instruction	Students are assisted in accurately monitoring their arousal states, recognizing situations that typically provide intense feelings of anger and frustration, and using inhibitory self-directives to slow down the automaticity of their response. For example, the school social worker models and teaches students specific skills (either individually or in small groups) and enlists the support of the parents/guardians to observe and reinforce those behaviors through the use of a weekly chart.
Problem-solving training	Students are taught to describe the problem, determine the goals, generate alternative solutions, evaluate the solutions, choose a solution, design and practice a plan, and implement the plan.

Source: Adapted from *Multisystemic Treatment of Antisocial Behavior in Children and Adolescents*, (pp. 194–203), by S. W. Henggeler, S. K. Schoenwald, C. M. Borduin, M. D. Rowland, and P. B. Cunningham, 1998, New York: Guilford Press; and "Cognitive-Behavioral Therapies with Youth," by P. C. Kendall, 1993, *Journal of Consulting and Clinical Psychology, 61,* pp. 235–247.

School Survival Group

The school survival group is for middle/junior high school students with school behavior problems. The school survival group is based on several tenets of social cognitive theory. According to this theory, all human beings are doing the best that they can, given what they know about themselves and their world; all behavior is the result of people's best effort to interpret events and solve problems as they interact with their environment (Brower & Nurius, 1993). The primary goal of the school survival group is to increase participant's conscious awareness of the distorted social cognitions that underlie their unproductive school behavior. This group treatment program focuses on changing students' perceptions about the amount of personal control they have over their school behavior. The notion of choice is emphasized throughout the group sessions. Group members learn that there are a number of ways they can respond to conflictual situations involving peers and adults at school and that the ways in which they respond result in certain consequences, both positive and negative. It is emphasized that students, given their relatively low status in the school, will always "lose" if they engage in power struggles with teachers and school administrators. Consequently, group members are taught to think before they act. They also learn to recognize and label feelings and to recognize the difference between having feelings and acting on feelings.

Each of the 10 group sessions is highly structured with specific content to be taught and discussed. The groups meet once a week for 40 to 50 minutes over a period of 10 consecutive weeks. The first phase of the school survival group, sessions 1 through 5, focuses on increasing students' cognitive awareness of unproductive ways of thinking and acting in conflictual school situations. To accomplish this, group members are taught the transactional analysis (TA) concepts of "life scripts," "games," and "ego states" and the Adlerian goals of misbehavior (i.e., attention, power, revenge, to be left alone, and excitement). These concepts are especially helpful because they are easy to understand and they provide a means for analyzing destructive communication patterns. It is assumed that once group members understand the patterns and motivations underlying their thoughts and behaviors, they will feel empowered to change their unproductive ways of thinking and behaving. The second phase of this group, sessions 6 and 7, focuses on learning and implementing a structured problem-solving process that emphasizes choices and options. The third and final phase of this group, sessions 8 through 10, focuses on the acquisition of specific school survival skills. A number of role-plays are used to model how to work through conflictual situations involving peers or adults in schools. Group members are also given homework (e.g., completion of a self-monitoring checklist) to complete between group sessions. As an incentive, students who attended each weekly session are invited to a pizza party at the conclusion of the final group session. See Appendix for a detailed, session-by-session description of the school survival group.

Findings from an initial experiment supported the short-term effectiveness of the school survival group (Dupper & Krishef, 1993). A second field experiment further developed and tested the effectiveness of the school survival group (Dupper, 1998). It was discovered that students who participated in this group reported a shift from a more external to a more internal locus of control. This finding is important because a shift to a more internal locus of control has been shown to be positively correlated with school success in other studies.

Source: Excerpted from "An Alternative to Suspension for Middle School Youths with Behavior Problems. Findings from a 'School Survival' Group," by D. R. Dupper, 1998, *Research on Social Work Practice, 8,* pp. 354–366.

programs were included because they were specifically designed for culturally diverse student populations, an important focus of school social work practice. For more specific information on the methodology used (e.g., sample size, ethnicity of participants) to determine the effectiveness of programs discussed in the following section, refer to the original source cited for each program.

Interpersonal Cognitive Problem Solving (ICPS)

One of the best-known cognitive-behavioral programs is *Interpersonal Cognitive Problem Solving* (ICPS). Also known as "I Can Problem Solve," ICPS is a 12-week interpersonal cognitive problem-solving program designed for children from preschool to sixth grade. ICPS uses games, didactic discussion, and group interaction techniques to teach children communication and decision-making skills (Greenberg, Domitrovich, & Bumbarger, 2000). According to Greenberg el al. (2000), the program consists of eight weeks of daily 20-minute lessons combined with teacher (or parent) training in "problem-solving dialoguing," an informal style of communication meant to foster the exercise of newly learned problem-solving skills. The core skills of ICPS are the ability to generate multiple solutions to interpersonal problems, the ability to consider consequences to decisions or actions, and the ability to consider others' perspectives as a consideration in decision making. ICPS has been widely replicated, and several independent studies have supported the cognitive and behavioral gains of students trained in the curriculum (Callahan, 1992; Weddle & Williams, 1993). Shure (1997) reports that ICPS is effective in reducing children's impulsiveness and disruptiveness and in increasing their cooperativeness and prosocial behaviors in the classroom, at home, and with peers.

Second Step

Second Step is a violence-prevention social skills curriculum designed to help children develop empathic skills, impulse control skills, and anger management skills to increase social competence and reduce impulsiveness and aggressive behavior (Larson, 1994). The Second Step curriculum consists of 30 lessons, 35 minutes each, taught once or twice per week in a classroom setting. Lessons consist of photograph lesson cards accompanied by a scenario that forms the basis for discussion and role-plays. A team of researchers from the University of Washington recently concluded, "The Second Step violence prevention curriculum appears to lead to a moderate observed decrease in physically aggressive behavior and an increase in neutral and prosocial behavior in school" (D. C. Grossman et al., 1997). Second Step is currently being implemented in more than 10,000 schools in the United States and Canada (Portner, 1997).

Multisystemic Therapy (MST)

Multisystemic Therapy (MST) is an intensive family- and community-based treatment that addresses the known causes of serious antisocial behaviors in youth and their families (Henggeler, 1997). MST has met a set of rigorous scientific standards and has been designated as an effective, model "blueprint" program in preventing violence by the Center for the Study and Prevention of Violence at the University of Colorado at Boulder. The MST approach is significantly different from more traditional strategies developed to treat serious antisocial behavior in adolescents because MST "focuses first on improving psychosocial functioning for youth and their families so that the need for out-of-home child placements is reduced or eliminated" (Henggeler, 1997, p. 1). The goal of the MST approach is to provide an integrative, cost-effective family-based treatment that results in positive outcomes for adolescents who demonstrate serious antisocial behavior. It accomplishes this goal by treating those factors in the youth's environment that are contributing to his or her behavior problems. These factors may include individual characteristics (e.g., poor problem-solving skills), family relations (e.g., inept discipline), peer relations (e.g., association with deviant peers), and school performance (e.g., academic difficulties)

(Kumpfer, 1999). MST measures success "in terms of reduced re-cidivism rates among participating youth, improved family and peer relations, decreased behavioral problems, and decreased rates of out-of-home placements" (Henggeler, 1997, p. 2). Re-search has shown that MST is more effective than usual commu-nity treatment for inner-city juvenile offenders. Specifically, youth who received MST "had fewer arrests, reported fewer criminal offenses, and spent an average of 10 fewer weeks in de-tention during a 59-week follow-up" (Henggeler, 1997, p. 2).

Promoting Alternative Thinking Strategies (PATHS)

The *Promoting Alternative Thinking Strategies* (PATHS) curriculum is another model "blueprint" program that has met a rigorous set of scientific standards established by the Center for the Study and Prevention of Violence at the University of Colorado at Boulder (Greenburg, Kusche, Cook, & Quamma, 1995). Ac-cording to Greenberg, Domitrovich, and Bumbarger (2000), PATHS is implemented, over a period of up to five years, by trained teachers with entire classrooms using a 131-lesson cur-riculum. The curriculum consists of three major units:

1. The Readiness and Self-Control Unit consisting of 12 les-sons.
2. The Feelings and Relationships Unit consisting of 56 lessons.
3. The Interpersonal Cognitive Problem-Solving Unit consist-ing of 33 lessons.

PATHS also intersperses lessons on building positive self-esteem and improving communications throughout these three major units. Parent letters and home activity assignments are used to encourage generalization of the skills to the home environment. Greenberg and Kusche (1997) found that second and third grade regular education students who participated in PATHS showed significant improvements in social problem solving and understanding of emotions; they continued to

show one-year follow-up improvements on a number of outcome measures related to social competencies. Studies of PATHS
have indicated that it is effective across both regular and special
needs children in both urban and rural settings (Greenberg et al.,
2000).

Positive Adolescents Choices Training (PACT)

Positive Adolescents Choices Training (PACT) is "unique in that it is
culturally relevant and aimed at reducing aggression and victimization in high-risk youths" (Jenson & Howard, 1999,
p. 153). According to U.S. Departments of Education and Justice (1999), PACT targets high-risk youth between the ages of
12 and 16 who have serious behavior problems or have a history of violence, victimization, or exposure to violence. PACT
was developed with sensitivity to the needs of African American youth; however, the techniques used in PACT are applicable
to multiethnic groups. PACT teaches skills in the areas of giving
constructive criticism, receiving negative feedback, and negoti-
ating in lessons that are delivered one or more times a week for
19 weeks to groups of no more than 10 students. Yung and
Hammond (1998) reported that PACT was found to be effective
in improving participants' ability to provide negative feedback
and in significantly reducing physical aggression in school. Another study reported that students receiving PACT instruction
reduced their antisocial and violent behavior by 38 percent relative to a comparison group (U.S. Departments of Education
and Justice, 1999).

Gang Resistance Education and Training (G.R.E.A.T.)

Gang Resistance Education and Training (G.R.E.A.T.) is a program
designed to reduce youth violence and gang membership
through a nine-lesson curriculum taught by law enforcement
officers to students in grades three through eight. G.R.E.A.T.
students learn about the consequences of gang and youth violence through structured exercises and interactive approaches

(U.S. Departments of Education and Justice, 1999). Arnette and Walsleben (1998) reported that students who received G.R.E.A.T. training demonstrated more prosocial behaviors and attitudes and were more attached to school and their parents than nonparticipants. Other researchers found a 4 percent reduction in drug use, a 3 percent reduction in total delinquency, and a 4.5 percent reduction in minor offenses in students who received G.R.E.A.T. training compared to students who did not

Table 3.3   **Contact Information for Student-Focused Interventions for Externalizing Behaviors**

- *Interpersonal Cognitive Problem Solving (ICPS)*
  Myrna Shure, PhD
  Telephone: (215) 762-7205
  E-mail: mshure@drexel.edu
  Ordering information:
  Research Press
  Telephone: (800) 519-2707
  E-mail: rp@researchpress.com
  www.researchpress.com
- *Second Step*
  Committee for Children
  Telephone: (800) 634-4449
  Fax: (206) 343-1445
  www.cfchildren.org
- *Multisystemic Therapy (MST)*
  Scott W. Henggeler, PhD
  (Contact) Keller Strother, President
  MST Services, Inc.
  Telephone: (843) 856-8226
  Fax: (843) 856-8227
  E-mail: keller@mstservices.com
- *The Promoting Alternative THinking Strategies (PATHS)*
  Mark T. Greenberg, PhD
  Telephone: (814) 863-0112
  E-mail: prevention@psu.edu
  www.psu.edu/dept/prevention/PATHS

- *Positive Adolescent Choices* Training (PACT)
  Betty R. Yung, PhD
  Telephone: (937) 775-4300
  Fax: (937) 775-4323
  E-mail: betty.yung@wright.edu
- *Gang Resistance Education and Training (G.R.E.A.T.)*
  Telephone: (800) 726-7070
  E-mail: great@atfhq.atf.treas.gov
  www.atf.treas.gov/great/great.htm
- *Anger Coping Program*
  John Lochman, PhD
  Telephone: (205) 348-5083
  Fax: (205) 348-8648
  E-mail: jlochman@gp.as.ua.edu
- *Brain Power Program*
  Cynthia Hudley, PhD
  Telephone: (805) 893-8324
  Fax: (805) 893-7264
  E-mail: hudley@education.ucsb.edu
- *Think First*
  Jim Larson, PhD
  Telephone: (414) 472-5412
  Fax: (414) 472-1863

receive this training (U.S. Departments of Education and Justice, 1999).

Several other programs have been ranked among the top 50 percent in terms of strong program effects by at least one of three groups of researchers, according to the *1999 Annual Report on School Safety* by the U.S. Departments of Education and Justice (1999). These programs include the Anger Coping Program, the BrainPower Program (1999), and Think First. Contact information for programs discussed in this section can be found in Table 3.3. Readers may obtain more detailed information about each program by contacting the program director or publisher.

Alternatives to Out-of-School Suspension and Expulsion

School shootings over the past several years, especially the carnage at Columbine High School in Littleton, Colorado, have made the issue of school violence a major public concern across communities in the United States. Under the Improving America's Schools Act, to receive Title I funds from the U.S. Department of Education, a state must have a law requiring the expulsion, for a period of not less than one year, of students who bring weapons to school (Ingersoll & LeBoeuf, 1997). While this immediate removal of students who pose an immediate danger to others in school is justifiable, there has been a near epidemic of suspensions and expulsions for nonweapon-related student offenses such as interpersonal conflicts (Skiba & Peterson, 1999). In fact, "zero tolerance" discipline policies resulted in more than 3.1 million suspensions and 87,000 expulsions during the 1998 school year (Civil Rights Project, 2000). Of particular concern to school social workers is the fact that African American and Latino children tend to be suspended in disproportionate numbers for more discretionary offenses, such as "defiance of authority" and "disrespect of authority." According to information from this project, "this damage is particularly acute for children who are considered 'at-risk' for school failure, and often has the effect of pushing them out of school completely" (p. 7). School social workers should oppose the wholesale application of zero-tolerance discipline policies because these policies create a school environment that exacerbates those very behaviors that school officials seek to alleviate. These policies further alienate students and result in situations in which excluded youth often lack parental supervision and repeat the same disruptive behaviors in the home and community (Ingersoll & LeBoeuf, 1997). The challenge for school social workers is to assume a greater role in advocating discipline policies designed to eliminate certain behaviors rather than the students themselves. In addition to pushing students out of school through suspensions and expulsions, many states rely on physical discipline as a response to student misbehavior. While it gets little attention, corporal punishment remains legal in 23 states with African American students 2.5 times more likely to be paddled than White students (Wilgoren, 2001). School social workers need to advocate more humane and rational discipline policies and work to eliminate corporal punishment in those states where it is legally sanctioned. Several Web sites dedicated to the elimination of corporal punishment in schools can be found in the Additional Resources section at the end of this chapter.

Findings from one study (Dupper, 1994a) indicated nearly unanimous support for school social workers' involvement in the development (99 percent) and implementation (83 percent) of alternatives to suspension. However, only 39 percent of the school social work respondents stated that they were actually involved in these activities. Two major barriers to their involvement identified in this study were:

1. Lack of time.
2. The need for additional training and information.

Based on these findings, it appears that school social workers need more information about alternatives to suspension that are effective and congruent with social work values. Fortunately, a growing number of alternatives to out-of-school suspension and expulsion, congruent with social work values, show promise in increasing appropriate behavior or decreasing the frequency or intensity of student misbehavior. These alternatives include in-school suspension programs, conflict resolution and mediation programs, and school-based mentoring programs.

Rather than isolating students for punishment, the most effective *in-school suspension programs* include counseling components, conflict resolution strategies, and computer tutorial programs (Ingersoll & LeBoeuf, 1997). *Conflict resolution* and *mediation programs* have also been shown to be effective in resolving the inevitable conflicts that emerge among peers in schools. The essence of conflict resolution and mediation programs is to "teach students to listen carefully and respectfully to another person's point of view, accept that there are meaningful differences, and develop creative, mutually satisfactory solutions" (Cornell, 1999, p. 6). Peer mediation relies on an impartial third party to help students use problem-solving steps to negotiate and reach a mutually beneficial agreement (Chittooran, 2000). According to Chittooran, the peer mediator's role is to oversee the process, remain unbiased, and help the disputants work together to solve problems. Peer mediators are usually nominated by peers or teachers because they are respected and trusted by their peers and have demonstrated leadership and communication skills. A study by the Ohio Commission on Dispute Resolution and Conflict Management (1994) found conflict resolution and mediation programs to be effective in improving student attitudes toward conflict, increasing understanding of nonviolent problem-solving methods, and enhancing communication skills. Conflict resolution and mediation programs have also been shown to significantly reduce the number of school suspensions for fighting (Lam, 1989) and to improve students' ability to manage conflicts (Deutsch et al., 1992).

Another student-focused intervention that has been shown to be effective in dealing with students with behavioral problems are *school-based mentoring programs*. School-based mentoring is one of the most promising and rapidly expanding approaches to mentoring. The goal of successful mentoring programs is the formation of an ongoing, one-on-one relationship with a caring adult that will benefit the younger person (School Safety Update, 1997). To facilitate the building of strong relationships with adult role models, schools must recruit adults as mentors/advocates/tutors for students with behavior problems. Mentors may be recruited formally or informally from corporations or local businesses, professional organizations, faith communities, law enforcement, college faculties, or retirement communities. Teachers and counselors can also be assigned as mentors to students (McPartland & Slavin, 1990). Since African American and Hispanic males are disproportionately at-risk of being suspended or expelled, it is particularly important that African American and Hispanic men be recruited as mentors. Big Brothers/Big Sisters of America (BBBSA), the largest mentoring program operating in the United States, projects that by 2003 it will have established 100,000 school-based matches, about one-third of the agency's total (Herrera, 1999). Findings from an evaluation of the Big Brothers/Big Sisters Program, indicate that mentored youth were less likely to engage in drug or alcohol use, resort to violence, or skip school and were more likely to improve their grades and their relationships with family and friends (Grossman & Garry, 1997).

School social workers can assume a number of roles and tasks in implementing any of the programs and interventions discussed in this chapter. As advocates, school social workers must inform school officials about the detrimental impact of exclusionary policies and practices, such as suspension and expulsion, and encourage school boards to implement proven or promising alternatives to suspension and expulsion, particularly targeting disadvantaged and culturally diverse students. These advocacy efforts may involve meeting the school administrative team or testifying before the school board about the goals and effectiveness of a given intervention program. School social workers, in collaboration with other professionals, may also find it necessary to write grants to fund new programs. (A number of resources on grant writing can be found in the Additional Resources section at the end of this chapter.) Once funded, school social workers can be directly involved in delivering the program to students either as a group leader or coleader. School social workers may also be indirectly involved by providing ongoing consultation (see Chapter 9 for a detailed description of school social workers as consultants) and guidance to teachers or other school professionals involved in the delivery of the program. For more detailed information and guidelines on successfully planning, implementing, and evaluating new programs, see Chapter 12.

Summary

Classroom behavior problems, bullying, and peer sexual harassment are three forms of externalizing behavior problems commonly found in schools today. While it is essential that school social workers be able to identify and intervene with potentially violent students, they should also be aware and make other school professionals aware of the fact that any assessment tool designed to identify students who may be at risk of violence can be misused and even abused. Cognitive-behavioral interventions have been shown to be particularly effective in reducing externalizing behavior problems in school settings. School social workers should be aware of and advocate the implementation of exemplary student-focused interventions that have been shown to be effective in reducing a number of externalizing behaviors such as those discussed in this chapter. School social workers may be directly or indirectly involved in the delivery of a given program.

Questions for Discussion

1. Why might students exhibit behavior problems in classrooms?
2. What negative effects result from chronic bullying? From peer sexual harassment?

3. What concrete steps can school social workers take to protect victims of bullying?

4. What concrete steps can school social workers take to minimize peer sexual harassment in schools?

5. What programs have been shown to be effective in helping students manage their anger?

Refer to the case study at the beginning of this chapter:

1. What immediate action can be taken to help Sam?

2. What interventions may be helpful to reduce this bullying behavior on the school bus?

3. How can the lack of supervision on the bus best be addressed?

4. In what ways should Sam's parents be involved in addressing this problem?

Additional Resources

Grant Writing

Chavkin, N. F. (1997). Funding school-linked services through grants: A beginner's guide to grant writing. *Social Work in Education, 19*, 164–175.

Mathis, E. D. & Doody, J. E. (1994). *Grant proposals: A primer for writers*. Washington, DC: National Catholic Educational Association.

White, G. & Morgan, N. (1992). A coordinated development program for K-12 schools. *Phi Delta Kappan, 74*, 260–262.

Bullying

- *Preventing bullying: A manual for schools and communities* can be obtained from the U.S. Department of Education at:
  www.ed.gov/pubs/index.html
- Mullin-Rindler, N. (1998). Selected bibliography of children's books about teasing and bullying for grades K-5. Available through Center for Research on Women.
- The Center for Effective Collaboration and Practice (CECP) supports and promotes the production, exchange, and use of knowledge about effective practices for children and

youth with emotional and behavioral problems at risk of school and social failure. See "Safeguarding our children: An action guide" available at:
www.air.org/cecp/guide/actionguide

- American Academy of Pediatrics (AAP) & American Psychological Association. (1995). *Raising Children to Resist Violence: What You Can Do* (brochure). Available on-line at:
www.aap.org/family/parents/resist.htm

Peer Sexual Harassment

- "Sexual harassment guidance: Harassment of students by school employees, other students, or third parties" U.S. Department of Education available by calling: (202) 205-5413 or(800) 421-3481
- U.S. Department of Education, Office of Civil Rights. (1999). *Protecting students from harassment and hate crime: A guide for schools.* Washington, DC: U.S. Department of Education. (ED 422 671)

Alternatives to Out-of-School Suspension and Expulsion

- The National Center for the Study of Corporal Punishment and Alternatives (NCSCPA) conducts research and consults about physical and emotional maltreatment of students, and about school discipline and school violence. Staff provide clinical and psychoeducational evaluations of victimized students, offer expert testimony, and conduct advocacy activities in workshops for educators, parents, and mental health professionals. Publications list available at:
www.temple.edu/education/pse/NCSCPA.html
- Project NoSpank is a resource for students, parents, educators, health care professionals, policymakers, and everyone who believe that children's optimal development occurs in nurturing and violence-free environments and that every child has the right to grow and learn in such an environment. Project NoSpank is the Web presence of Parents and Teachers Against Violence in Education (PTAVE). Contact by e-mail or see Web site at:
ptave@nospank.org
www.nospank.org
- Center for Effective Discipline
www.stophitting.com
- National Institute for Dispute Resolution
e-mail: nidr@nidr.org
- The National Resource Center for Youth Mediation has extensive training materials. (800)249-6884

Internalizing Behavior Problems

In this chapter, we discuss:

- *Anxiety and fearfulness.*
- *Loneliness/shyness.*
- *Grieving.*
- *Depression and suicide.*
- *Proven or promising student-focused interventions designed to address internalizing behavior problems.*

4

Chapter

Lakesha is a fourth-grade student. She was referred to Lori, the school social worker, because of an increase in absences and falling grades over the past several months. While interviewing Lakesha, Lori discovers that she appears to be very anxious about taking tests and has been having stomachaches on those days when she has to take a test. Lori also discovered that Lakesha is avoiding homework assignments out of fear of not doing them "well enough." Lori infers that Lakesha's perfectionism has become so crippling that she is now avoiding school altogether. Lori also discovers that Lakesha's teachers interpret her behavior as apathy and have adopted a punitive attitude toward her when she is at school. During their latest session, Lori finds out that Lakesha's mother is an alcoholic who refuses to seek any help. Lakesha begs Lori not to contact her mother.

A t any one time, between 10 and 15 percent of the child and adolescent population have some symptoms of depression. (Shaffer et al., 1996)

Introduction

While school officials focus most of their attention on students with acting out or externalizing behavior problems, many students "suffer quietly" in our schools with little or no assistance. This chapter highlights several forms of internalizing behaviors found in schools today including anxious and fearful students, lonely/shy/withdrawn students, grieving students, and depressed/suicidal students. It also discusses a number of standardized instruments that can be used to assess these behaviors. The chapter concludes with a discussion of proven or promising student-focused interventions that have been shown to prevent or minimize internalizing behaviors.

Anxiety and Fearfulness

Today's preteens and teens exhibit a higher level of anxiety compared to children treated for psychiatric disorders 50 years ago (Twenge, 2000). Anxiety impacts students' physical, mental, emotional, social, and spiritual health. A number of factors may cause or exacerbate anxiety in students including illness, injury, inadequate nutrition, low levels of physical fitness, dysfunctional family lives, and an inability to find purpose in life or to understand how individual lives contribute to a much larger and grander universe (Brophy, 1996; Massey, 1998). As the case vignette illustrates, many children in school are anxious about home problems, and this anxiety is exacerbated by pressures in school. School conditions that may contribute to anxiety in students include being asked to answer academic questions, being asked to perform in public, engaging in activities that they know will be evaluated, changing schools or changing classes, pressures to excel in extracurricular activities, peer pressure, school size, lighting, temperature and ventilation, noise, crowding, sanitation and cleanliness, accessibility, and the personality and behavior of a teacher (Massey, 1998).

While many children experience some anxiety, an estimated 1 percent of all school-age children suffer from a type of anxiety that is largely irrational and out of proportion to the threat. These children are labeled "school phobic" (Terry, 1998). According to King and Ollendick (1989), all school phobias have the following basic characteristics: severe difficulty attending school; severe emotional upset including feeling ill when faced with the prospect of going to school; staying home from school with the parent's knowledge; and the absence of antisocial behaviors such as stealing, lying, and destructiveness.

A number of parent and teacher rating scales and checklists have been developed to help school social workers and other school professionals determine if a child's anxiety and fear are part of normal development or if an intervention is needed. The most frequently used instruments are *Achenbach's Child Behavior Checklist* (Achenbach, 1979), the *Behavior Problems Checklist* (Quay & Peterson, 1983), the *Fear Survey Schedule for Children* (Ollendick, 1983), the *Children's Manifest Anxiety Scale* (Reynolds & Richmond, 1978), the *Test Anxiety Scale for Children* (Sarason, Davidson, Lighhall, & Waite, 1958), and the *Preschool Observation Scale of Anxiety* (Glennon & Weisz, 1978). The *Preschool Observation Scale of Anxiety* helps in determining the conditions that contribute to fear and anxiety. For example, if a child's anxiety occurs only with a certain teacher, an intervention may consist of consultation with that particular teacher or a request to change teachers (King & Ollendick, 1989).

Loneliness/Shyness

Numbers of students experience feelings of loneliness that often result in poor peer relationships or exclusion from peers (Asher,

Parkhurst, Hymel, & Williams, 1990; Bullock, 1998). As a result of these poor peer relationships, lonely children may miss out on many opportunities to interact with peers and learn important lifelong skills; they may also be at increased risk for later problems (Bullock, 1998). Bullying and other forms of peer harassment may lead to feelings of loneliness. For example, in one study, kindergarten children who were victimized by peers (e.g., picked on, or physically or verbally attacked or taunted) reported higher levels of loneliness, distress, and negative attitudes toward school than nonvictimized children (Kochenderfer & Ladd, 1996).

Closely related to lonely students are those who are shy and withdrawn. Many relatively quiet students are well-adjusted academically and socially and content to work independently. Shyness becomes problematic when it leads to a pattern of behavior that includes a reluctance to enter social situations, discomfort and inhibition in the presence of others, exaggerated self-concern, unresponsiveness, an increasingly negative social self-concept, or a combination of these (Honig, 1987; Thompson & Rudolph, 1992). Bullock (1998) described a number of factors that may contribute to feelings of loneliness and problematic shyness in young children including: moving to a new school or neighborhood, losing a friend, losing an object or possession, experiencing the divorce of parents, experiencing the death of a pet or significant person, being rejected by peers, lacking the social skills to make friends, or possessing personal characteristics (e.g., shyness, anxiety, and low self-esteem) that contribute to difficulties in making friends.

Grieving

Death is a part of life and children will experience the deaths of loved ones, including pets, through illness or accidents. Separation from loved ones in any form results in grieving. Children who have suffered a loss often have difficulty coping with the school environment and may exhibit the following symptoms: a lack of concentration, an inability to complete tasks, fatigue, excessive displays of emotion, or a combination of these (McGlauflin, 1998).

Several standardized instruments have been developed to measure grief responses in children and adolescents. The *Hogan Parent /Sibling Inventory of Bereavement (HSIB)* is the preeminent grief instrument for adolescents. It has also been successfully applied to assessing aspects of children's grief. The *Loss Response List* measures physical, emotional, social, and cognitive responses to grief (Wheeler & Austin, 2000). N. B. Webb (1993) developed a comprehensive assessment for working with bereaved children that includes the following three categories of factors:

1. Individual factors (age, developmental stage, cognitive functioning, temperamental factors, past coping behaviors).
2. Death-related factors (type of death, contact with the deceased, expression of farewell, relationship to deceased, grief reactions).
3. Family/social/religious/cultural factors.

School social workers and other school professionals give students the opportunity to grieve their losses; they also work to create a school climate that is sensitive to the significant number of children experiencing loss on a regular basis (McGlauflin, 1998).

Depression and Suicide

Epidemiological studies have reported that up to 2.5 percent of children and up to 8.3 percent of adolescents in the United States suffer from depression (Birmaher et al., 1996). It also appears that depression is occurring earlier in life today than in past decades (Klerman & Weissman, 1989) and that early onset depression often persists, recurs, and continues into adulthood (Weissman, Wolk, & Goldstein, 1999).

In childhood, boys and girls appear to be at equal risk for depressive disorders; but during adolescence, girls are twice as likely as boys to develop depression (Birmaher et al., 1996). Children who develop major depression are more likely to have a family history of the disorder; they often have a parent who experienced depression at an early age (Harrington, Rutter, & Weissman, 1997). Depression in young people often co-occurs with anxiety, disruptive behavior, or substance abuse disorders (Angold & Costello, 1993), and with physical illnesses, such as diabetes (Kovacs, 1997). Depression in adolescents is of particular concern because clinically depressed adolescents are five times more likely to attempt suicide that their nondepressed peers (Portner, 2000a). Depressed adolescents are also at increased risk for substance abuse and suicidal behavior (Birmaher, Brent, & Benson, 1998; Ryan, Puig-Antich, & Ambrosini, 1987; Weissman et al., 1999).

In 1996, more teenagers and young adults died from suicide than from cancer, heart disease, AIDS, birth defects, stroke, pneumonia, influenza, and chronic lung disease combined ("Surgeon General's Call to Action," 1999). Suicide is now the second leading cause of death among youths 15 to 19 years of age and the third leading cause of death among youths 15 to 24 years of age (Hoyert, Kochanek, & Murphy, 1999). It has been estimated that one in 13 high school students attempts suicide and that for every teenager who commits suicide, 100 more will try (Kann et al., 1998). While teenage girls attempt suicide three times as often as boys, males are four times more likely to be successful in their attempts (Portner, 2000a). Several subgroups of students are at particular risk. The suicide rate among African American adolescent males, ages 15 to 19, increased 105 percent between 1980 and 1996. Thirty percent of all attempted or completed youth suicides are related to issues of sexual identity; gay and lesbian youth are two to three times more likely to commit suicide than other youth ("Surgeon General's Call To Action," 1999).

What factors account for this escalating rate of suicide among our youth? Sociologists and mental health experts point to a tangled web of cultural, psychological, and medical factors. These factors include a general sense of isolation and alienation from caring adults both at home and at school, a high divorce rate, parental abuse, poor impulse control stemming from exposure to television, the lack of access to mental health services, and the ready availability of handguns. According to the federal Bureau of Alcohol, Tobacco, and Firearms, there were 90 million guns in circulation in 1960 while today there are an estimated 200 million firearms in private hands. Substance abuse also plays a significant role. Autopsies of adolescent suicide victims show that one-third to one-half of them were under the influence of drugs or alcohol shortly before they killed themselves (Portner, 2000a).

Because depression in children and adolescents is associated with an increased risk of suicidal behaviors, it is essential that school social workers and other school professionals be alert to the symptoms of depression in children and adolescents (Shaffer et al., 1996; Weissman et al., 1999). Unfortunately, recognizing and diagnosing childhood and adolescent depression is difficult because the way in which symptoms of depression are communicated varies with the developmental stage of the child (Birmaher et al., 1998). For example, sulking and other behaviors typical of the adolescent years may be normal or may be symptoms of depression. The length and severity of any one or combination of symptoms is a critical factor in assessing childhood and adolescent depression. Table 4.1 lists some typical signs associated with depression in young children and in older children and teenagers.

Several standardized assessment tools have been designed to screen children and adolescents for possible depression. The *Children's Depression Inventory (CDI)* assesses symptoms of depression in children ages 8 to 17 years. The *Beck Depression*

Table 4.1   Signs That May Be Associated with Depression

Young children
- Pretending to be sick.
- Overactivity.
- Clinging to parents and refusing to go to school.
- Worrying that parents may die.

Older children and teenagers
- Sulking.
- Refusing to participate in family and social activities.
- Getting into trouble at school.
- Using alcohol or other drugs.
- Stop paying attention to their appearance.
- Becoming negative, restless, grouchy, aggressive, or feeling that no one understands them.

Source: Adapted from The Center for Mental Health Services, n.d., *Major Depression in Children and Adolescents.* Retrieved September 5, 2001, from www.mentalhealth.org/publications/allpubs/CA-0011/default.asp

Inventory (BDI) and the *Center for Epidemiologic Studies Depression (CES-D) Scale* assess symptoms of depression in adolescents. Contact information for each of these depression scales can be found in Table 4.2. If a child or youth screens positive on any of these standardized instruments, a referral to a specialist for a comprehensive diagnostic evaluation is warranted (Center for Mental Health Services, n.d.).

Table 4.2   Depression Scales for Children and Adolescents

Children's Depression Inventory
Developed by Kovacs, M. Available from Multi-Health Systems (MHS, Inc.), 65 Overlea Blvd., Suite 10, Toronto, Ontario M4H1P1 Canada; telephone: (800) 456-3003.

Beck Depression Inventory
Developed by Beck, A. Available from Psychological Corporation, 555 Academic Court, San Antonio, TX 78204; telephone: (210) 299-1061.

Center for Epidemiologic Studies Depression Scale
Developed by NIMH. Available from NIMH, 6001 Executive Boulevard, Room 8184, MSC 9663, Bethesda, MD 20892-9663; telephone: (301) 443-4513.

Proven or Promising Student-Focused Interventions Designed to Address Internalizing Behavior Problems

The following section discusses proven or promising student-focused interventions designed to address anxiety and fearfulness in students, loneliness and shyness, grieving students, and depressed/suicidal students.

One of the oldest and most respected school-based programs designed to identify and intervene with children who are at-risk for emotional and behavioral problems is the *Primary Mental Health Prevention (PMHP)* project (Cowen et al., 1996). (See the Primary Mental Health Prevention (PMHP) Project box on page 76 for a description of this exemplary program.)

Anxiety and Fearfulness

Several cognitive-behavioral (C-B) procedures (i.e., modeling, systematic desensitization, and flooding and implosive therapy) have been shown to be effective in reducing anxiety and fear in children and adolescents. All of these C-B procedures focus on helping students develop specific thinking skills and apply those skills whenever confronted with a particular feared stimulus event or object (Morris & Kratochwill, 1985). According to King and Ollendick (1989), modeling entails demonstrating nonfearful behavior in anxiety-producing situations and desired responses for handling the feared stimuli. Systematic desensitization consists of progressive relaxation training, the development of a hierarchy of fear-producing stimulus, and the systematic pairing of items that are feared with relaxation techniques (King & Ollendick, 1989). According to Morris and Kratochwill, flooding and implosive therapy call for a prolonged exposure to the most anxiety-evoking stimuli. However, ethical concerns have been raised about using such potentially aversive procedures with children.

One program developed specifically to reduce anxiety in children shows promise. The *Queensland Early Intervention and*

Primary Mental Health Prevention (PMHP) Project

PMPH has been teaching social problem-solving skills, assisting children with divorced parents, facilitating peer relationships, and encouraging cooperative learning for almost 40 years. *PMPH* is based on the premise that the traditional school-based mental health professional alone is inadequate to provide substantial assistance to the large number of children who require additional supports. *PMPH* addresses this problem by restructuring the role of the mental health professional and by using a cadre of paraprofessional child associates to work more intensively with children exhibiting early signs of maladjustment in a structured playroom environment. For each identified child, the core intervention component is the development of an ongoing interactive relationship with a trained paraprofessional child associate. Child associates are carefully selected and receive an intensive 24- to 36-hour training followed by continuing education workshops. The child associate meets with the child alone or in small groups once per week, over a period of 20 to 25 weeks, for 25 to 45 minutes per session. These meetings take place in a structured playroom equipped with items designed to encourage expressive play. The expression and exploration of all emotions is encouraged, with limits placed on inappropriate behavior. Child associates take advantage of opportunities for teaching life skills such as taking turns, following rules, and attending to a task. Weekly or biweekly supervisory meetings are held between the mental health professional and child associates. The *PMPH* project has been shown to be particularly successful with children who exhibit internalizing behaviors.

Source: Excerpted from "Preventing Mental Disorders in School-Age Children: A Review of the Effectiveness of Prevention Programs," by M. T. Greenberg, C. Domitrovich, and B. Bumbarger, 2000, Pennsylvania State University: Prevention Research Center for the Promotion of Human Development, College of Health and Human Development. Reprinted with permission.

Prevention of Anxiety Project is designed to "prevent the onset and development of anxiety problems in children by teaching them to utilize cognitive, behavioral, and physiological coping strategies while exposing them to increasingly fearful situations. The program is primarily focused on the individual child but includes three sessions with parents" (Greenberg et al., 2000, p. 32). A large-scale, longitudinal evaluation of the *Queensland Early Intervention and Prevention of Anxiety Project* found that anxious but nondisordered students who received this program had developed significantly fewer internalizing disorders compared to controls at six-month postintervention (Greenberg et al., 2000).

Another program that shows promise is *Stress Inoculation Training I*. This 13-session school-based program is designed to reduce "negative emotional arousal" and other psychological problems associated with stress by using cognitive restructuring, problem solving, and anxiety management (Greenberg et al., 2000). An evaluation of this program with a sample of high school youth who had anxiety problems found that students "with higher levels of stress before the intervention reported the most significant changes in anxiety and depressive symptoms [following the intervention]" (Greenberg et al., 2000, p. 33).

Loneliness/Shyness

Research that supports specific practices to assist lonely and shy children in school is weak (Brophy, 1996). However, a number of researchers (Brophy, 1995; Honig, 1987; McIntyre, 1989; Thompson & Rudolph, 1992) have generated lists of several very practical strategies that can be used to help shy students. As seen in Table 4.3, most of these strategies are best carried out by teachers. However, several strategies can be implemented by school social workers, including role playing where children are asked to interact with others in social situations in which they might otherwise be shy, and by using bibliotherapy materials such as "The Shy Little Girl" by P. Krasilovsky.

Table 4.3   Strategies for Helping Shy or Withdrawn Students

- Use interest inventories to determine interests of shy students, then follow up by using these interests as bases for conversations or learning activities.
- Display their (good) artwork or assignments for others to see in the classroom.
- Assign them as a partner to, or promote their friendship with, a classmate who is popular and engages in frequent contact with peers.
- Check with these students frequently if they are prone to daydreaming.
- Help shy children set social development goals and assist them by providing training in assertiveness, initiating interactions with peers, or other social skills.
- Provide them with information needed to develop social insight (e.g., explaining that new students often have trouble making friends at first, or that teasing does not necessarily mean that peers do not like you), suggesting ways for them to initiate productive peer contacts or to respond more effectively to peer initiations.
- Provide them with a designated role that will give them something to do and cause them to interact with others in social situations in which they might otherwise become shy and retreat to the fringes of the group.
- Teach them social "door openers" for greeting others and speaking to them in person or on the telephone, especially assertive requests ("Can I play, too?").
- Make time to talk with them each day, even if just for a few minutes, and listen carefully and respond specifically to what they tell you.
- Use bibliotherapy materials such as "The Shy Little Girl," a story by P. Krasilovsky about a sad and shy girl who becomes more outgoing. Shy children may need direct instruction in social skills, such as those included in various social skills training programs intended for elementary school students.

Source: From *"Working with Shy or Withdrawn Students"* (pp. 2–3), by J. Brophy, 1996. ERIC Document Reproduction Service No. ED402070. This document is in the public domain.

Grief

McGlauflin (1998) offers a list of recommendations for school professionals to help individual students, as well as to integrate the grief process into the entire school (see Table 4.4). One of the recommendations calls for a school social worker or other school professional to share an empathic statement with a child who has experienced a death or loss soon after his or her return to school.

Table 4.4   Recommendations for Integrating the Grief Process into the School Setting

Look at grieving as a valuable life skill. Learning to grieve the many losses that persons inevitably face throughout life is a valuable life skill. Using historic occasions such as Veteran's Day to discuss death can become "teachable moments" when classes can learn about grieving and its importance in life.

Learn to recognize opportunities. School social workers and other school professionals can create a "memorial" bulletin board to remember anniversaries of importance to individuals or the school community. Other grief opportunities are more spontaneous, such as times when children and adults make comments about people who have died, about changes in their lives, or express their yearnings for a better time. Responding with acceptance by saying "you still think of your dad a lot" or "it is still hard getting used to all the changes" can be a great relief to a griever.

Respect the consciousness of grief. Bereavement is a time of disorientation and a very different consciousness than people normally maintain, one that should be treated with gentleness and respect. This means accepting random thoughts that may seem unrelated to present reality, expecting silly mistakes, and allowing sudden shows of emotion. Communicating that all these responses are normal and to be expected is tremendously supportive.

Speak from a place of compassion, not pity. To create a climate of emotional safety in a school, staff and children should reach out to one another with compassion— a deep understanding between equals. While it is common for caring people to pity a grieving person, especially a grieving child, pity often feels condescending and removed.

Do not be afraid to show emotion. Showing and sharing emotion are the greatest gifts one person can give another. While it may be uncomfortable, it is a meaningful and human time.

Offer children outlets for their grief. For example, teachers and other school professionals might allow journal writing about loss; allow students to do a research topic pertinent to their losses (e.g., looking up a disease); create a "special area" in a room where a child can go for a predetermined period of time if needed; and/or encourage expression through painting, drawing, dancing, and so forth.

Honor every possible goodbye in the school. Usually people hope to leave without saying goodbye in order to avoid pain. Ironically, people still experience the pain of separation but experience it alone. Perhaps the best grief education a school can do is to honor all good-byes that occur during the year—students leaving, changing grades, pets dying, family changes, losing friends. By

(continued)

Table 4.4 *(Continued)*

acknowledging the importance of every good-bye (creating ceremonies for transitions, writing a good-bye song when there is a loss, attending memorial services), the school community acknowledges the process of grief in all aspects of life.

Speak to children about death or loss. When a student has experienced a loss, a school professional should speak to him or her soon after his or her return to school. This may seem obvious but there are times when a child returns to school after a loss and no one mentions it for fear of saying the "wrong" thing. A comment can simply be "I was sad to hear your brother died,; this must be a hard time for you." Even if a child does not immediately respond, it is still very important that an empathic statement be shared.

Be as honest as possible. Being as honest as possible means that school professionals should share what they know, what they do not know, and what they are not able to discuss, and why. This honesty respects both the children's need to know and the school's valid limitations.

Continue with the routines, discipline, and high expectations. For many grieving students, school may be the most stable and predictable place in their lives. While schools can communicate respect for the grieving process by making allowances, grieving students benefit from functioning as normally as possible and by having limits placed on inappropriate behavior.

Never forget about a loss, even years later. Losses are part of the fabric of each person's identity. To remember the anniversary of a death or divorce, to remember a quality of a person who died, or the love a child had for a pet is to continue to honor those relationships.

Support one another. Supporting healthy grief in a school is not easy work. It is natural to be deeply moved, deeply saddened, and heavy of heart after being with a grieving child. Ideally, each school professional should have at least one other person he or she can look to for on-going support—this will greatly enhance the warmth and empathy that school professionals can offer grieving children.

Source: From *Helping Children Grieve at School* (p. 46), by H. McGlauflin, 1998, Alexandria, VA: American School Counselor Association. Copyright 1998 by American School Counselor Association. Reprinted with permission.

Depression and Suicide

Research indicates that certain types of short-term psychotherapy, particularly cognitive-behavioral therapy (CBT), can help relieve depression in children and adolescents (Birmaher et al., 1998; Jayson, Wood, Kroll, Fraser, & Harrington, 1998; Reinecke, Ryan, & DuBois, 1998). For example, a study comparing CBT, supportive therapy, and family therapy found that CBT led to a reduction in depressive symptoms in nearly 65 percent of cases, a higher rate than in either supportive therapy or family therapy alone (Brent et al., 1997).

One school-based program, the *Suicide Prevention Program*, uses a cognitive-behavioral approach to teach students how to think about stress and distress, to provide them with coping and problem-solving skills, and to help them identify and use a peer support network (Greenberg et al., 2000). According to Greenberg et al., the *Suicide Prevention Program* consists of seven distinct topical units based on three phases: an educational-conceptual phase, an exercise-training phase, and an implementation-application phase. This program is implemented in groups of about 18 students over 12 weekly sessions of about 50 minutes each. A study involving 237 low- to middle-class eighth graders in Israel showed that males who participated in the program, compared to a waiting-list only control group of students, showed significant improvements on the Index of Empathy for Children and the Adolescents Israeli Index of Potential Suicide (IIPS) and (Klingman & Hochdorf, 1993).

One study in particular indicated strong support for the involvement of school social workers in the assessment and treatment of students who may be contemplating suicide. A 10-month University of Washington study involving 14 Seattle schools concluded that one of the most promising places to prevent suicides may be the school social worker's or school nurse's office. In this study, at-risk students were interviewed in two-hour sessions by a school social worker or school nurse who asked them a series of questions about their mood and called their parents or a hospital if they expressed suicidal intentions.

The authors of this study reported that 54 percent of those who participated in the psychological interview program were less likely to have suicidal thoughts or act on them in the months following than those who did not participate (Portner, 2000b).

Despite the fact that students who are contemplating suicide often exhibit a number of warning signs (e.g., having a sustained case of the blues, discarding valuable possessions, displaying emotional volatility, making suicidal statements, or a combination of these), teachers often fail to notice these warning signs and take appropriate action. This may be because many high school teachers may not have enough time to develop personal relationships with all students due to large class sizes and the continuous changing of classes (K. King, Price, Telljohann, & Wahl, 1999). To address this problem, school social workers should take several additional steps. Because students may be the individuals who possess the most intimate knowledge about their peers, school social workers should make sure that all students are educated about the risk factors for adolescent suicide and receive instruction on the importance of sharing this information with the school social worker or counselor if they suspect that a friend may be at risk. The importance of peers' sharing this information with an adult in school cannot be overemphasized. Research indicates that in 70 percent of all teen suicides, another teen knew about the victim's plans and did nothing because, many times, peers view sharing any information about each other with an adult as "tattling" (Portner, 2000b).

If a suicide does occur, school social workers can initiate several steps to minimize problems and "copycat" suicides. First, schools should construct a "calling tree" immediately to spread the news to school staff and parents of friends of the deceased. Next, a school professional should be assigned to talk to students, to call the family to offer assistance, and to keep the principal and superintendent informed. It is also important to not glamorize the act by constructing shrines for the dead, as well as to minimize exposure to media reports about the suicide (Portner, 2000a).

Summary

Many students who are anxious, fearful, lonely, shy, grieving, or depressed are underserved or not served at all in our schools. A number of standardized instruments have been developed to assess these problems. Several cognitive-behavioral (C-B) techniques (e.g., modeling, systematic desensitization, flooding and implosive therapy) have been shown to be effective in reducing anxiety, fear, and depression in children and adolescents. One of the oldest and most respected school-based programs designed to identify and intervene with children who are at-risk for emotional and behavioral problems is the Primary Mental Health Prevention (PMHP) project. School social workers should be aware of a number of proven or promising *student-focused* interventions that have been developed to address these internalizing behaviors and advocate their implementation in schools.

Questions for Discussion

1. What school conditions may contribute to stress and anxiety?
2. What are some long-term consequences for children who have poor peer relationships?
3. What behavior do grieving children typically exhibit?
4. Why is it often difficult to diagnose depression in children and adolescents?
5. Identify and describe several cognitive-behavioral techniques that have been shown to be effective in reducing anxiety, fear, and depression in children and adolescents.

Refer to the case study at the beginning of this chapter:

1. How could the school social worker address Lakesha's problems at home without breeching confidentiality?
2. What steps can the school social worker take to help Lakesha deal with her need to be "perfect"?

Additional Resources

Anxiety and Fearfulness

- Clegg, L. B. (1996). Using children's literature to help children cope with fear. *Educational Horizons, 74*(3), 134–138.
- Robinson, E., Rotter, J., Fey, M., & Vogel, K. (1992). *Helping children cope with fears and stress.* Ann Arbor: University of Michigan (ERIC Document Reproduction Services, ED 348625). A source for activities that help students learn more about their own interests and personal strengths and can enhance self-confidence and feelings of self-worth.
- Miller, S., & McCormick, J. (1991). Stress: Teaching children to cope [Special feature]. *Journal of Physical Education, Recreation, and Dance, 62*(2), 53–70 (EJ 425 072). Offers suggestions for teaching stress management and relaxation skills to preschool and elementary children that can be implemented by classroom teachers and parents.
- Quackenbush, Robert M. (1982). *First grade jitters.* New York: Lippincott. Ages 5–7. In this short, simple tale of apprehension about school, the young rabbit narrator feels defensive when his parents try to define his "jitters."
- Tester, Sylvia Root. (1979). *We laughed a lot my first day of school.* Children's Press. Ages 3–6. A Hispanic boy discovers that his fears about kindergarten are unfounded, and he enjoys a positive first-day experience.

Loneliness/Shyness

- Sheridan, S., Kratochwill, T., & Elliott, S. (1990). Behavioral consultation with parents and teachers: Delivering treatment for socially withdrawn children at home and school. *School Psychology Review, 19*(1), 33–52.

Grieving

- Teen Age Grief, Inc., is a nonprofit organization that provides grief support to bereaved teens. TAG professionals primarily train school personnel, health professionals, law enforcement, and organizations serving "at risk" youth. www.smartlink.net/~tag
- The Touchstone Center for Grieving Children and Adolescents was established to promote and support the special needs of grieving children and adolescents. It is a place where families can join together and find guidance and support in coping with the pain and confusion of grief. www.touchstonecenter.org

■ "A Child's Simple Guide Through Grief" by A. Cunningham (2000). Aims to help children through the grieving process after losing a loved one. Jalmar Press.

Depression/Suicide

■ The NIMH publication entitled: "Depression in children and adolescents: A Fact Sheet for Physicians" summarizes some of the latest scientific findings on child and adolescent depression and lists resources where physicians can obtain more information. This publication can be found online at:
www.nimh.nih.gov/publicat/depchildresfact.cfm
■ National Institute of Mental Health (NIMH) Suicide Research Consortium
www.nimh.nih.gov/research/suicide.htm
■ King, K.A. (1999). High school suicide postvention: Recommendations for an effective program. *American Journal of Health Studies, 15,* 217–222. This article provides a comprehensive review of the professional literature of the appropriate steps school professionals should carry out before a student suicide occurs and after a student suicide occurs.

Social Problems

5

Chapter

In this chapter, we discuss:

- Truancy.

- Dropouts/pushouts.

- Homelessness.

- Foster care.

- Abuse and neglect.

- Divorce and separation.

- Substance abuse.

- Teen sexual behavior/pregnancy/parenthood.

- Proven or promising student-focused interventions targeting children and youth experiencing social problems.

Amanda is a first-grade student referred to Kathy, the school social worker, by her teacher. The reason for the referral was "poor hygiene." Amanda enters the school social worker's office crying. Amanda says that the other kids have been teasing her for wearing the same clothes day after day. Amanda's clothes look wrinkled and dirty. Kathy knows that Amanda's family has limited resources but that Amanda has, until recently, had a neat and clean appearance. Kathy asks Amanda how her family has been doing. Amanda tells her that her mom's boyfriend left and that she and her mom and her two brothers have been living in their van. Amanda says that she and her mom sleep in sleeping bags in the van and that her brothers usually sleep at their friends' houses. At the end of the session, Amanda begins to sob, stating that she does not want to return to class.

Our behavior is shaped by conditions in our environment, particularly as we grow. This is the essential piece to the puzzle. The way our children are treated within their important environments will largely determine the shape they will be in and how they will behave. (Pransky, 1991, p. 7)

Introduction

Social problems do not stop at the schoolhouse door. Social problems will impact, to a greater or lesser extent, a child's academic performance and behavior in school. For example, a homeless child may not be able to study or sleep while residing in the chaotic environment of a homeless shelter. Foster children may have to adjust to frequent school changes, and they may fear school and anticipate failure. An abused child may be depressed and may have a difficult time interacting with his or her peers in school.

While some social problems are highly correlated with income and ethnicity, others cut across all income levels and ethnic groups. This chapter discusses a number of social problems that impact students' social, emotional, and academic functioning in school. It highlights exemplary student-focused interventions that have been shown to be effective in addressing the specific needs of students experiencing these social problems. While this chapter concentrates on student-focused interventions, a number of system-focused interventions have also been developed and shown to be effective in preventing or minimizing truancy rates, sexual abuse, and teen pregnancy. These comprehensive school-based prevention programs are discussed in Chapter 7.

Truancy

Truancy is a critical problem in many school districts across the United States with some daily absentee rates as high as 30 percent (Ingersoll & LeBoeuf, 1997). In addition to being detrimental to students' academic progress, promotion, graduation, self-esteem, and employment potential (DeKalb, 1999), truancy is one of the most powerful predictors of delinquency (Garry, 1996).

Ingersoll and LeBoeuf (1997) discussed a wide variety of reasons that may explain why students are truant from school. Students may fear becoming victims of school violence, they may be bored with the way teachers present the curriculum, or they may become discouraged by constantly having to struggle to keep up with their peers academically. Some youth miss school because they have to take care of younger siblings. Some students stop coming to school because every time they return to school, they are suspended for interpersonal problems with their teachers or peers. Some students do not attend school because their parents neglect their educational needs while other children are school phobic and cannot function outside the security of their home. (See Chapter 4 for a discussion of interventions with students who are school phobic.) Chronic truancy is a precursor to dropping out of school, which is described in the next section.

Dropouts/Pushouts

Despite the increased importance of a high school education in an increasingly technological society, the high school completion rate has shown limited gains over the past 25 years. Overall, in 1999, 11.2 percent of the 34 million 16- through 24-year-olds in the United States were classified as dropouts (Kaufman, Kwon, Klein, & Chapman, 2000). The dropout rate in large urban districts remains particularly high. For example, nearly two-thirds of school dropouts leave before the tenth grade, 20 percent drop out by the eighth grade, and 3 percent do not even complete the fourth grade. Hispanic students are slightly more likely to drop out than African Americans. Nearly 40 percent of Hispanic students drop out before the eighth grade. The social and personal costs of dropping out of school are staggering. Dropouts comprise nearly half of the heads of households on welfare and a similar percentage of the prison population (Schwartz, 1995a). Dropping out also leads to increased health care costs and lowered tax revenues for states (Catterall, 1985), and dropouts earn about one-third less in wages than high school graduates (Schwartz, 1995a).

Interviews with dropouts have uncovered a variety of reasons for leaving school early. Several reasons are outlined in Table 5.1. As shown in the table, a number of personal factors, such as getting pregnant, getting a job, or having a drug or alcohol problem, were mentioned. However, a number of school factors such as not getting along with teachers or peers, a lack of academic assistance due to large classes, or the humiliation of repeating classes were also mentioned. Also reported were having disciplinary problems, being suspended, or expelled. Suspension and expulsion are especially problematic because many students are suspended for relatively minor offenses.

In a study exploring the reasons that students were suspended in a school district in Illinois, it was discovered that most school suspensions resulted from preventable minor offenses such as repeated tardiness, insubordination, profanity, and dress code violations rather than serious offenses such as weapons violations, physical confrontations with teachers, theft, and alcohol or drug-related offenses (Dupper & Bosch, 1996). These findings were consistent with an earlier study of Boston middle schools that found that most school suspensions were for "school disruption"—a catch-all category that can include behaviors ranging from name calling and talking back to a teacher to fighting (Massachusetts Advocacy Center, 1986). These findings call into question the use of the term *dropout* for early school leavers who are continually suspended from school. A more accurate term for this subcategory of early school leavers should be *pushouts* rather than *dropouts*. While

Table 5.1   **Dropouts' Reasons for Leaving School Early**

School factors	Impersonal schools.
	Poor preparation for high school.
	Classes were too large.
	Humiliation of repeating classes and being surrounded by younger students.
	Received failing, poor grades, or couldn't keep up with schoolwork.
	Didn't get along with teachers and/or students.
	Had disciplinary problems, was suspended or expelled.
	Didn't fit in.
	Didn't feel safe.
	Not enrolled in a college preparatory program.
	Missed at least 10 days of school or cut class at least 10 times.
Personal factors	Got a job, had a family to support, or had trouble managing both school and work.
	Got married, became pregnant or became a parent, wanted to have a family, or had a family to take care of.
	Family conflict.
	Had friends who dropped out.
	Wanted to travel.
	Had a drug or alcohol problem.
	Believed that they didn't have control over their lives, that chance and luck were important, and that something always seemed to stop them from getting ahead.
	Felt "useless at times," "no good at all," and/or "didn't have much to be proud of."

Source: Adapted from *Not-so-simple reasons for dropout rate*, by A. Hartocollis, 2001; *The New York Times, New York Times on the Web*. Retrieved from www.nytimes.com/2001/; and "A profile of parents of eighth graders," *National Educational Longitudinal Study of 1988* by L. Horn and J. West, 1992, Washington, DC: National Center for Educational Statistics. (ERIC Document Reproduction Service No. ED 350341)

the term *dropout* connotes individual dysfunction and pathology, the term *pushout* focuses attention on those school conditions that may exacerbate or even cause youth to leave school prior to graduation (Dupper, 1994b). Despite the fact that some youth leave school as a result of entirely personal factors, school social workers must be careful not to limit their conceptualization of the dropout problem to personal factors alone. By broadening their conceptualization of early school leavers to include pushouts as well as dropouts, school social workers are able to focus their attention on detrimental school factors (e.g., overly harsh and discriminatory school discipline policies and procedures) in assessing and developing interventions to address the dropout/pushout problem.

Homelessness

The *Stewart B. McKinney Homeless Assistance Act* defines a homeless person as "any individual who lacks a fixed, regular, and adequate nighttime residence, or has a primary nighttime residence that is a publicly operated shelter, an institution providing temporary shelter, or a public or private place not designed for the accommodation of human beings." This last category includes cars and park benches, as in Amanda's case in the vignette at the beginning of this chapter.

The homeless youth population is estimated to be about 300,000 young people each year, or about 3 percent of the urban homeless population (Institute for Health Policy Studies, 1995). Families with children are among the fastest-growing segments of the homeless population groups in the United States, constituting about 40 percent of people who become homeless (Shinn & Weitzman, 1996). Highly correlated with these growing numbers of homeless children is a U.S. child poverty rate that is among the highest in the developed world. Despite its enormous wealth, child poverty in the United States has hovered at or above 20 percent for more than a decade (Annie E. Casey Foundation, 1998).

A study of the educational problems of homeless children and youth in Illinois revealed that the most immediate concerns to school social workers and educators are a number of barriers that preclude homeless children and youth from even enrolling in school. These barriers include guardianship requirements, delays in transfer of school records, lack of a permanent address, immunization records, or a combination of these (Dupper & Halter, 1994). Often, homeless children and youth who are able to enroll in school cannot attend school because homeless families may not have a family car or money for public transportation, and many shelters are unable to provide transportation (National Coalition for the Homeless, 1999). Even if they have transportation, it is difficult for homeless children to attend school regularly because homeless families are often forced to move frequently due to length-of-stay restrictions in shelters, short stays with friends and relatives, or relocation to seek employment (Dupper & Halter, 1994). Other school-related problems facing homeless children include a chaotic shelter environment that is not conducive to studying or sleeping (Kozol, 1989; Nord & Luloff, 1995); limited educational resources available for homeless children (Eddowes & Hranits, 1989); disproportionately high levels of depression and developmental delays (Menke, 1998); taunting by classmates and teachers once their homelessness is known (Bassuk, 1990); feelings of shame, embarrassment, humiliation about being homeless (Dupper & Halter, 1994); and problems in evaluating homeless children for special education services (Zima, Bussing, Forness, & Benjamin, 1997).

Foster Care

More than half a million children currently live with foster families, the majority of which are children of color and residents of urban areas (Noble, 1997). Nearly all foster children have suffered traumatic experiences and many have had multiple homes. Similar to homeless children, foster children must face frequent school changes and adjust repeatedly to different educational expectations, curricula, and educators. Foster children may be truant because they fear school and anticipate failure or because their biological parents did not enforce attendance (Schwartz, 1999). Foster children may not care about schoolwork because it seems inconsequential in comparison with their other problems such as abuse and neglect and other turmoil in their lives (Altshuler, 1997; Ayasse, 1995;

Noble, 1997). A major obstacle in meeting the educational needs of children and youth in foster care is the lack of collaboration between school personnel and the child welfare system (Altshuler, 1997). According to Schwartz, foster parents also face a number of challenges. They must address their children's many needs without adequate preparation or training, they must conform to the demands of a social welfare system that provides too little money and support, and they must live with the fact that the children may leave at any time.

Abuse and Neglect

It has been estimated that more than 3 million children are maltreated each year in the United States (Mental health: A report of the Surgeon General, 1999). According to a report of the Surgeon General (1999), physical and sexual abuse is associated with a host of mental health problems including insecure attachment, posttraumatic stress disorder, conduct disorder, attention deficit disorder with hyperactivity (ADHD), depression, and impaired social functioning with peers (Mental health: A report of the Surgeon General, 1999). Psychological maltreatment is believed to occur more frequently than physical abuse (Mental health: A report of the Surgeon General, 1999). Children who are abused may experience a broad array of adverse short- and long-term mental health difficulties depending on the child's developmental level, the context of the abuse (including the perpetrator's use of force, threats, and weapons), the duration and frequency of abuse, or the extent of parental support upon disclosure (Henggeler et al., 1998).

School social workers play a key role in informing school personnel about the signs and symptoms of physical and sexual abuse. This is especially important since teachers may lack this knowledge. For example, in a study that asked teachers about their knowledge of various forms of abuse, only 4 percent of the polled teachers stated that they were "very aware" of the signs of sexual abuse, 17 percent said they would be able to recognize signs that were "very obvious," and 75 percent reported that they would not recognize signs at any point (McIntyre, 1987). In addition to physical abuse, teachers and school personnel should also be made aware of the "soft" sign indicators of child sexual abuse. (See Table 5.2 for the "soft" as well as physical indicators of child sexual abuse.) It is important to note that just because a child exhibits some of the symptoms outlined in

Table 5.2   **Signs and Symptoms of Sexual Abuse**

Sexual abuse victims may show the following "soft" sign indicators:

- Difficulty with walking, sitting, and playing.
- Extreme modesty and unwillingness to change clothes or expose any body parts in the presence of others.
- Extreme fear of being approached, touched, or examined by others.
- Extreme fear of going home, to school or day care, or to a friend's or relative's home.
- Extreme fear of travelling with parents, relative, or friend's parent.
- Running away from school, day care, or a relative's or friend's home.
- Adolescent prostitution.
- Sexual references or vocabulary that are atypical or unusual for a child's age.
- Sexual knowledge that is too sophisticated for the child's age.
- Sexual behavior that appears to be inappropriate for the age of the child.
- Withdrawn, infantile, or fantasy-filled behavior.
- Attempted suicide or talk of suicide.
- Extreme changes in school performance and behavior.
- Unaccountable accumulations of money, objects, clothing, candy, or other material items.
- Indirect allusions of the child's fears, worries, concerns, or anxieties.

Other signs of sexual abuse include physical indicators such as:

- Stained or bloody clothing or underwear, either torn or not torn.
- Blood or semen in or around the mouth, anus, or genital area of a victim.
- The presence of inanimate or foreign objects in the anus or vagina.
- Genitalia/anus that are swollen, inflamed, infected, bloody, bruised, torn, lacerated, or have a lax muscle tone that suggests stretching or forcing.
- Scars, scabs, cuts, or bite marks around the genitals, buttocks, mouth, breasts, neck, or thighs.
- Sexually transmitted diseases in children.
- Irritations, rashes, discharges, or unusual odors around the genital area.
- Pregnancy (especially in young adolescent girls).

Source: From *Child Sexual Abuse: An Administrator's Nightmare* (p. 4), by H. R. Cellini, B. K. Schwartz, and S. Readio, 1993, Westlake Village, CA: Pepperdine University's National School Safety Center, www.nsscl.org. Copyright 1993 by National School Safety Center. Reprinted with permission.

this table, school social workers and educators must not automatically jump to the conclusion that the child is being physically or sexually abused. Often signs are ambiguous and other stressors in a child's life can produce similar symptoms (Lumsden, 1991).

In addition to failing to recognize the signs and symptoms of physical and sexual abuse, several other factors may affect the reporting of child abuse in schools. Teachers may be unaware of the fact that if they make a report in "good faith," they have immunity from civil or criminal liability. The reporting philosophy of the school principal may also exert an important influence on teacher reporting of child abuse. For example, if a principal encourages it, teachers are more likely to report; when principals are reluctant to report in an effort to maintain good parental relations and school image, teachers report abuse less often (Lumsden, 1991). It is essential that school social workers make teachers and other school personnel aware of the fact that, despite the reporting philosophy of the principal, adults are *required by law* in all 50 states to report suspected child abuse.

Divorce and Separation

American families have changed in dramatic ways over the past decade. Children are increasingly likely to have single mothers, unmarried couples, and grandparents as caretakers (D. Cohn & Cohen, 2001). The percentage of children living with one parent increased to 27 percent in 1999 ("America's Children: Key National Indicators of Well-Being," 2000) with 60 percent spending some time in their childhood without a father present (DADS of Tennessee, Inc., 2000). This trend is troublesome because research indicates that children who grow up without a father present, even when adjustments are made for income, are more likely to suffer a wide variety of other disorders including anxiety, peer conflict, hyperactivity; are 75 percent more likely to need professional assistance for emotional problems; and are twice as likely to repeat a grade of school (DADS of Tennessee, Inc., 2000).

Increasing numbers of grandparents are assuming the role of surrogate parents to their grandchildren with more than 2 million taking on this responsibility, according to the latest Census figures (D. Cohn & Cohen, 2001). Reasons behind this trend include the death of one or both parents, parental abandonment, divorce, an increase in the number of unmarried mothers, drug addiction, mental illness, or parental imprisonment (Rothenberg, 1996). In fact, between 1991 and 2000, there has been a 60 percent increase (1.5 million children) in the number of children who had a mother or father in federal or state prison with more than 58 percent of these children younger than 10 years old (Sniffen, 2000). Having a parent in prison is a significant risk factor since children with parents in prison are five times more likely to become incarcerated themselves (Sniffen, 2000).

Substance Abuse

Today over half of young people in America have tried an illicit drug by the time they finish high school (Monitoring the future, 2000). Eighty percent of students have consumed alcohol by the end of high school with 62 percent of twelfth graders and 25 percent of eighth graders reporting being drunk at least once by the time they graduate (Monitoring the future, 2000). Rates of illicit drug use continue to increase as the quantity of drinking rises (Millennium Hangover: Keeping Score on Alcohol, 1999) with marijuana being the most widely used illicit drug— 38 percent of high school seniors reported that they have tried it (Monitoring the future, 2000). These statistics are cause for concern because adolescent drug and alcohol use is associated with declining grades, absenteeism, and dropping out (Crowe, 1998). It has also been estimated that 20 to 25 percent of children and youth are impacted by their caretakers' drug and alcohol problems and that 95 percent of children and youth living with an alcoholic are never identified and never receive any intervention at school (Morey, 1999). This is another important gap in services that needs to be addressed by school social workers. Moreover, nearly two-thirds of seniors have tried cigarettes with more than one-third identifying themselves as current smokers (Monitoring the future, 2000). In addition to the health concerns over smoking cigarettes, there is a correlation between smoking cigarettes and alcohol and substance abuse. Specifically, youth between the ages of 12 and 17 years old who smoked were 9 times as likely to use illicit drugs and 16 times as likely to drink heavily as compared to nonsmoking youth (Gfroerer, 1997).

Teen Sexual Behavior/Pregnancy/Parenthood

According to the Alan Guttmacher Institute (1999), four out of five young people have sex as teenagers. Just over 7 percent of students nationwide report having sex before the age of 13, 42.5 percent by grade 10, and 60.9 percent by grade 12. Slightly over half of those surveyed reported using a condom during their last experience of sexual intercourse, with African American students significantly more likely than Hispanic or White teens to report condom use at last intercourse.

The rate of teenage pregnancy in the United States remains the highest in the developed world. Approximately one million American teenage girls become pregnant each year with 78 percent of these pregnancies unintended (Alan Guttmacher Institute, 1999). Since the average age of menarche has reached an all-time low of 12 or 13 years, a greater proportion of teenage girls are at risk of becoming pregnant than ever before (Potts, 1990). The negative consequences of teenage pregnancy and childbearing impact both the mother and child . For example, teen mothers are less likely to graduate from high school and more likely to live in poverty and to rely on welfare than their peers who delay childbearing (Annie E. Casey Foundation, 1998). The children of teenage mothers are often born at low birth weight; experience health and developmental problems; and are frequently poor, abused, neglected, or a combination of these (Annie E. Casey Foundation, 1998). Furthermore, teenage pregnancy poses a substantial financial burden to society, estimated at $7 billion annually in lost tax revenues, public assistance, child health care, foster care, and involvement with the criminal justice system (Annie E. Casey Foundation, 1998). It is important to target young men in reducing teenage pregnancy since teen fatherhood has been shown to be associated with engaging in delinquent and other problem behaviors (Thornberry, Wei, Stouthamer-Loeber, & Van Dyke, 2000).

Proven or Promising Student-Focused Interventions Targeting Children and Youth Experiencing Social Problems

Truancy

While there is no evidence to suggest that punitive approaches alone are effective, most schools and communities appear to be leaning heavily toward punitive approaches to combat truancy. Schools give detentions and suspensions or academic consequences (i.e., lowering grades, removing students from the regular school program) for nonattendance. Communities have passed ordinances that result in fining or jailing parents, suspending a truant youth's driver's license, or a combination of these (National School Safety Center, 1994). However, there is evidence to suggest that programs that combine "carrot and stick" approaches have been shown to be effective in reducing truancy rates. One proven program, the *Truancy Intervention Program (TIP)*, in Dade County, Florida, combines early intervention with prosecutorial enforcement of compulsory education laws. According to the School Safety Update (1997), *TIP* uses computerization to identify students after they have five unexcused absences from school and then follows up with a strongly worded letter from the state attorney. This letter notifies parents or guardians of their legal responsibility to ensure regular school attendance under state law and the potential for prosecution for disobeying such laws. Program outcomes for *TIP* are quite impressive. According to the School Safety Update, after 145 assigned students and their parents/guardians attended their first *TIP* conference, 94 percent of the students had fewer unexcused absences, unexcused absences for the overall group decreased by 86 percent, 60 percent of the students improved their academic grades, 45 percent improved their effort grades, and the total number of violations of the code of student conducts decreased by 90 percent.

Another program that uses a "carrot and stick" approach is the *Truancy Abatement and Burglary Suppression (TABS)*. The *TABS* program was established in 1993 as a collaborative effort of the Milwaukee County sheriff's office, police department, and public schools, and the Boys and Girls Club of Greater Milwaukee. According to the School Safety Update (1997), law enforcement officers pick up juveniles who are not in school and take them to the *TABS* center. At the *TABS* center, their parents are contacted and a school counselor helps the parents and students set goals for regular school attendance. If social services are needed, the counselor arranges them and any follow-up conferences. For chronic truants, police may issue citations to the parents and require the student to participate in counseling programs (School Safety Update, 1997). A police department's evaluation of *TABS*, over a 30-day tracking period, indicated that daytime juvenile crime rates and violent juvenile crime rates declined while student attendance improved (School Safety Update, 1997). Based on this description of the *TABS* program, there appears to be a substantial role for school social workers in assisting parents in setting goals and connecting parents with needed social services.

In addition to providing direct services to parents and truant students, school social workers should advocate greater flexibility in disciplinary policies and practices involving truant students (e.g., changing discipline policies that mandate the suspension of students for being truant). They should also support programs that recognize and reward truant students who are making efforts to attend school more frequently. Taking the parents of truant students to court should be used only as a final alternative (Rohrman, 1993).

Dropouts/Pushouts

Over the past 10 years, the percentage of youth completing high school through an alternative program such as the GED has increased (Kaufman et al., 2000). While a number of students will require such alternatives to graduate from high school, it is important for school social workers to also focus their efforts on changing those school conditions that contribute to or even cause students to leave school prior to graduation (see Table 2.1). Reducing the impact of these school risk factors should lead to a reduction in the rate of early school leavers, both dropouts and pushouts. Several innovative programs designed to transform the culture and climate of schools from places of intimidation and zero tolerance into places of learning are discussed in Chapter 7.

Homelessness

In response to the mandates of the Stewart B. McKinney Homeless Assistance Act Amendments, most urban schools have implemented a number of strategies to help homeless children and youth succeed in school (Schwartz, 1995b). Schwartz has outlined a number of these strategies including:

- Leaving brochures at local shelters that explain school enrollment procedures and transportation options.
- Moving classes to homeless shelters.
- Establishing "transition rooms" for homeless students in schools.
- Making teachers aware of the fact that homeless children and youth may be more tired than other children.
- Implementing one-on-one tutoring programs for homeless children and youth.

- Educating all students about the reasons for poverty and homelessness in an effort to lessen the stigma that homeless students feel at school.

Some schools have addressed the basic needs of homeless children by providing special meal programs, storage space, clothing, and health services. Separate schools for homeless children and youth, such as the Pappas School in Phoenix, have also been established. Pappas School has an enrollment of about 800 students and includes a school-based health clinic, clothing room, and provides two meals per day (Woods, 1997). It should be recognized that the establishment of separate schools for homeless children and youth is controversial since many advocates believe that homeless children should not be segregated from other children and that services for homeless children should be provided in regular public schools. School social workers have a pivotal role to play in advocating more programs to meet the educational needs of homeless children and youth and in enlisting the support of school personnel and the larger community in implementing these strategies.

Foster Care

In an attempt to address the lack of collaboration between the school system and the child welfare system, a number of communities across the United States are making concerted efforts to forge closer working relationships to better serve the educational needs of foster children. For example, in New York City and Seattle, the school districts and the child welfare agencies are working together to design a database that will allow officials to more closely monitor the school attendance and academic progress of foster children (Jacobson, 2000). School social workers can advocate programs such as these in their communities and assist in their implementation. Several authors have proposed a number of concrete steps that school personnel, including school social workers, can take to assist children in foster care. For example, school social workers can:

- Develop and implement specific plans for enrolling and integrating foster students on short notice (Noble, 1997; Stahl, 1990; Stufft, 1989).

- Help teachers become more knowledgeable about the unique problems facing children in foster care and their families and how these problems may impact their learning and behavior (Schwartz, 1999).

- Advocate placing children who are in foster care with the most experienced teachers to increase their chances for school success (Noble, 1997; Rothenberg, 1996).

- Assist teachers and administrators in critically reviewing books and curriculum materials for possible insensitivities about children living in nontraditional families (Schwartz, 1999).

- Invite foster parents to participate in a meaningful way in their foster child's education (Altshuler, 1997).

Abuse and Neglect

School social workers can address the problem of child abuse and neglect in a number of ways. Since cooperation between school personnel and child protective services workers is vitally important (Lumsden, 1991), school social workers should work to establish and maintain cooperative relationships between the schools they serve and the child welfare agency. School social workers can also participate as key members of community child protection teams that bring together a team of community professionals (e.g., educators, doctors, lawyers, police, and other mental health professionals) to collaborate and make team decisions about child abuse cases (McEvoy, 1990). In addition, school social workers can train teachers and school staff how to identify the various forms of child abuse, the procedures for reporting suspected cases of child abuse, and their legal responsibility for making these reports. School social workers can also provide direct interventions to victims of abuse and work toward alleviating the faulty belief that the victim was responsible for the abuse. See Henggeler et al. (1998) for a description of anxiety management and cognitive techniques for abused children and youth.

Divorce and Separation

The Children of Divorce Intervention Program (CODIP) and the Child Support Group (CSG) have been found to be effective in working with children of divorce. CODIP is a school-based group intervention program designed to alleviate the behavioral and emotional problems resulting from divorce (Greenberg et al., 2000). According to Greenberg et al. and Alpert-Gillis, Pedro-Carroll, and Cowen (1989), CODIP targets children in kindergarten through eighth grade and is designed to create a support network that facilitates discussion of divorce-related feelings and attitudes, discusses divorce-related issues and misconceptions surrounding a divorce, develops relevant coping skills as well as positive self- and family perceptions, and reduces the likelihood that the child will engage in self-blame for the events taking place related to the divorce. CODIP has been found to improve children's self-reported anxiety, parent-reported adjustment, and teacher ratings of problem behavior for children in the program (Greenberg et al., 2000).

The Child Support Group (CSG), is a 14-week school-based program for children of divorce. According to Stolberg and Mahler (1994) and Greenberg et al. (2000), CSG consists of three major components: support or special topics, skill building, and skills transfer. The discussion of specific themes in the support or special topics component is carried out through cartoons and pictures, newspaper articles, and games. The skill building component consists of teaching children to label feelings and to associate feelings with causal events, and to be able to combine feelings and events into statements to others. The skills-transfer component consists of teaching children how to apply self-control and problem-solving skills to divorce-related problems. CSG also includes four parental workshops and materials for families to use at home. An evaluation of CSG found that a sample of children who met *Diagnostic and*

Statistical Manual of Mental Disorders, 3rd Edition (*DSM-III*; American Psychiatric Association, 1987) diagnosis and were randomly assigned to the intervention were less likely to have adjustment problems (Stolberg & Mahler, 1994).

Substance Abuse

A series of treatment improvement protocols (TIPs) for treating substance abuse disorders has been developed by the Substance Abuse and Mental Health Services Administration's (SAMHSA) Center for Substance Abuse and Treatment (CSAT). TIP Series 32 focuses on best practice guidelines for the treatment of adolescents with substance abuse disorders. This protocol discusses how adolescent substance abusers differ from adults including how substance use is often an integral part of an adolescent's identity. This protocol also discusses how to tailor treatment to the adolescent, assessment guidelines, staffing issues, program components, treatment planning, and includes a detailed discussion of 12 step-based programs (including the Minnesota Model approach), therapeutic communities (TCs), and family therapy. This protocol also discusses the distinctive treatment needs of youth in the juvenile justice system, homeless youth, gay and lesbian youth, and youth with coexisting physical, behavioral, and psychiatric disorders. This protocol concludes with a discussion of the legal end ethical issues of providing substance abuse treatment to adolescents. Of particular interest to school social workers is the discussion of the schooling component of treatment and the need for treatment programs to work closely with other entities, such as school systems, and to designate a liaison (e.g., the school social worker) between the school and treatment program staff. Contact information for the TIPs series can be found in the Additional Resources section at the end of this chapter.

Teen Sexual Behavior/Pregnancy/Parenthood

Given the dimensions of teenage sexual activity, together with the accompanying risks of STD's, HIV, and unwanted pregnancies, the question is no longer "Should sex education be taught in schools?" but rather "How should sex education be taught?" (Kirby, 1994). According to Frost and Forrest (1995), sexuality education programs that encourage students to postpone sex until they are older, but also promote safer sex practices for those who choose to become sexually active, have been proven effective at delaying first intercourse and increasing use of contraception among sexually active youth. Sex education programs that teach communication, negotiation, and refusal skills and combine abstinence education with medically accurate information on contraception, safe sex, and the risks of unprotected intercourse have been shown to delay the onset of sexual initiation among younger adolescents by as much as 15 percent and to increase contraceptive use among older adolescents by as much as 22 percent (Brindis, 1999; Frost & Forrest, 1995). Easy and confidential access to family planning services through clinics, school-linked health centers, and condom availability programs have also been found to help prevent unintended pregnancy (Kahn, Brindis, & Glei, 1999). Abstinence-only programs, supported by the Bush administration, are ineffective because they fail to delay the onset of intercourse and often provide information that is medically inaccurate and potentially misleading (Berne & Huberman, 1999; Kirby, 1997). Proven and promising teenage pregnancy and sexually transmitted disease prevention programs are discussed in Chapter 7.

Summary

Truancy, dropouts/pushouts, homelessness, foster care, abuse and neglect, divorce and separation issues, substance abuse, and teen sexual behavior/pregnancy/parenthood are some of the major social problems that impact children and youths' functioning in school. As a result of their training and ecological approach, school social workers are uniquely qualified to assume a leadership role in designing, implementing, and evaluating interventions to meet the needs of children and youth impacted by these social problems. A number of student-focused interventions have been developed to address the social, emotional, and academic needs of these children and youth. In addition, school social workers must also advocate the implementation of the truancy, sexual abuse, and teen pregnancy prevention programs described in Chapter 7.

Questions for Discussion

1. Truancy is a powerful predictor of delinquency. Why?
2. What school factors may contribute to early school leaving? What is meant by the term *push out*?
3. Describe several steps that school social workers can take to better serve homeless children in schools.
4. What challenges do foster children and their foster families face in educational settings?
5. What factors affect school personnel's reporting or failing to report child abuse?

Refer to the case study at the beginning of this chapter:

1. What role should the school social worker play to help this family obtain needed resources?
2. How might the school social worker handle Amanda's refusal to return to class?
3. How might the school social worker help Amanda improve her peer relationships?

Additional Resources

Divorce and Separation

- Single Parent Central provides online resources for single parents. www.singleparentcentral.com/factstat.htm

- Parents and Children Together, Inc. (P.A.C.T.) was established in 1984 to preserve and strengthen families of incarcerated persons.
  www.fcnetwork.org/programs/pact.html

Substance Abuse

- Treatment Improvement Protocols (TIPs) can be accessed via the Internet on the National Library of Medicine's home page at:
  text.nlm.nih.gov

Teen Sexual Behavior/Pregnancy/Parenthood

- *Whatever happened to childhood? The problem of teen pregnancy in the United States* may be obtained from the National Campaign to Prevent Teen Pregnancy at:
  www.plannedparenthood.org/library/TEEN-PREGNANCY/Reducing.html

Students with Disabilities

Chapter

In this chapter, we discuss:

- Overview of Individuals with Disabilities Education Act (IDEA) and IDEA Amendments of 1997.

- The Individualized Educational Program (IEP).

- Functional Behavioral Assessment (FBA) and Positive Behavioral Interventions and Supports (PBIS).

- The Social Developmental Study (SDS).

- Attention Deficit Disorder with Hyperactivity (ADHD).

- Emotional Disturbance (ED).

- Learning Disabilities (LD).

- Autism.

- Promising interventions targeting students with disabilities.

Mia, a social worker for the West View School System received a referral for John. John, age 10, was diagnosed as having attention deficit disorder with hyperactivity (ADHD) and an emotional disturbance. According to John's teacher, he consistently refused to do his work, cried often, and began to fall asleep in school. His teacher described him as a "manipulator" and "chronic liar" and produced her grade book, pointing at a string of almost straight zeros for the last four-week period. In addition, John's classmates began to ostracize him. The multidisciplinary team decided to add "weekly individual counseling with the school social worker" to John's individualized educational program (IEP). Mia began to see John individually on a weekly basis.

W e have been extremely pleased with the results of Positive Behavioral Interventions and Supports [PBIS]. Teaching appropriate behaviors is much more effective than punishing inappropriate behaviors. It allows the child to know the expectations of our school and accept responsibility of his or her actions. (Judi Hunter, Principal, Julius Marks Elementary School, Lexington, Kentucky)

Introduction

During 1995 and 1996, 8.6 percent, or 5,796,833 U.S. public school students between the ages of 0 and 21 years received special education and related services under the Individuals with Disabilities Education Act (IDEA; Knoblauch & Sorenson, 1998; U.S. Department of Education, 1998). Because school social workers provide a number of services to students with disabilities, such as John in the case vignette, they must have a working knowledge of the requirements and mandates of the IDEA and its accompanying regulations. School social workers should inform parents of children with suspected disabilities of their legal rights under IDEA. School social workers should also know how to write an effective social developmental study (SDS), have a working knowledge of individualized education programs (IEP), know how to conduct functional behavioral assessments (FBA), and know how to implement behavior intervention plans that include positive behavioral interventions and supports (PBIS). All these topics are discussed in this chapter.

In addition, this chapter describes several categories of disabilities that often involve the services of the school social worker including attention deficit disorder with hyperactivity (ADHD), emotional disturbance (ED), learning disabilities (LD), and autism. This chapter concludes with a discussion of several effective interventions targeting students with disabilities. A number of additional resources and Web sites related to children with disabilities can be found under the Additional Resources section at the end of the chapter.

Overview of IDEA and IDEA Amendments of 1997

The IDEA Amendments of 1997 require every state and the District of Columbia to provide every youth who has a disability, as defined by IDEA, with a free, appropriate public education (FAPE) and, to the maximum extent appropriate, educate them with youth who are not disabled (Burrell & Warboys, 2000). Under IDEA, schools may place children with disabilities in separate classrooms or schools only when supports and services are not sufficient to help the child learn in a regular classroom. Although some states use different terminology, states may not provide fewer rights than those afforded under federal law (Burrell & Warboys, 2000). Table 6.1 contains definitions of the 13 federal categories of disabilities as specified under IDEA.

The IDEA Amendments of 1997 have resulted in a number of substantial changes in the education of children with disabilities. First, these amendments require more parental involvement in the continuum of special education services. States are required to maximize parental involvement in all educational decisions as well as implement a formal system to settle any disputes between the parents/guardians and the school (Whitted & Constable, 1999). Second, the amendments state that the student's regular education teacher and related personnel (including school social workers) be members of the team that develops a student's individualized education program (IEP; Hare & Rome, 1999). Third, the amendments allow school authorities greater flexibility in disciplining special education students with behavioral problems (Hare & Rome, 1999). Specifically, schools are authorized to remove a student for up to 10 school days for minor disciplinary infractions and for up to 45 days for situations involving weapons or drugs. For any suspension longer than 10 consecutive days, the school system must hold a *manifestation hearing* to determine whether the triggering misconduct was related to the student's disability (IDEA Amendments of 1997).

The IDEA Amendments of 1997 provide important procedural safeguards and substantive protections to students and

Table 6.1   **Federal Categories/Definitions of Disabilities under IDEA**

Autism: A developmental disability significantly affecting verbal and nonverbal communication and social interaction, generally evident before age 3, that adversely affects a child's educational performance. Other characteristics often associated with autism are engagement in repetitive activities and stereotyped movements, resistance to environmental change or change in daily routines, and unusual responses to sensory experiences. The term does not apply if a child's educational performance is adversely affected primarily because the child has a emotional disturbance as defined below.

Deafness: A hearing impairment so severe that the child cannot understand what is being said even with a hearing aid.

Deaf-Blindness: A combination of hearing and visual impairments causing such severe communication, developmental, and educational problems that the child cannot be accommodated in either a program specifically for the deaf or a program specifically for the blind.

Hearing impairment: An impairment in hearing, whether permanent or fluctuating, that adversely affects a child's educational performance but that is not included under the definition of deafness as listed above.

Mental retardation: Significantly subaverage general intellectual functioning existing concurrently with deficits in adaptive behavior. And manifested during the developmental period that adversely affects a child's educational performance.

Multiple disabilities: A combination of impairments (such as mental retardation-blindness, or mental retardation-physical disabilities) that causes such severe educational problems that the child cannot be accommodated in a special education program solely for one of the impairments. The term does not include deaf-blindness.

Orthopedic impairment: A severe orthopedic impairment that adversely affects educational performance. The term includes impairments such as amputation, absence of a limb, cerebral palsy, poliomyelitis, and bone tuberculosis.

Other health impairment: Having limited strength, vitality, or alertness due to chronic or acute health problems such as a heart condition, rheumatic fever, asthma, hemophilia, and leukemia, which adversely affect educational performance.

Emotional disturbance: This term includes schizophrenia, but does not include students who are socially maladjusted, unless they have a serious emotional

(continued)

Table 6.1   *(Continued)*

disturbance. A condition exhibiting one or more of the following characteristics, displayed over a long period of time, and to a marked degree that adversely affects a child's educational performance:

- An inability to learn that cannot be explained by intellectual, sensory, or health factors.
- An inability to build or maintain satisfactory interpersonal relationships with peers or teachers.
- Inappropriate types of behavior or feelings under normal circumstances.
- A general pervasive mood of unhappiness or depression.
- A tendency to develop physical symptoms or fears associated with personal or school problems.

Specific learning disability: A disorder in one or more of the basic psychological processes involved in understanding or in using language, spoken or written, that may manifest itself in an imperfect ability to listen, think, speak, read, write, spell, or do mathematical calculations. This term includes such conditions as perceptual disabilities, brain injury, minimal brain dysfunction, dyslexia, and developmental aphasia. This term does not include children who have learning problems that are primarily the result of visual, hearing, or motor disabilities; mental retardation; or environmental, cultural or economic disadvantage.

Speech or language impairment: A communication disorder such as stuttering, impaired articulation, language impairment, or a voice impairment that adversely affects a child's educational performance.

Traumatic brain injury: An acquired injury to the brain caused by an external physical force, resulting in total or partial functional disability or psychosocial impairment, or both, that adversely affects a child's educational performance. The term applies to open or closed head injuries resulting in impairments in one or more areas, such as cognition; language; memory; attention; reasoning; abstract thinking; judgment; problem solving; sensory, perceptual and motor abilities; psychosocial behavior; physical functions; information processing; and speech. The term does not apply to brain injuries that are congenital or degenerative, or brain injuries induced by birth trauma.

Visual impairment, including blindness: An impairment in vision that, even with correction, adversely affects a child's educational performance. The term includes both partial sight and blindness.

Source: Adapted from *IDEA's definition of disabilities*, by B. Knoblauch and B. Sorenson, 1998, Reston, VA: ERIC Clearinghouse on Disabilities and Gifted Education. (ERIC Document Reproduction Service No. ED429396). This document is in the public domain.

parents/guardians. However, school systems often do not fully comply with these IDEA provisions, and many parents/guardians of children with special needs do not have access to attorneys with expertise in this complex area of law (Burrell & Warboys, 2000). Therefore, it is incumbent on school social workers to inform parents of children with suspected or confirmed disabilities of their legal rights under the IDEA Amendments of 1997 and to actively advocate for these parents. One invaluable resource is the federally funded parent training and information centers in each state that provide training and information to parents of infants, toddlers, school-aged children, and young adults with disabilities and professionals who work with their families. Contact information for parent training and information centers can be found in the Additional Resources section at the end of this chapter.

The Individualized Education Program (IEP)

By law, each public school child who receives special education and related services must have an individualized education program (IEP). Because it guides the development and delivery of special education supports and services, the IEP is the foundation of a quality education for children with disabilities. The IEP serves as an agreement between the school and the family on the educational goals of a particular student. It outlines the specific skills a student needs to develop as well as appropriate learning activities that build on that student's strengths. Because parents know their child best, they should play an important role in identifying those specific skills needed most in developing the IEP (Constable, 1999; National Institute of Mental Health [NIMH], 1997; Office of Special Education and Rehabilitative Services, 2000).

School social workers are involved in the attainment of IEP goals by mobilizing a variety of services both in and outside the school. For example, school social workers may provide individual and group counseling to students with disabilities or work to resolve difficulties in the school, home, or neighborhood that impact the student's educational performance (Constable, 1999). See Constable (1999) for a detailed description of the contents of the IEP and the process involved in setting annual goals and short-term objectives, as well as a description of the individualized family plan (IFP) and the individualized family service plan (IFSP).

Functional Behavioral Assessments (FBA) and Positive Behavioral Interventions and Supports (PBIS)

According to Dunlap and Fox (1999), school teams charged with developing an IEP for students with disabilities are required to conduct a functional behavioral assessment (FBA) and to implement behavior intervention plans that include positive behavioral interventions and supports (PBIS). The FBA process gathers information about the purpose of the behavior and the environmental and instructional factors associated with its occurrences and nonoccurrences. The results of the FBA contribute to the individualized behavior support plan, which usually includes procedures for teaching alternatives to the behavior problems as well as making changes to those factors associated with the problems. In essence, positive behavioral interventions and supports (PBIS) help the student acquire more effective, desirable ways of interacting with the environment. See Table 6.2 for a brief summary of positive behavioral interventions and supports (PBIS).

The Social Developmental Study (SDS)

The SDS is a comprehensive assessment of a child's functioning that includes a student's prenatal and birth history, family functioning, personal strengths, stressors that may be contributing to his or her problem, and current social functioning. To prevent inappropriate labeling of students, an assessment of adaptive

Table 6.2 **Positive Behavioral Intervention and Supports: A Brief Summary**

- Positive behavior support is the application of positive behavioral interventions and systems to achieve positive change.
- Positive behavior support is an approach to discipline and intervention that is proving both effective and practical in schools.
- Positive behavior support is the application of the science of behavior to achieve socially important change. The emphasis is on behavior change that is durable, comprehensive, and linked to academic and social gains.
- As a general matter, positive behavior support should be applied before any child is excluded from school due to problem behavior.
- The development of positive behavioral interventions and plans that are guided by functional behavioral assessment (FBA) is a foundation on which positive behavioral support is delivered.
- Functional behavioral assessment (FBA) is a systematic way of identifying problem behaviors and the events that predict occurrence, nonoccurrence, and maintenance of those behaviors.
- Strong, active administrative leadership, support, and participation is needed for effective efforts.
- Positive behavior support considers multiple contexts: community, family, district, school, classroom, nonclassroom, and individual.
- A proactive perspective is maintained along a continuum, using primary (what we do for all), secondary (what we do for some), and tertiary (what we do for a few) prevention and interventions.

Source: From the U.S. Department of Education, 2001, *Prevention Research and the IDEA Discipline Provisions: A Guide for School Administrators.* Retrieved December 5, 2001, from www.ed.gov/offices/OSERS/OSEP. This document is in the public domain.

behavior, as well as any environmental or cultural factors that may be contributing to or exacerbating a child's learning or behavior problems in school, should be included in the SDS. The SDS is used to aid in the "selection of an educational environment conducive to optimum learning and development . . . " (Tiefenthal & Charak, 1999, p. 279).

Assessment information included in the SDS is based on direct observations, interviews with parents/guardians, interviews with teachers, and sometimes interviews with the student. A major component of the SDS is a valid and reliable measure of adaptive behavior. Adaptive behavior assesses the extent to which a student is able to function independently and meet "culturally imposed standards of personal and social responsibility" in those various environments in which students must function (Tiefenthal & Charak, 1999, p. 284). A measure of adaptive behavior is important in identifying students with "cognitive impairments, emotional disturbance, and mental impairments" (Van Acker, 1999, p. 258). Social workers are uniquely qualified to conduct assessments of adaptive behavior given their training in interviewing skills and their focus on the assessment of the "goodness-of-fit" between individuals and their environments (Van Acker, 1999, p. 259). See Tiefenthal and Charak (1999) for a detailed description of the various components of the social developmental study. Van Acker (1999) lists and discusses several widely used measures of adaptive behavior.

According to the authors of the National Association of Social Workers (NASW) publication "Individuals with Disabilities Education Act Amendments of 1997 (IDEA): Implications for Social Workers," school social workers can meet the challenges of educating children with disabilities in a number of important ways. First, the reauthorized legislation expands the authority of school personnel to discipline students for behavior not related to their disability in the same manner as they discipline students without disabilities. Therefore, school social workers must monitor this expanded authority and be aware that inappropriate and unwarranted suspensions and expulsions may occur. Second, since the reauthorized IDEA expands the membership of the IEP team by adding the regular classroom teacher and "related services personnel" as appropriate, school social workers can maximize these new opportunities for participation in the IEP process. Third, under IDEA, each student's needs must be addressed in the least restrictive environment. School social workers can assist in successfully including students with disabilities in mainstream classrooms by facilitating communication and collaboration among mainstream teachers, special education personnel, and parents. Fourth, the reauthorized IDEA requires more parental involvement in the evaluation process, IEP development, and placement decisions.

Therefore, the law boosts the importance of school social work activities that promote and sustain such parental involvement. Fifth, school social workers must become skilled in the development and provision of behavioral management plans and interventions that prevent violent and disruptive behaviors in school and "market" themselves as having this expertise (National Association of Social Workers [NASW], 1997).

Several categories of disabilities that frequently involve the services of school social workers are discussed next. While students must receive one of the following labels to be eligible for special education services, the label itself may impact an individual student's self-esteem, teachers' expectations of that student's ability or behavior, or parental expectations. Therefore, it is essential that school social workers be sensitive to the impact of labels, both positive and negative.

Attention Deficit Disorder/Hyperactivity Disorder (ADHD)

According to Donovan (2000) and NIMH (1996), attention deficit disorder with hyperactivity (ADHD), once referred to as "hyperkinesis" or "minimal brain dysfunction," is one of the most common mental disorders identified among children. ADHD affects perhaps as many as 2 million American children with ten percent of grade school boys and 5 percent of grade school girls having been diagnosed with ADHD. It has been estimated that at least one child in every classroom in the United States needs help for this disorder. This statistic is not surprising since classrooms demand that children sit still, pay attention, and stick with a task. While students with ADHD are fully capable of learning, their hyperactivity and inattention make learning difficult.

An ADHD assessment should involve a complete medical, family, social, psychiatric, and educational history (NIMH, 1996). To rule out other causes, it is important to assess the extent to which the home and classroom environment may be stressful or chaotic and the way the student's parents and teachers deal with him or her. This is done by asking the child's teachers, past and present, to rate their observations of the child's behavior on standardized inventories to compare the student's behaviors with those of other students the same age. A diagnosis of ADHD should be made *only if the child exhibits such behaviors substantially more than other children of the same age.* Several commonly used inventories provide valuable information on the student's behavior in different settings and situations (NIMH, 1996). These inventories include the parent and teacher versions of the Conners Rating Scales, and the parent and teacher versions of the Child Behavior Checklist (CBCL; Cowan, 2000). It is important to note that these inventories are subjective in that they assess only the parent's or teacher's personal perception of the student and that the student's actual behavior may be under- or overreported. Tests of intelligence and learning achievement may also be given to determine whether the student has a learning disability. It is also important to observe the child in the classroom and to pay special attention to the child's behavior in noisy or unstructured settings such as the lunchroom and playground, or in situations that require sustained attention, such as playing board games (NIMH, 1996). A medical doctor may also examine a child for allergies or nutrition problems that might make the child seem overly active. School social workers are frequently involved in gathering this information from parents or guardians and teachers. Because ADHD is a disability that affects a child's ability to learn and interact with others, it can be a disabling condition; and many children with ADHD are able to receive special education services under the IDEA. However, students who do not qualify for services under IDEA can receive help under Section 504, often referred to as "504 eligibility," which defines disabilities more broadly than IDEA (McKethan, 2001; NIMH, 1996).

Psychosocial therapy, usually combined with medications (i.e., Ritalin, Dexedrine or Dextrostat, Cylert) is the treatment approach of choice to alleviate ADHD symptoms. However, it is important to note that the use of Ritalin and the other stimulants has sparked a great deal of controversy in the United

States. This is largely due to the fact that despite having only 5 percent of the world's population, the United States consumes 90 percent of the world's Ritalin (Donovan, 2000). An alarming trend is the growing number of young children being diagnosed with ADHD and being prescribed Ritalin. For example, data from a Midwestern state indicates that between 1991 and 1995, prescriptions of stimulants for children under age 5 increased by 78 percent for boys and 107 percent for girls (Donovan, 2000). To keep up with this demand, production of the stimulant methylphenidate (Ritalin) increased seven times between 1991 and 1998 (Donovan, 2000). These data suggest that children who do not have a true attention disorder are being medicated as a way to control their disruptive behaviors. An important role of the school social worker is to ensure that a systematic and comprehensive assessment of ADHD is carried out so that other possible causes of a student's behavior can be ruled out. School social workers should also help parents understand the potential benefits and potential risks of using Ritalin and other drugs used to treat ADHD.

Behavior modification therapy and cognitive-behavioral therapy are often used with children and youth with ADHD. Behavior modification therapy uses a reward system to reinforce appropriate behavior and the completion of tasks and can be implemented in the classroom as well as the home (Cowan, 2000). Cognitive-behavioral therapy has been shown to decrease impulsive behavior by getting the child to recognize the connection between thoughts and behavior and by changing negative thinking patterns (Cowan, 2000). NIMH (1996) outlines a number of special accommodations that can be made to help children with ADHD learn in the classroom. For example, the student may be seated in an area with few distractions or in an area of the classroom where the student can move around and release excess energy. The student may also keep a card or a picture on his or her desk to serve as a visual reminder to raise a hand instead of shouting out or to stay in a seat instead of wandering around the room. Other ways of helping students focus include telling students in advance what they will learn, providing visual aids, and giving written, as well as oral, instructions. School social workers can assist the classroom teacher in implementing many of these special accommodations.

Emotional Disturbance (ED)

The IDEA Amendments of 1997 changed "serious emotional disturbance" to "emotional disturbance" in an effort to reduce negative connotation of the term "serious." It has been estimated that approximately 4 million to 6 million children and youth have ED (Housewright, 1999; Quindlen, 1999). However, only 1 percent are identified by schools as ED and only two-thirds of those receive any type of mental health treatment (Housewright, 1999; Quindlen, 1999). Students identified with an emotional disturbance are more likely to be African American, economically disadvantaged, and live in single parent families (Wagner, 1995).

Students identified with an emotional disturbance face problems far different from students with other types of disabilities. For example, they often have teachers who are ill equipped to meet their unique needs (Montague, McKinney, & Hocutt, 1996). Moreover, many general education teachers believe that their classroom is an inappropriate placement for students with an emotional disturbance (Schumm & Vaughn, 1992). As a result, students with emotional disturbances are at substantial risk for a number of educational problems including poor overall academic achievement, high rates of absenteeism and suspension, and significantly higher rates of dropout (Montague et al., 1996). In addition, students identified with an emotional disturbance are more likely to have difficulty finding and keeping a job after high school and to have arrest rates of 58 percent five years after leaving school (Wagner, 1995). As a result, educating students identified with an emotional disturbance has been referred to as "one of the most stressful, complex and difficult challenges facing public education today, and perhaps one of our greatest failures" (Osher, Osher, & Smith, 1994, p. 7).

One of the most widely used standardized scales to identify students with an emotional disturbance is the child behavior checklist (CBCL). According to Achenbach (1996), the CBCL was developed to meet the need for "standardized, quantifiable, psychometrically sound, and economical procedures" that can be used to assess behavioral and emotional problems under varied conditions. Separate versions of the CBCL have been designed to obtain parents' ratings of children at various ages, teachers' ratings of students at various ages, self-ratings of adolescents, and direct observations.

A number of behavior management techniques (i.e., positive reinforcement, token economies, contracting, and time-out) are commonly used with students identified with an emotional disturbance (Zabel, 1988). Other interventions used with these students include the teaching of social skills through modeling, discussion, and rehearsal. Music, art, exercise, and relaxation techniques, as well as individual and group counseling, have also been used with students identified with ED (Zabel, 1988). A school social worker often provides these related services, as spelled out in the student's IEP.

Learning Disabilities (LD)

According to the NIMH (1993), nearly 4 million school-age children have been identified as having learning disabilities (LD). LD is a disorder that affects people's ability to either interpret what they see and hear or to link information from different parts of the brain. Legally, LD is defined as a significant gap between a person's intelligence and those skills the person has achieved at each age. However, in reality, children with above-average intelligence who manage to maintain passing grades in spite of their disability are less likely to be identified (NIMH, 1993). Another complicating factor in identifying LD students is the difficulty in distinguishing LD students from students labeled as "slow learners" because of learning difficulties in some aspects of their lives. To further complicate the matter, students who are at risk due to cultural, linguistic, medical, social, and economic factors often appear to have LD (Lokerson, 1992).

A diagnosis of LD uses standardized tests that compare the child's level of ability to what is considered normal development for a person of that age and intelligence (NIMH, 1993). However, there are variations between states and among school systems in identifying learning disabilities. For example, some states specify an intelligence range while other states examine the discrepancy between potential and achievement (Lokerson, 1992). These different criteria indicate a lack of consensus about what exactly is meant by "learning disabilities." Careful assessment by a multidisciplinary team using a variety of standardized instruments, informal tasks, and observation is an important part of verifying the existence of LD (Lokerson, 1992).

In working with students with LD, teachers should draw on as many of the child's senses as possible since many experts believe that the more senses children use in learning a skill, the more likely they are to retain that skill (NIMH, 1993). For example, if one of the short-term goals in an LD student's IEP is learning to spell and recognize words, the teacher may ask the student to say, write, and spell each new word and also ask the student to write new words in sand to engage the sense of touch. (NIMH, 1993). School social workers can be written into an LD student's IEP as a related service to provide direct counseling to help LD students develop greater self-control and develop a more positive attitude toward their own abilities. School social workers can also work with family members to allow them to vent their feelings as well as receive support and reassurance.

Autism

Autism was added as a separate category of disability in 1990 under the IDEA (Knoblauch & Sorenson, 1998). A small but growing number of children are being diagnosed with autism. Autism currently affects about one or two people out of every thousand and occurs in four times as many boys as girls (NIMH, 1997). Most children with autism appear to have considerable difficulty learning to engage in everyday human interaction (NIMH, 1997). Research indicates that about half of the children diagnosed with autism remain mute throughout their lives (NIMH, 1997). About 75 percent to 80 percent of people with autism are mentally retarded to some extent, with 15 percent to 20 percent considered severely retarded (i.e., IQs below 35). However, at least 10 percent of people with autism have an average or above average IQ (NIMH, 1997). There are no known racial, social, economic, or cultural differences in children with autism, although girls with autism tend to have more severe symptoms and lower intelligence (Dunlap & Bunton-Pierce, 1999; NIMH, 1997). About one-third of the children with autism develop seizures, starting either in early childhood or adolescence (NIMH, 1997). In addition to loss of personal potential, the cost of health and educational services to those affected exceeds $3 billion each year (NIMH, 1997).

Since several conditions can cause symptoms that resemble those of autism, the child's pediatrician should rule out other disorders, including hearing loss, speech problems, mental retardation, and neurological problems (NIMH, 1997). According to Dunlap and Bunton-Pierce (1999), a specialist should make a diagnosis of autism only if there is clear evidence of poor or limited social relationships, underdeveloped communication skills, repetitive behaviors, or a combination of these, by age three years.

Researchers have begun to identify certain interventions that are effective in reducing or reversing symptoms associated with autism (NIMH, 1997). For example, it appears that treatment programs that produce the greatest gains are those that build on the child's interests, provide a predictable and structured schedule, teach tasks as a series of simple steps, and provide regular reinforcement of behavior (NIMH, 1997). The Treatment and Education of Autistic and Related Communication Handicapped

Children (TEACCH) program has been shown to result in short-term gains for preschoolers with autism (Ozonoff & Cathcart, 1998). While some antipsychotic drugs have been shown to be effective in the treatment of autism, it must be noted that a significant number of children develop serious side effects (Campbell et al., 1997).

Promising Interventions Targeting Students with Disabilities

A number of promising interventions targeting students with disabilities have been published. This section describes two intervention programs: One focuses on improving attention in young children with ADHD, and the other is a behavioral treatment program for an adolescent with autism. Kerns, Eso, and Thomson (1999) investigated the effectiveness of a set of child-oriented direct intervention materials from the *Pay Attention!* program in 14 children diagnosed with ADHD. Both treatment and control groups were matched for age, sex, and medication status. The treatment group worked with *Pay Attention!* materials. These materials, which include both visual and auditory activities, are designed to train different levels of attention (e.g., sustained, selective, alternating, and divided attention) in young children. The control group engaged in a variety of computer-based activities, including computer puzzles and games. Both groups completed pre- and posttraining assessment batteries that included psychometric measures of attention, a measure of academic efficiency, and behavioral rating scales completed by parents and teachers. According to Kerns et al. (1999), children who were involved in *Pay Attention!* improved performance on several psychometric measures of sustained, selective, and higher levels of attention. A significant decrease in inattention and impulsivity of the control group was also noted by schoolteachers. These authors suggest that direct interventions aimed at improving attention may be a valuable treatment option for improving cognitive efficiency in children with ADHD.

Gerdtz (2000) described an intervention program that a social worker designed for an autistic student who had behavioral problems not only at school but also at home. After assessments were performed, it was discovered that most problem behaviors occurred when there were unexpected changes in the student's classroom routine. Consequently, the intervention included a plan to make unexpected changes less stressful, to increase the student's tolerance for unexpected changes, and to increase the student's social skills. Data sheets were used by the school staff and by the student to record behavior each day. Gerdtz (2000) reported that the intervention was successful at school, and disruptive behaviors also decreased at the student's home despite the fact that behavior at home was not targeted. The cooperation among the family, staff, and student was identified as the most helpful component of the treatment.

Summary

School social workers should have a working knowledge of the requirements and mandates of the Individuals with Disabilities Education Act (IDEA) and its accompanying regulations. In addition, school social workers should know how to write an effective social developmental study (SDS) that focuses on students' strengths and abilities as well as their deficits. They should also have a working knowledge of individualized education programs (IEP), know how to conduct functional behavioral assessments (FBA), and know how to implement behavior intervention plans that include positive behavioral interventions and supports (PBIS). School social workers are frequently involved in providing services to students with ADHD, students identified with an emotional disturbance, students with learning disabilities, and students with autism. It is essential that school social workers be sensitive to the impact of labels, both positive and negative.

School social workers are able to assist in meeting the challenges of educating children with disabilities in a number of ways. School social workers must ensure that parents of children with disabilities understand their rights and support these parents, as well as engage in activities that promote and sustain parental involvement. School social workers should also monitor the expansion of the discipline provisions contained in IDEA; maximize new opportunities for participation in the IEP process; facilitate communication and collaboration among mainstream teachers, special education personnel, and parents; and become skilled in the development and provision of behavioral management plans and interventions that prevent violent and disruptive behaviors in school. School social workers should also be familiar with the most current assessment tools and proven or promising interventions for students with disabilities such as the *Pay Attention!* program for students diagnosed with ADHD.

Questions for Discussion

1. What substantial changes have resulted from the passage of the IDEA Amendments of 1997 (Pub. L. No. 105–17) in relation to the education of children with disabilities?

2. What is the IEP and why is it considered the foundation of a quality education for each child with a disability?

3. Define and describe functional behavioral assessments (FBAs) and positive behavioral interventions and supports (PBISs).

4. What is an SDS? Why is adaptive behavior such an important component of the SDS?

5. In what specific ways can school social workers assist in meeting the challenges of educating children with disabilities?

Refer to the case study at the beginning of this chapter:

1. How might the school social worker approach John's teacher in an effort to improve John's relationship with his teacher?

2. What should the school social worker do to improve John's relationship with his peers? Why is this important?

3. Who should be involved in John's IEP meetings?

Additional Resources

- Parent Training and Information Centers
  www.taalliance.org/PTIs.htm
- Children with disabilities
  www.childrenwithdisabilities.ncjrs.org
- 504 Plan and IDEA Information Links
  www.adprima.com/specialed.htm
- Parent's Guide to Section 504 of the Rehabilitation Act of 1973
  www.wistech.org/Sec504/contents.html
- The National Information Center for Children and Youth with Disabilities (NICHCY) is the national information and referral center that provides information on disabilities and disability-related issues for families, educators, and other professionals.
  www.nichcy.org
- *A Guide to the Individualized Education Program* assists educators, parents, and state and local educational agencies in implementing the requirements of Part B of the Individuals with Disabilities Education Act (IDEA) regarding Individualized Education Programs (IEPs) for children with disabilities, including preschool-aged children.
  www.ed.gov/offices/OSERS/OSEP/IEP_Guide
- *Technical Assistance Guide: Applying Positive Behavioral Support and Functional Behavioral Assessment in Schools* provides educators, parents, policymakers, and others with guidance on positive behavioral interventions and supports and functional behavioral assessment.
  www.pbis.org/english/index.html
- IDEA Web site and E-Newsletter for teachers and families interested in advances in special education.
  www.ideapractices.org
- The Center for Appropriate Dispute Resolution (CADRE) in Special Education provides technical assistance to states, jurisdictions, and others on implementation of the mediation requirements under IDEA 1997.
  www.directionservice.org/cadre
- Service Providers (Teachers and Related Services) Association of Service Providers Implementing IDEA
  www.ideapractices.org

- Families and Advocates
  www.fape.org
- CHADD is a national nonprofit organization representing children and adults with ADHD that was founded by a group of concerned parents in 1987. This organization works to improve the lives of people with ADHD through education, advocacy, and support. The site offers legislative information, news releases, research studies, and information concerning relevant conferences.
  www.chadd.org
- The Center for Effective Collaboration and Practice facilitates the production, exchange, and use of knowledge about effective practices for children with, or at risk of developing, emotional disturbance.
  www.air.org/cecp/cecp.html
- Gehret, J. (1990). *Learning disabilities and the don't give up kid.* Fairport, NY: Verbal Images Press. (For classmates and children with learning disabilities and attention difficulties, ages 7 to 12.)
- Learning Disabilities Association (LDA; www.ldnatl.org) is a national nonprofit organization with chapters in all 50 states. Its Web site offers families and professionals information on advocacy, research, legal developments, and access to local LDA chapters. LDA has a broad range of fact sheets, news alerts, and other publications on specific learning disabilities, legal issues, and advocacy for youth with disabilities.
- Autism Society of America, 7910 Woodmont Avenue, Suite 650, Bethesda, MD 20814-3015
  www.autism-society.org
- Readings and Resources on Autism, ERIC Minibibliography No. E13. Autism Center
  www.patientcenters.com/autism/news/pdd4 7990601.htm
- Autism Resources
  www.autism-resources.com
- Autism Society of America
  www.autism-society.org

SYSTEM-FOCUSED
INTERVENTIONS

Possessing clinical skills is necessary but insufficient for effective school social work practice. While direct practice with students is an important aspect of school social work practice, the preamble of the National Association of Social Workers (NASW) Code of Ethics states that "fundamental to social work is attention to environmental forces that create, contribute to, and address problems in living." Therefore, interventions with those larger systems that impact students is also an important aspect of all social work practice. The preamble also states that *clients* is used inclusively to refer to individuals, families, groups, organizations, and communities." Therefore, the school itself can and should be viewed as a potential *client*. This also holds true for families, neighborhoods, and communities.

Several decades ago, Alderson (1972) presented several models of school social work practice. In the school-change model, Alderson challenged school social workers to move beyond a psychopathological view of student problems by working to change dysfunctional conditions in the school. Alderson also discussed the community school model of practice that focused on working with disadvantaged communities. Costin's school-community-pupil relations model also emphasized the interactions among students, school, and community and the modification of harmful school policies and practices (Costin, 1975).

While targeting schools, neighborhoods, and communities for change appears to be a daunting task, the knowledge base of proven or promising interventions designed to bring about systemic changes in schools, neighborhoods, and communities has grown dramatically over the past decade. This knowledge base is reflected throughout all the chapters in this section of the book.

Chapter 7 discusses a number of exemplary school-based programs designed to prevent or minimize problems commonly found in school settings including violence, bullying, substance abuse, truancy, teenage pregnancy, and teenage substance abuse as well as innovative programs designed to transform entire schools. Chapter 8 focuses on interventions on behalf of students who are victimized because of known or presumed gay or lesbian sexual orientation, or because they are children of color or students who are being reintegrated into school from residential and juvenile justice settings. Chapter 9 discusses the emerging school social work role of consultant and how they can, as consultants, be effective and efficient in meeting the varied needs of at-risk students. Chapter 10 describes the emerging school-community collaboration movement and the challenges facing school social worker in developing, enhancing, and maintaining successful school-community collaborations and how to increase "parental connectedness" with schools.

School-Based Prevention Programs

In this chapter, we discuss:

- Exemplary school-based prevention programs.
- Programs for prevention of violence.
- Programs for prevention of bullying.
- Programs for prevention of substance abuse.
- Programs for prevention of truancy.
- Programs for prevention of sexual abuse.
- Programs for prevention of teenage pregnancy and sexually transmitted disease.
- Innovative programs designed to transform schools.

Chapter

Jim, a high school student, came to see Ms. Cory, the school social worker, complaining of pressures at school that included a classmate who was harassing him. Jim said that this kid had been bullying him and everyone else since first grade but that he could usually deal with it. Currently, other pressures were so great that the harassment was really getting to him. What bothered Ms. Cory most was that Jim had been bullied since first grade. She decided to spend some time in the elementary school observing classroom behavior. It did not take long for her to notice early forms of bullying. Some pushing took place in hallways, and teachers were inconsistent with consequences. Ms. Cory noticed kids grabbing things from others or verbally harassing each other when teachers' backs were turned. As a result of her observations, Ms. Cory realized that the culture of the school would have to change to reduce the prevalence of bullying, and that this cultural change would need to begin in elementary school. Ms. Cory set up a time to meet with the elementary school principal to discuss her concerns about the problem and the need to implement a bullying prevention program.

Our nation is at a "critical crossroad" as we begin the twenty-first century. We can continue to react to youth violence by becoming increasingly punitive and building and locking more and more of our youth in adult prisons, or we can be more proactive by implementing effective violence prevention programs in our schools and communities. (Elliott, 1998)

Introduction

As more federal and state funds are directed at prevention programs rooted in scientific research, schools will turn increasingly to those professionals, including school social workers, with expertise to prevent problems commonly found in school settings today. Like Ms. Cory in the case vignette, school social workers are professionals who not only provide clinical services to individual students and their families but also have the knowledge and expertise to implement interventions designed to target larger systems for change, such as school-based prevention programs.

Several decades of prevention research has greatly expanded the knowledge base of "what works" in school-based programs (Sloboda & David, 1997) and yielded those essential elements found in successful school-based prevention programs (see Table 7.1). As shown in this table, the most successful school-based prevention programs do more than reach the individual child; they also seek to change the total school environment. Individual-change strategies use experiential techniques rather than a lecture format, and school-change strategies are designed to impact the culture and climate of the

Table 7.1   **Essential Elements Employed in Successful School-Based Prevention Programs**

- Includes both individual-change and school-change strategies.
- Individual-change strategies attempt to develop social competence by changing students' knowledge, skills, attitudes, beliefs, or behaviors by using interactive teaching techniques (e.g., role plays and practice with peers) rather than lectures or one-way communications.
- School-change strategies include programs aimed at changing the culture of the school and clarifying and communicating behavioral norms (e.g., the use of alcohol and drugs is not the norm for teenagers).
- Individual-change and school-change strategies consist of multiple years of intervention using a well-tested, standardized intervention with detailed lesson plans and student materials.

Source: Adapted from *Drug Abuse Prevention,* by K. Bosworth, 1997, Washington, DC: ERIC Document Reproduction Service No. ED409316; "School-Based Violence Prevention," by W. DeJong, 1994, *Forum, 25,* Spring; "School-Based Crime Prevention," by D. C. Gottfredson, 1997, in L. W. Sherman, D. Gottfredson, D. MacKenzie, J. Ech, P. Reuter, and S. Bushway (Eds.), *Preventing Crime,* College Park: University of Maryland; and *Preventing Drug Use Among Children and Adolescents,* by Z. Sloboda and S. L. David, 1997, Washington, DC: National Institute on Drug Abuse.

school. Moreover, successful school-based prevention programs are not "one-shot" undertakings. Successful programs require multiple years of intervention (e.g., booster sessions) using standardized, detailed lesson plans.

This chapter provides an overview of a number of proven or promising school-based prevention programs that employ both individual- and school-change strategies. Included are programs designed to prevent violence, bullying, substance abuse, truancy, sexual abuse, and teenage pregnancy and sexually transmitted diseases. In addition, this chapter highlights several innovative programs designed to transform schools to "reach out" rather than "push out" at-risk students (Civil Rights Project, 2000).

Exemplary School-Based Prevention Programs

Each of the school-based prevention programs described in this chapter reflects these essential elements of successful school-based prevention programs. The primary criterion for inclusion was strong empirical support. For example, a number of these programs rank among the top 50 percent in terms of strong program effects by at least one of three groups of researchers (U.S. Departments of Education and Justice, 1999), several have been named *exemplary* or *promising* programs by the U.S. Department of Education's Expert Panel on Safe, Disciplined and Drug-Free Schools, while others have been named *blueprint programs* by the Center for the Study and Prevention of Violence at the University of Colorado at Boulder because they met a very high scientific standard of program effectiveness and provided a nucleus for a national violence prevention initiative. For more specific information on the methodology used (e.g., sample size, ethnicity of participants) to determine the effectiveness of individual programs, refer to the original source cited for each program. Contact information for many of the school-based prevention programs discussed in this chapter can be found in Table 7.2.

Programs for Prevention of Violence

Resolving Conflicts Creatively Program

Resolving Conflicts Creatively Program (RCCP) is the most extensively researched school-based violence prevention program and is widely regarded by public health experts as one of the most promising violence prevention programs in operation today (DeJong, 1999). According to DeJong, the goal of RCCP is to create school change so that students have a safe environment in which to explore peaceful ways of resolving conflict. RCCP is based on the assumption that students who engage in violent acts often do not know how to manage conflict in their lives, and conflict education is important because it provides youth with tools to deal with the inevitable daily conflicts that can result in violent behaviors. The primary objectives of the RCCP are to achieve a long-term reduction in violence and violence-related behavior, promote cooperative behavior among students and adults, promote intercultural understanding and positive

Table 7.2   **Partial Listing of Contacts for Effective School-Based Prevention Programs**

Violence Prevention Programs	*Substance Abuse Prevention Programs*
Resolving Conflicts Creatively Program (RCCP)	Life Skills Training
Mariana Gaston	Telephone: (800) 636-3415
Phone: (212) 260-6290	www.lifeskillstraining.com
Linking the Interests of Families and Teachers (LIFT)	Project ALERT
J. Mark Eddy PhD	G. Bridget Ryan
Telephone: (541) 485-2711	Telephone: (800) 253-7810
Fax: (541) 485-7087	Fax: (213) 623-0585
E-mail: marke@oslc.org	E-mail: info@projectalert.best.org
www.oslc.org	www.projectalert.best.org
Metropolitan Area Child Study	Know Your Body (KYB)
Patrick H. Tolan, PhD	Telephone: (212) 551-2509
Telephone: (312) 413-1893	Fax: (212) 697-4374
Fax: (312) 413-1703	E-mail: KYBprogram@aol.com
E-mail: Tolan@uic.edu	www.ahf.org
Teaching Students to be Peacemakers	*Truancy Prevention Programs*
Linda Johnson	At School, ON Time, Ready to Work
Telephone: (612) 831-7060	Sheryl A. Beagley
Fax: (612) 831-9332	Telephone: (316) 431-5750
Bullying Prevention Programs	Project Helping Hand
The Bullying Prevention Program	Sally Ann Williams or Colleen Denelsbezk
Dan Olweus, PhD, Principal Investigator	Atlantic County Division of Intergenerational
E-mail: Olweus@psych.uib.no	Services
www.colorado.edu/cspv/blueprints/model	101 South Shore Road
/bully_materials.html	Northfield, NJ 08225
Sue Limber	Operation Save Kids
Telephone: (864) 656-6271	Terry Bays Smith
Steps to Respect	Telephone: (602) 412-7347
Telephone: (800) 634-4449	
Fax: (206) 343-1445	
www.cfchildren.org	

relations, and promote greater student academic achievement and a reduction in the absentee rates for both students and teachers (Aber, Brown, Chaudry, Jones, & Samples, 1996). An evaluation of RCCP found that almost 71 percent of responding teachers observed students demonstrating less physical violence in the classroom to a moderate or great extent, and almost 72 percent of responding teachers observed that students have increased skills in understanding others' points of view (Metis Associates, Inc., 1990). See Aber et al.'s and Metis Associates' studies for more detailed evaluation results of RCCP.

Linking the Interests of Families and Teachers

Linking the Interests of Families and Teachers (LIFT) is a multicomponent program that targets the individual child, school, classroom, peer group, and home to reduce the antecedents for conduct disorder (Greenberg et al., 2000, p. 108). LIFT is a 10-week intervention consisting of parent training, a classroom-based social skills program, a playground behavioral program, and routine school-parent communication. According to Greenberg et al., the school component consists of 20, one-hour sessions provided over a 10-week period. The school component includes:

1. Developmentally appropriate classroom instruction on social and problem-solving skills.
2. Opportunities to practice social and problem-solving skills in large and small group settings.
3. Free play in the context of a group cooperation game (adapted from the Good Behavior Game; see Chapter 9).
4. Skills review and presentation of rewards.

The school-parent communication component consists of a telephone and answering machine for each classroom on which teachers leave daily messages about class activities, homework assignments, and special events. Parents may call to hear these messages. Additionally, a parent intervention focuses on teaching parents how to create and sustain a home environment marked by consistent and effective discipline practices and close supervision. LIFT has been shown to "virtually stop aggressive behavior" in elementary school children (see Reid, Eddy, & Fetrow, 1999).

Metropolitan Area Child Study

Metropolitan Area Child Study (MACS) "seeks to affect the child's thinking and behavior, while also affecting the major influences on development (teachers, peers, and parents)" (U.S. Departments of Education and Justice, 1999, p. 40). According to the U.S. Departments of Education and Justice (1999), MACS is designed to be implemented in elementary schools with one version designed for second and third grades and one version designed for fifth and sixth grades. The most basic program, implemented for 20 weeks over two years, combines teacher training in classroom behavior management and instructional techniques with a classroom-based social-skills, social problem-solving curriculum. A 20-session, small group component for children at high risk for aggression can be added on a weekly basis for between six and eight children. A third component that involves families in 22 weekly meetings can also be added. MACS has been carefully and extensively evaluated using a multiethnic, economically disadvantaged population. The full/integrated program has been shown to be effective in "reducing aggression, improving academic functioning, and lessening rates of later delinquency" (U.S. Departments of Education and Justice, 1999, p. 37).

Teaching Students to be Peacemakers

Teaching Students to be Peacemakers is described as a peer mediation and school discipline program that teaches students how to resolve disagreements peacefully (U.S. Departments of Education and Justice, 1999). Students in the *Teaching Students to be Peacemakers* program are "taught what is and what is not a conflict, how to mediate schoolmates' conflicts, and how to negotiate agreements" (U.S. Department of Education and Justice, 1999, p. 38). Students learn six-step negotiation procedures and four-step mediation procedures. "Evaluators observed a 63 percent reduction in antisocial and violent behaviors in students who participated in this program compared to students who did not participate" (U.S. Departments of Education and Justice, 1999, p. 38).

Programs for Prevention of Bullying

Bullying Prevention Program

The *Bullying Prevention Program* is the first and best-known intervention that specifically targets bullying in schools. It has been designated as a model blueprint program by the Center for the Study and Prevention of Violence, Institute of Behavioral Science, at the University of Colorado at Boulder. The *Bullying Prevention Program* is described as a comprehensive prevention program consisting of schoolwide interventions, classroom-level interventions, and individual-level interventions (Limber & Nation, 1998). According to Olweus (1993), the *Bullying Prevention Program*, implemented in Norway and Sweden in the early 1980s, has as its major goal the reduction of victim/bullying problems among primary and secondary school children. It achieves this goal by increasing the awareness of the bullying problem, actively involving teachers and parents, developing clear rules against bullying behavior, and providing support and protection to the victims of bullying. The *Bullying Prevention Program* has been shown to result in substantial reductions in the frequency with which students report being bullied and bullying others, significant improvements in the "social climate" of the class, and significant reductions in students' reports of vandalism, fighting, theft, and truancy (Olweus, Limber, & Mihalic, 1999, p. 19). See the Bullying Prevention Program box on page 141 for a description of this exemplary program.

Steps to Respect

Steps to Respect is a school-based program designed to decrease bullying in elementary schools and help children build more respectful, caring peer relationships. According to information

Bullying Prevention Program

The *Bullying Prevention Program* is a multilevel, multicomponent program designed to reduce victim/bully problems among primary and secondary students by restructuring the existing school environment to reduce opportunities and rewards for bullying behavior. All students participate in most aspects of the program, while students identified as bullies or victims receive additional individual interventions. Core program components are implemented at the school, classroom, and individual levels.

School-level components include an anonymous student questionnaire assessing the nature and prevalence of bullying at a school; a school in-service day for discussing bullying problems, increasing awareness and knowledge of the problem, and planning the implementation of the program; the formation of a Bullying Prevention Coordinating Committee to coordinate all aspects of a school's program; and the development of a coordinated system of supervising students during break periods.

Classroom-level components include establishing and enforcing classroom rules against bullying, holding regular classroom meetings with students to increase knowledge and empathy, and encouraging prosocial norms and behavior. Meetings with parents are also scheduled to foster more active involvement on their part. *Individual-level components* include interventions with children identified as bullies and victims, support and protection for the victims of bullying, and discussions with the parents of involved students.

The *Bullying Prevention Program* provides a 32-page informational booklet on bullying, bullies, and victims; a folder of information and recommendations for parents about bullies and victims; a video of vignettes about bullying for classroom use; and a school questionnaire to assess the level of bully/victim problems in a particular school that can serve as a catalyst for schoolwide discussion.

Source: Excerpted from "Bullying Prevention Program" by D. Olweus, S. Limber & S. F. Mihalic, 1999. In D. S. Elliott (Series Ed.), *Blueprints for Violence Prevention* (Book 9). Boulder, CO: Institute of Behavioral Science, Center for the Study and Prevention of Violence. Reprinted with permission.

provided by the Committee for Children (n.d.), *Steps to Respect* is based on research demonstrating that teaching certain skills is an effective method of reducing bullying behavior. The entire school staff attends a three-hour all-staff training. Because it is designed to increase adult awareness of bullying at school and teach adults how to respond effectively to children's reports of bullying, this staff training is an essential component of *Steps to Respect*. Skill lessons focusing on building students' skills in making and keeping friends, solving problems, managing emotions, and responding to bullying are taught once a week, followed by one 15- to 20-minute booster session taught later during the same week. An eleventh lesson reviews, summarizes, and concludes each level.

Programs for Prevention of Substance Abuse

Life Skills Training

Life Skills Training (LST) is "designed to provide middle school students with the motivation and skills necessary to resist peer and media pressure to use drugs" (U.S. Departments of Education and Justice, 1999, p. 42). *Life Skills Training* has been recognized as a program that "works" by the Centers for Disease Control and Prevention, the American Medical Association, and the American Psychological Association (O. Mayer, 1999) and has been recognized as one of ten model blueprint programs that has met the scientific standards set by the Center for the Study and Prevention of Violence at the University of Colorado at Boulder. According to the U.S. Departments of Education and Justice (1999), *Life Skills Training* is a three-year, sequential intervention consisting of 15 sessions for seventh-grade students followed by a two-year booster component of 10 sessions in the second year and 5 sessions in the third year (U.S. Departments of Education and Justice, 1999). The program teaches students general self-management skills and skills related to avoiding substance abuse through training techniques such as instruction, demonstration, feedback, reinforcement, and practice. *Life Skills Training* has been shown to dramatically reduce tobacco, alcohol, and marijuana use across a wide-range of adolescents, and to maintain these changes over a period of time. For example, evaluations of *Life Skills Training* "have found a 31 percent reduction in alcohol use, a 32 percent reduction in alcohol and marijuana use after four months, and a 4 percent reduction in alcohol and marijuana use after 16 months for program students" (U.S. Departments of Education and Justice, 1999, p. 43).

Project ALERT

Project ALERT has been named an exemplary program by the U.S. Department of Education's Expert Panel on Safe, Disciplined and Drug-Free Schools, one of only nine programs to receive this designation out of more than 130 programs evaluated. *Project ALERT* was also named winner of the Exemplary Substance Abuse Prevention Programs Award by the United States Department of Health and Human Services, Center for Substance Abuse Prevention. According to Ellickson and Bell (1990), *Project ALERT* is a 14-lesson program designed to prevent or curb the use of alcohol, tobacco, marijuana, and inhalants. The program uses experiential activities and videos to help students establish nondrug norms, understand the benefits of being drug-free, recognize that most people don't use drugs, recognize alternatives to substance use, counter advertising appeals, resist internal and social pressures to use drugs, communicate with parents, and support others in making nonuse decisions. Guided classroom discussions and small group activities encourage peer interaction and challenge students, while intensive role playing helps students to master resistance skills. Homework assignments enhance the learning process. *Project ALERT* also seeks to establish schoolwide norms against drug use. An evaluation found that the curriculum delayed or reduced cigarette and marijuana use during the middle school years and was equally effective in schools with higher minority populations (Ellickson & Bell, 1990).

Know Your Body

Know Your Body (KYB) is a skill-based health education program for children in grades K through 6. According to the U.S. Departments of Education and Justice (1999), KYB involves 35 hours of classroom instruction each year in addition to performance assessments, workshops, brochures, and a parent and community component. To address a wide range of health and social-issue related topics, the KYB curriculum "combines developmentally appropriate health instruction, in addition to building cognitive and behavioral skills" (p. 42). The KYB curriculum is multiethnic and has even been translated into seven languages. An evaluation of the program using a sample of Black and White students in an urban setting found that fifth- and sixth-grade program youth had a "prevalence rate for tobacco that was 23 percent lower than youth who did not participate in the program" (U.S. Departments of Education and Justice, 1999, p. 42).

Programs for Prevention of Truancy

The school environment is an integral factor in student attendance and performance, and school social workers and others interested in increasing attendance must create invitational and welcoming schools. For example, one Kentucky high school *requires* that teachers compliment marginal students as well as offer academic incentives for good attendance (Rohrman, 1993). Other ways of creating invitational schools is helping teachers to minimize verbal reprimands and other forms of punishment, and to deemphasize competition in the classroom.

Several schoolwide programs have been developed to prevent truancy. Garry (1996) described three of these programs. The *At School, ON Time, Ready to Work* program, recognizing that many truant children are placed in the custody of social service agencies, focuses on preventing children's removal from home. *Project Helping Hand* is an early identification and intervention program that provides counseling for parents and elementary students at risk of developing chronic truancy problems. *Operation Save Kids* addresses truancy through a broad-based coalition of citizens and businesses in an Arizona community.

Programs for Prevention of Sexual Abuse

According to Tutty (1995), the *Who Do You Tell?* program uses discussion, pictures, short videos, and developmentally appropriate role plays to provide children, from kindergarten to sixth grade, with information and permission to say no to unwanted touch. Two leaders work with groups of between 15 to 20 children for two sessions of 45 to 60 minutes each, presented on consecutive days. Following the presentations, children are given the opportunity to ask for individual time to talk to the presenters. Parental permission is required. An evaluation of the *Who Do You Tell?* program, involving 231 children, found that participants were more likely to know the difference between appropriate and inappropriate touch than nonparticipants (Tutty, 2000).

Programs for Prevention of Teenage Pregnancy and Sexually Transmitted Disease

Contrary to the fears of many parents, it has been shown that programs that focus on sexuality (including HIV education programs, school-based clinics, and condom availability programs) *do not* increase any measure of sexual activity (Kirby, 1997). Despite the fact that the Bush Administration is boosting funding for abstinence-only programs, scientifically proven programs include information about both abstinence *and* contraception. It has also been shown that broad-based community support and parental involvement are critical to the implementation and success of adolescent pregnancy prevention efforts (Arnold, Smith, Harrison, & Springer, 1999). Since a number of myths surround this issue and since it is such an emotionally laden issue, it is essential that school social workers present the facts to educators and the general public about what approaches are effective in preventing teen pregnancy and sexually transmitted diseases. To counteract community resistance, school social workers must also build a broad-based community coalition to assist in the design and implementation of these programs. See Chapter 12 for a detailed discussion of guidelines for successfully planning, implementing, and evaluating programs such as these.

Several programs have been found to be successful in reducing the initiation of sexual activities, reducing unwanted pregnancies, increasing contraceptive use, and increasing the proportion of students abstinent before the program to successfully remain abstinent following the program. *Postponing Sexual Involvement* is a program for African American eighth graders that uses older peers (eleventh and twelfth graders) to help youth understand social and peer pressures to have sex and to develop and apply resistance skills (Ekstrand et al., 1994). *Healthy Oakland Teens* (HOT) uses health educators to teach basic sex and drug education and peer educators to lead experiential exercises focusing on values, decision making, communication, and condom-use skills (Ekstrand et al., 1994). *Reducing the Risk* is a high school program that uses role playing and experiential activities to enhance skills and to reduce unprotected intercourse by avoiding sex or using protection (Kirby, Barth, Leland, & Fetro, 1991). The *Carrera* program offers not only traditional sex education, but also tutoring, SAT preparation, job skills, medical and dental care, sports, and creative arts (Lewin, 2001). *AIDS Prevention for Adolescents in School* is a program for ninth and eleventh graders that focuses on providing accurate information about AIDS, evaluating risks of transmission, increasing knowledge of AIDS-prevention resources, exploring personal values, understanding external influences, and teaching skills to delay intercourse (Walter & Vaughn, 1993).

Innovative Programs Designed to Transform Schools

Too many schools are places of fear, intimidation, and zero tolerance rather than places of learning (Civil Rights Project, 2000). Making our schools safe havens would go a long way to counteract the negative home and community experiences of many at-risk children and youth (Garbarino et al., 1992). The more that youth feel bonded to schools, the less likely they are to engage in antisocial behavior (Hawkins & Weis, 1985). The innovative programs described in this section have been shown to transform schools in a number of creative ways.

School Development Program

The *School Development Program* (SDP) seeks to transform the culture of elementary schools composed of primarily low-income, African American students. It accomplishes this goal by forming a "representative governance and management team composed of school administrators, teachers, support staff, and parents" (Gottfredson, 2001, p. 129–130). This school management team identifies "goals for the school, plans activities to meet these goals, monitors activities, and takes corrective action to keep the activities on track" (Gottfredson, 2001, p. 130). The school management team oversees the establishment and implementation of a parent program and a multidisciplinary mental health team designed to address student behavior problems. By encouraging these supportive relationships, SDP builds a school community that promotes the social, emotional, and academic development of students (Corbin, 2001). SDP is based on the assumption that significant adults play a major role in children's learning and that congruence in goals and values between home and school is very important, particularly for children at risk for educational failure (Catalano, Loeber, & McKinney, 1999). It has been found that students participating in the SDP had significantly higher grades, academic achievement test scores, and self-reported social competence as compared to a similar group of students who did not participate in the program (Catalano et al., 1999).

School Transitional Environment Project

The *School Transitional Environment Project (STEP)* focuses on changing the school culture and climate to be less threatening and overwhelming to students during their transition from elementary to middle or from middle to high school. According to Greenberg et al. (2000), STEP's core components include:

1. Creating "cohorts" of transitioning students who remain together as a group during core classes and home room.
2. Restructuring classes to create smaller "learning communities" within the larger school.
3. Redefining the role of the homeroom teacher to that of "advisor" to students in his or her cohort and "liaison" between the students, their families, and the rest of the school.

The homeroom teacher also helps students select classes and addresses truancy issues with families (Greenberg et al., 2000). Felner and colleagues (Felner, Ginter, & Primavera, 1982; Felner et al., 1993) found in a series of evaluations that "STEP's restructuring of the school environment produced significantly lower levels of stress and reductions in anxiety, depression and delinquent behavior" (Greenberg et al., 2000, p. 14).

Seattle Social Development Project

The *Seattle Social Development Project* (SSDP) is designed to develop children's communication, conflict resolution, and problem-solving skills by targeting multiple risk factors across several settings (Hawkins, Von Cleve, & Catalano, 1991). In the classroom component, teachers are trained in proactive classroom management, interactive teaching (Brophy, 1986), and cooperative learning (Slavin, 1991). Teachers also teach refusal skills related to substance abuse and peer pressure in sixth-grade classes. The parent training component consists of parent classes offered in collaboration with local school and parent councils (Hawkins et al., 1991). Students who participated in

SSDP had reduced rates of teacher-reported aggression and externalizing behavior in second grade, had more proactive family management by parents and greater family communication in fifth grade, spent less time with deviant peers at the end of sixth grade, and had statistically significant positive outcomes related to commitment and attachment to school by age 18 (Hawkins et al., 1991).

Child Development Project

The *Child Development Project* (CDP) is designed to transform schools into "caring communities of learners" (Greenberg et al., 2000). The CDP is "based on research showing that school contexts in which children feel valued and accepted by teachers and peers and in which students are granted greater autonomy are associated with higher levels of prosocial behavior, greater intrinsic motivation in learning, and fewer conduct problems" (Hughes, 2000, p. 321). Program components include school staff training in cooperative learning strategies, cross-grade "buddying" activities, and involving students in classroom decision-making (Greenberg et al., 2000, p. 78). Longitudinal research on the CDP supports its "effectiveness in enhancing prosocial competencies and reducing substance abuse and delinquent behaviors" (Hughes, 2000, p. 322).

As with the student-focused interventions described in Chapters 3 and 4, the implementation of these school-based prevention programs poses a number of challenges for school social workers. To meet these challenges, school social workers must develop "political savvy" (see Chapter 2) because the work involved in bringing about systemic changes is a "daunting task that requires a steadfast commitment from the principal, teachers, staff, parents, and community. Specifically, it is difficult to "sell" the concept of prevention to school administrators, school board members, and a skeptical public concerned about how their tax dollars are being spent. The public is much more willing to spend money on prison construction than prevention programs. As John Calhoun, from the National Crime

Prevention Council, so powerfully stated, "If you're in trouble, we are ready to spend $20,000 to $30,000 a year on a prison cell for you. We need a companion promise that we will address problems before they get out of control." Consequently, school social workers must become familiar with recent advances in prevention research (as described in this chapter) and those specific prevention programs that have been shown to be effective in minimizing and preventing a host of school problems such as those described in this chapter. School social workers need to share this knowledge with school administrators, school board members, and a skeptical public. To assist with these advocacy efforts, it may be helpful to enlist supportive teachers and community members. Another major challenge in starting a new program is finding adequate funding. School social workers will often find it necessary to collaborate with community agencies or a nearby university to write grants. (A number of grant writing resources can be found in the Additional Resources section at the end of Chapter 3.) Once funded, school social workers can be directly involved in delivering the program to students or indirectly involved by providing ongoing consultation (see Chapter 9 for a detailed description of school social workers as consultants) and guidance to other school professionals involved in the delivery of the prevention program. Additional guidelines and steps for overcoming resistance and successfully planning, implementing, and evaluating new programs can be found in Chapter 12.

Summary

Several decades of prevention research have greatly expanded our knowledge base of "what works" in school-based programs. Several essential elements can be found in successful school-based prevention programs. Successful school-based prevention programs do more than reach the individual child; they also seek to change the total school environment. Individual-change strategies use experiential techniques rather than a lecture format, and school-change strategies are designed to impact the culture and climate of the school. Successful prevention programs require multiple years of intervention using standardized, detailed lesson plans.

A number of proven or promising school-based prevention programs employ both individual- and school-change strategies. Included are programs designed to prevent violence, bullying, substance abuse, truancy, sexual abuse, and teenage pregnancy and sexually transmitted diseases. Several innovative programs have been designed to transform schools so that they reach out to at-risk students rather than pushing them out. Since school leaders will increasingly turn to those professionals with expertise in implementing successful school-based prevention programs, school social workers should seize this opportunity by marketing themselves as professionals who not only provide clinical services to individual students and their families but also have knowledge of and expertise in implementing successful school-based prevention programs such as those discussed in this chapter.

Questions for Discussion

1. What essential elements have been found in successful school-based prevention programs?

2. What school-based violence prevention program is widely regarded by public health experts as one of the most promising violence prevention programs in operation today?

3. What is the first and best-known intervention that specifically targets bullying in schools?

4. What can school social workers do to change a school's culture and climate to reduce truancy and dropouts?

5. Name several challenges that await school social workers in attempting to implement school-based prevention programs. What steps can school social workers take to meet these challenges?

Refer to the case study at the beginning of this chapter:

1. What should Ms. Cory do to prepare for her meeting with the principal? How can she inform and persuade the principal that there is a problem and action needs to be taken?

2. What steps could Ms. Cory take to begin to change the climate of this particular school?

3. Who are several important "players" that Ms. Cory needs to reach out to in order to bring about changes in this school?

Additional Resources

Violence Prevention

- In the Spotlight: School Safety
  www.ncjrs.org/school_safety/school_safety.html
- The National Youth Gang Center assists state and local communities in the collection, analysis, and exchange of information on gang-related demographics, legislation, literature, research, and promising program strategies; telephone: (850) 385-0600. www.iir.com/nygc

Truancy Prevention Programs

- *Manual to Combat Truancy* (Prepared by the U.S. Department of Education in cooperation with the U.S. Department of Justice).
  www.ed.gov/pubs/Truancy

Teenage Pregnancy and Sexually Transmitted Disease Prevention Programs

- The Surgeon General's Call to Action to Promote Sexual Health and Responsible Sexual Behavior (June 2001).
  www.surgeongeneral.gov/library/sexualhealth/call.htm
- Kirby, D. (2001). Emerging Answers: Research finding on programs to reduce teen pregnancy.
  www.teenpregnancy.org/iresearc.htm

Interventions on Behalf of Vulnerable Groups of Students

In this chapter, we discuss:

- Victimization based on known or presumed gay or lesbian sexual orientation.
- Children of color.
- Students being reintegrated into school from residential and juvenile justice settings.
- Interventions designed to enhance the school success of these vulnerable groups of students.

Tom is a gay high school student who has "come out" recently to a female bisexual friend, Amy. Tom cannot imagine telling anyone else in his school about his sexual orientation. Just the other day he overheard several students call him a "faggot" because of the way he was standing. He has even heard several of his teachers making derogatory comments about homosexuality. Amy suggests that they talk to the school social worker. After some hesitation, Tom agreed. During the course of their discussion with Mary, the school social worker, Tom and Amy ask about forming a school support group for gay and lesbian students. Mary enthusiastically supports this idea and tells them that she will check into it. Mary approaches a school counselor and tells him about the idea. The counselor's reaction is disheartening. He says he agrees that the school needs such a group but warns that another staff member initiated such a support group a few years ago and is no longer employed by the school.

Educators have a social responsibility to provide an environment that supports the ability of all students—including lesbians and gays—to learn and that is free from physical and psychological abuse. (Sears, 1987)

Introduction

While the primary mission of the social work profession is to "enhance human well-being and help meet the basic human needs of all people," social workers are obligated to pay particular attention to the needs and empowerment of people who are vulnerable and oppressed (National Association of Social Workers [NASW] Code of Ethics, 1996). Several groups of students are particularly vulnerable—students who are victimized because of known or presumed gay or lesbian sexual orientation, children of color, and students who are being reintegrated into school from residential and juvenile justice settings. This chapter discusses the unique problems confronting each of these groups of vulnerable students and interventions designed to enhance the school success of these students. This chapter also discusses the importance of school social workers and the wide range of school social work roles necessary to implement systemic changes on behalf of these vulnerable groups of students.

Victimization Based on Known or Presumed Gay or Lesbian Sexual Orientation

Victimization based on known or presumed gay or lesbian sexual orientation is the most prevalent form of bias-related violence in the United States today (Pilkington & D'Augelli, 1995). Homophobic remarks in schools appear to be pervasive. For example, a 1999 survey of 496 lesbian, gay, bisexual, and transgender (LGBT) youth from 32 states found that more than 91.4 percent of LGBT youth sometimes or frequently heard homophobic remarks such as "faggot," "dyke," "queer" in their schools (Gay, Lesbian and Straight Education Network [GLSEN], 1999). In another study, 97 percent of students in public high schools reported hearing homophobic remarks from their peers on a routine basis (Massachusetts Governor's Commission on Gay and Lesbian Youth, 1993). Unfortunately, this harassment often extends beyond verbal abuse. A study by Pilkington and D'Augelli (1995) reported that 22 percent of gay males and 29 percent of lesbians were physically hurt by another student because of their sexual orientation.

This verbal, and sometimes physical, victimization has a devastating impact on the mental health and school performance of victims. Elia (1993) reported that 80 percent of gays and lesbians had declining school performance, almost 40 percent had problems with truancy, and 30 percent had dropped out of school. Nearly half of the youth in the GLSEN (1999) study reported that they did not feel safe in their schools.

To compound the problem, many school personnel have negative feelings about gay and lesbian students. Most disturbingly, school personnel are often perpetrators themselves, as illustrated in the case of Tom at the beginning of this chapter. Several studies bear this out. For example, two-thirds of guidance counselors in one study were found to harbor negative feelings toward gay and lesbian persons (Sears, 1992) and a majority of youth in another study reported hearing homophobic remarks from faculty or school staff (Massachusetts Governor's Commission on Gay and Lesbian Youth, 1993). As a result, school personnel rarely intervene when gay or lesbian students are victimized in schools. For example, in the GLSEN (1999) study, one-third of gay and lesbian students reported that no adult ever intervened in these circumstances. Even school professionals who do intervene are often ill-equipped to serve gay and lesbian students. For example, Sears found that less than 20 percent of a sample of guidance counselors received any training on serving gay and lesbian students, and only 25 percent of guidance counselors considered themselves to be "highly competent" in serving gay and lesbian youth. Given these findings, it is not surprising to discover that gay and lesbian students keep their sexual orientation hidden from teachers and other school professionals. They believe that an essential part of them is being dismissed or despised by other students and school personnel (Khayatt, 1994).

Children of Color

The United States is experiencing another great wave of immigration. However, this current wave is composed of children of color from the economically developing worlds of Asia and Latin America rather than Europe (Hare & Rome, 1999). As a result, public schools are faced with the challenge of educating a population of students who are more racially and ethnically diverse, as well as disadvantaged, than at any other time in our nation's history. While today 65 percent of the nation's school-age children are non-Hispanic Whites, that figure will drop to 56 percent by 2020 and to fewer than 50 percent by 2040 when a majority of school-age children in the United States will be members of minority groups (Olson, 2000). The largest growth will occur among Hispanics, who are projected to account for 43 percent of the total U.S. population growth between 1999 and 2010. By the year 2025, nearly one in four school-age students will be Hispanic (Olson, 2000).

This diversity already exists in a number of states. For example, in New Mexico, California, and Texas, the numbers of children under age eighteen years who are African American, Latino, Asian, Pacific Islanders, and Native American together far exceed the number of White children (Hare & Rome, 1999). In Broward County, Florida, the nation's fifth largest school district, young people come from at least 52 different countries and speak 52 different languages, ranging from Spanish and Haitian-Creole to Tagalog (Olson, 2000).

Educating an increasingly diverse and disadvantaged student population poses a number of challenges for educators. One of the most difficult challenges is closing the educational achievement gap for children of color and low-income children. For example, at the current time, only 13 percent of low-income children in fourth grade read proficiently at their grade level compared to 29 percent of all fourth-graders (Symonds, 2001). By the end of high school, a majority of African American and Hispanic children perform at only the level White children do in eighth grade (Symonds, 2001). What factors may account for these gaps? In one study, African American students, males in particular, were found to be "disidentified" with academics, as evidenced by low correlations between grades and self esteem (Osborne, 1997). Other factors found to be associated with academic underachievement include single parent families, lack of parental involvement, absenteeism, physical fights, and weapons possession (Horn & Carroll, 1997; Young & Smith, 1997). This educational achievement gap leads to a number of poor outcomes. Research shows that children of color and low-income children are more likely than others to drop out of school, to come into contact with the criminal justice system, or to leave school without the skills needed in an increasingly technological society (Olson, 2000).

Students Being Reintegrated into School from Residential and Juvenile Justice Settings

It has been estimated that more than 500,000 juvenile delinquency cases are disposed of each year that allow juvenile offenders to return to the community and attend school (H. N. Snyder & Sickmund, 1995). Many of these juveniles coming from juvenile justice facilities and residential placements have experienced physical or sexual abuse, have psychological problems and emotional disabilities, have experienced family or gang violence on a regular basis, have performed poorly in school, or a combination of these (H. N. Snyder & Sickmund, 1995). Because of the complexity of their situations, successful integration back into school and follow-up treatment is essential. However, it has proven to be particularly difficult to meet the educational needs of youth on probation or in aftercare status. The unique difficulties confronting these youth were discussed by Ingersoll and LeBoeuf (1997). For example, there is a lack of advance planning and coordination between the educational and justice systems. To illustrate, juvenile offenders may arrive at a school without any notice, educational documentation, or a reintegration plan. Moreover, these youth frequently must face parents who have given up on them, teachers and fellow students who fear them, and a general public who do not want them in the community (Ingersoll & LeBoeuf, 1997).

Interventions Designed to Enhance the School Success of Vulnerable Groups of Students

School social workers have an essential role to play in supporting these vulnerable groups of students and working to bring about systemic changes on behalf of these groups of students. The interventions discussed in this section call upon a wide range of school social work roles and tasks and require that the school social worker develop resources both in the school and in the community to better serve the needs of these highly vulnerable populations of students.

Victimization Based on Known or Presumed Gay or Lesbian Sexual Orientation

Over the past several decades, several communities have established separate schools for lesbian and gay students. For example, the Harvey Milk High School in New York City provides a supportive environment for students on the verge of dropping out of traditional school. However, interventions must extend beyond establishing separate schools for gay and lesbian students. Given the pervasiveness of the problem and the fact that the entire culture and climate of a school is impacted by homophobia and the hate accompanying heterosexuals' fear of being considered gay (Schwartz, 1994), all schools need to create a culture and climate that minimizes the victimization of gay and lesbian students (LeCompte, 2000).

This change effort demands interventions at both the micro- and macrolevels. *Project 10* is one such program. *Project 10* is the first public school program in the United States dedicated to providing on-site educational support services to gay, lesbian, bisexual, and questioning youth. *Project 10* began in 1984 at Fairfax High School in the Los Angeles Unified School District. On the microlevel, *Project 10* attempts to improve self-esteem among lesbian and gay youth by providing accurate information and nonjudgmental counseling on issues of sexual orientation. On the macrolevel, *Project 10* provides ongoing workshops to train counselors, teachers, and other staff members on issues related to institutional homophobia and the unique needs of gay and lesbian youth; provides assistance to librarians in developing fiction and nonfiction materials on gay/lesbian topics; and enforces antislur resolutions and codes of behavior with regard to name calling (*Project 10 Handbook*, 1993).

In addition to the interventions implemented as part of *Project 10*, Hart and Parmeter (1992) and Linsley (2001) have offered a number of concrete steps that can be carried out by school social workers and others in the school to minimize the victimization of gay and lesbian students. These steps include:

- Implementing bullying prevention programs (see Chapter 7) that focus on the verbal abuse of students who are considered "different."
- Extending a welcoming hand to gay and lesbian students by providing support groups and supportive services specifically targeting gay and lesbian youth and their families.
- Ensuring that the school library contains books and information about homosexuality.
- Locating and sharing information with teachers that focuses on the achievements of gays throughout history.

- Advocating for lesbian and gay student rights through commissions, task forces, PTAs, and community outreach programs, and networking with community agencies, parents, educational organizations, and teachers' unions.

- Bringing in the local chapter of Parents, Friends, and Families of Lesbians and Gays (PFLAG; see PFLAG contact information at the end of this chapter in the Additional Resources section).

- Advocating for school-based suicide prevention programs (see Chapter 7) since gay and lesbian students are disproportionately at risk of suicide.

Changing the culture and climate of the school for gay and lesbian students will require a slow, multifaceted process because many of these efforts will face stiff opposition from the school and community, as illustrated in the case of Tom at the beginning of this chapter. Fortunately, a recent Supreme Court decision is paving the way for change. *Davis v. Monroe County Board of Education* (1999) holds schools liable for student harassment of classmates. As a result, to prevent costly lawsuits, educators across the United States are making policy changes and informing their staffs of their legal responsibilities in protecting gay and lesbian students (Gorman, 2000).

Children of Color

A number of school factors influence the school success of children of color. These factors include a school's overall attitude toward diversity and the extent to which the curriculum is culturally responsive. However, the most influential factor appears to be the relationships between teachers and their students (Burnette, 1999). To create invitational, welcoming, culturally diverse schools in which *all* students feel acknowledged, appreciated, and respected (Glenn, 1989), school social workers should assume the role of multicultural educators and enlist others to serve in this role. Several studies have linked multicultural education and improved academic learning (Webb,

1990). Spears, Oliver, and Maes (1990) reported that, to some participants, multicultural education made school more relevant, contributing, they believed, to decreased rates of dropping out. Oliver and Howley (1992) reported a decrease in racial stereotyping, leading to better relationships among students. Among children of color, a cultural *grounding,* or sense of belonging, was also reported.

As multicultural educators, school social workers provide cultural awareness and sensitivity training on an ongoing basis for all teachers and school staff. For example, at the beginning of the school year, school social workers might arrange to take an entire school staff on a bus ride through the neighborhoods where their students are living. Throughout the school year, school social workers could invite teachers to accompany them on home visits. As multicultural educators, school social workers should consistently examine the extent to which different cultural groups are represented in pictures and posters that get displayed in the classrooms and hallways, in the texts being used in classrooms, and in how students are grouped in classrooms (Bennett, 1990; First, 1988). As multicultural educators, school social workers should also look for miscues that occur between teachers and students based on misinterpretations and generalizations made about cultural background (Bennett, 1990; First, 1988). School social workers should help teachers to understand that student behaviors such as attention-getting strategies, ways of responding to questions, and ways of interacting are often examples of actions influenced by cultural background. School social workers should encourage teachers to consider modifying traditional direct instruction to include different types of instruction from which all students can benefit. They should also assist teachers in recognizing that communication can be increased with students from diverse language backgrounds by providing written notices in both languages for those parents who have difficulty with English (Field & Aebersold, 1990).

One promising program that has infused and embraced the principles of multicultural education into the school culture is

Success for All

Success for All (SFA) has been the most extensively evaluated elementary schoolwide reform program serving disadvantaged students. In essence, SFA uses research-based innovations in curriculum and instruction and reorganizes instruction in the early elementary grades to teach all students to read at or near grade level by the third grade. SFA is composed of five major components:

1. The *Story Telling and Retelling* (StaR) reading curriculum, in which children are asked to retell and act out stories to increase comprehension.

2. *Cooperative Integrated Reading and Composition* (CIRC), in which students work in teams and get recognition for their teams' progress.

3. Regrouping for reading instruction where tests are used to shift students into a higher or lower reading group to better match the child's current reading level.

4. Reading tutors where one-on-one tutoring is provided to students who are not performing well on their reading assessments.

5. Family support, which often involves a school social worker who provides services to families on an as-needed basis.

Evaluations of SFA have found generally positive results on language development and reading. In relation to grade levels, differences between *Success for All* and control students averaged three months in the first grade, increasing to almost a full grade equivalent by fifth grade.

Sources: From "Schoolwide reform models: What works?" by O. Fashola and R. E. Slavin, 1998; *Phi Delta Kappan, 79,* 370–379; *Schools and delinquency,* by D. C. Gottfredson, 2001, Cambridge, MA; Cambridge University Press; "Success for some: An evaluation of a success for all program," by E. M. Jones, G. D. Gottfredson, and D. C. Gottfredson, 1997, *Evaluation Review, 21,* 643–670; and "Success for all: A summary of research," by Slavin et al., 1996, *Journal of Education for Students Placed at Risk, 1,* 41–76.

Success for All (SFA). See the Success for All box on page 162 for a description of this exemplary program.

To help ensure the school success of children of color, school social workers must also address racist behavior and nstitutional racism in schools. Pine and Hilliard (1990) have suggested several steps necessary to change racist behavior in schools:

- Challenging institutional racism.
- Increasing the pool of minority teachers.
- Improving pedagogical practices.
- Elevating the self-esteem of all children.
- Teaching character development.

Table 8.1 shows additional strategies designed to change racist behavior in schools.

Table 8.1   **How to Change Racist Behavior in Schools**

- Articulate a clear statement of expectations regarding racism.
- Establish and enforce a series of consequences for violations of those expectations.
- Respond to racial incidents quickly and fairly by gathering adequate evidence. Correction should be remedial.
- Discourage students from congregating on the school grounds according to race.
- Design seating assignments with a priority on integration.
- Rely on peer counseling whenever possible.
- Seek advice and support from parent and student advisory boards.
- Enlist the help and advice of key minority leaders in the community for teacher workshops, assemblies, and arbitration of racial incidents when appropriate.
- Reward those who strive to reduce racism in their schools and classrooms.
- Hire and assign an appropriate balance of minority faculty and staff to act as role models and provide an adequate base of authority for policies and discipline.

Source: From *Racism in America's Schools,* by R. Beswick, 1990, Eugene, OR: ERIC Clearinghouse on Educational Management. (ERIC Digest No. 320196). This document is in the public domain.

Students Being Reintegrated into School from Residential and Juvenile Justice Settings

Several prerelease strategies appear to be important in successfully reintegrating youth from more restrictive to less restrictive settings. Ingersoll and LeBoeuf (1997) suggest that mental health, social services, probation, child protection, and educational agencies meet on a regular basis to share information and provide integrated services to the youth and his or her family. They also suggest using alternative schools as a transitional, interim placement for youths who are leaving a detention facility or a residential placement. Several additional steps, outlined in Table 8.2, can be taken to fully transition a student from an alternative school placement into a less restrictive regular education program. As shown in Table 8.2, students need to be made aware of school policies and procedures with a particular emphasis on zero tolerance discipline policies that will result in a long-term suspension or expulsion if violated. In addition, parents or guardians must be made aware of their responsibilities and accountability. School social workers can play a key role in meeting with students and parents/guardians in sharing this information and in developing academic, behavioral, and vocational goals with students.

Table 8.2   **Steps in Transitioning a Student from a More Restrictive to a Less Restrictive Educational Setting**

- Conduct a student admission interview.
- Review policies and procedures.
- Provide a clear explanation of the school's zero tolerance policies for substance abuse and other behaviors.
- Develop a violence elimination contract.
- Notify parents of their accountability.
- Assign a cluster or interagency representative.
- Identify target academic, behavioral, and vocational goals.

Source: From *Reaching out to Youth out of the Educational Mainstream* by S. Ingersoll and D. LeBoeuf, 1997, Washington, DC: Office of Juvenile Justice and Delinquency Prevention. This document is in the public domain.

In 1996, the Arizona Department of Juvenile Corrections Education System developed an efficient and effective approach in handling the transitions of 12- to 17-year-old youths from secure care to the appropriate public school or work environment. According to Griller-Clarck (2001), this approach involved the hiring of full-time transition specialists and housing them at each parole office with the responsibility of assisting in the development of an individualized vocational transition education plan (IVTEP), attending a transition staffing 30 days before the youth's release, and finding appropriate educational or vocational programs for the youth on release. Wright (1996) reported that participating youths, who were generally two to three years behind academically, scored an average of 40 percent higher on tests of readiness, writing, and math than they had previously.

Summary

Social workers are obligated to pay particular attention to the needs of people who are vulnerable. In schools, this includes students who are victimized because of known or presumed gay or lesbian sexual orientation, children of color, and students who are being reintegrated into school from residential and juvenile justice settings. Each of these groups of students are vulnerable and at risk of school failure. For example, the verbal, and sometimes physical, victimization of gay and lesbian students has a devastating impact on the mental health and school performance of victims. Children of color, particularly African American males have been found to be "disidentified" with academics, as evidenced by low correlations between grades and self-esteem. It is also difficult to meet the educational needs of youth on probation or in aftercare status because of the lack of coordination between the educational and justice systems.

To adequately address the problems impacting each of these vulnerable groups of students, school social workers must work at a number of levels. In addition to extending a welcoming hand to the students themselves, they must work to change the attitudes and beliefs of school administrators, teachers, students, parents, and the community. They must also advocate changes in those school policies and practices that negatively impact these vulnerable groups of students. Ultimately, school social workers must act to create schools that are welcoming and invitational to *all* students regardless of their sexual orientation, ethnicity, or previous involvement with the juvenile justice system.

Questions for Discussion

1. Why do school personnel rarely intervene when students are victimized because of their sexual orientation?

2. What are some examples of programs that schools have implemented to help gay and lesbian students?

3. What factors contribute to the educational gaps between White and minority children?

4. What is multicultural education? What do multicultural educators do?

5. What can school social workers do to help ensure the success of youths who are reintegrated into the school from residential and juvenile justice settings?

Refer to the case study at the beginning of this chapter:

1. How might the school social worker deal with the resistance he or she will encounter in establishing a gay/lesbian support group?

2. What other services might the school social worker implement to assist Tom?

3. Discuss how this school social worker might assume the roles of advocate, consultant, and liaison within the school and in the community to better serve the needs of Tom and other gay students at the school.

Additional Resources

Victimization Based on Known or Presumed Gay or Lesbian Sexual Orientation

- *Project 10.* This Web site includes links to a bill of rights for gay and lesbian students, how to deal with the opposition, and a teacher's self-evaluation of nonbiased behavior. www.project10.org
- Parents, Families and Friends of Lesbians and Gays (PFLAG). National support group for family and friends of gay and lesbian people. Operates more than 200 family groups and contacts nationwide.
  Telephone: (202) 467-8180
  www.pflag.org
- *The Gay, Lesbian, and Straight Education Network*'s mission is to combat antigay/lesbian prejudice in schools.
  121 West 27th St., Suite 804 New York, NY 10001.
- *It's Elementary. Talking About Gay Issues* (1996). Videotape is a 78-minute documentary that makes a case that children should be taught to respect all people, including lesbians and gay men, as part of their early education. It is designed to inspire teachers and administrators to take the next steps at their own schools to increase student knowledge and sensitivity for this aspect of diversity. This videotape may be obtained through Women's Educational Media, 2180 Bryant St., Suite 203, San Francisco, CA 94110.
  Telephone: (415) 641-4616
  E-mail: wemfilms@womedia.org
- Van Wormer, K., Wells, J. & Boes, M. (2000). *Social work with lesbians, gays and bisexuals: A strengths perspective.* Boston: Allyn & Bacon.

Children of Color

- Office for Equity Education, Washington Office of the State Superintendent of Public Instruction, Old Capitol Building, FG11, Olympia, WA 98504.
- Center for Research on Effective Schooling for Disadvantaged Students www.csos.jhu.edu

Students Being Reintegrated into School from Residential and Juvenile Justice Settings

- The National Center on Education, Disability, and Juvenile Justice is a collaborative research, training, technical assistance, and dissemination program designed to develop more effective responses to the needs of youth with disabilities in the juvenile justice system or those at risk for involvement with the juvenile justice system. www.edjj.org

The School Social Worker as Consultant and Team Member

In this chapter, we discuss:

- *Why consultation?*
- *Why teachers seek consultation.*
- *The defining characteristics of consultation in schools.*
- *Pitfalls to avoid in consultative relationships.*
- *School teams and effective collaboration.*
- *Strategies and programs designed to prevent classroom behavior problems.*

Linda, a school social worker at Marshall Middle School, was having lunch in the teacher's lounge when Mrs. Cooper, a seventh grade math teacher, sat down at a table and loudly joked about what a "mean" teacher she is and how her kids wish they weren't in her class. After everyone else left, however, Mrs. Cooper became serious and confided that this bothered her. She didn't know why she wasn't connecting with her students or what to do about it. Linda asked her if she just wanted her to listen or if she was asking for help. Mrs. Cooper said she would like help with this. Linda described the process of consultation and asked if Mrs. Cooper would like to meet with her for a few weeks to explore some possible changes in her classroom. Mrs. Cooper agreed, and they set up a time to meet after school that day.

Our primary means to assist students is by influencing the adults who control the environments of children and adolescents. (Gutkin & Conoley, 1990)

Introduction

The number of students labeled "mildly disabled," "difficult-to-teach," or "at risk" has increased dramatically over the past decade. Regardless of their label, these students respond poorly to traditional instructional and behavioral management methods (Rathvon, 1999). For example, teachers may limit themselves to didactic instructional techniques or, as illustrated in the case vignette, teachers may use discipline techniques based on fear and intimidation such as screaming, sarcasm, threats, and ridicule to control students in their classrooms (Hyman, 1997). Teachers, as well as other adults in authority, must be helped to understand how their expectations, attitudes, instructional techniques, and behavior impact students' behavior in and out of the classroom (Short & Short, 1987).

This chapter discusses the role of the school social worker as consultant and the various ways that he or she can support classroom teachers in meeting the needs of students who respond poorly to traditional instructional and behavioral management methods. It explores why teachers seek consultation as well as major pitfalls in consultative relationships. This chapter also discusses characteristics of effective collaboration in school teams, barriers to collaboration, and some new perspectives on collaboration. It concludes with a description of several strategies and programs that school social workers can draw on to assist teachers in preventing classroom behavior problems.

Why Consultation?

Consultation is becoming an increasingly important role for school social workers for a number of reasons. Many classroom problems can result when teachers unknowingly dominate communication in the classroom, rely on repetitive work, or lack insight into how their personal beliefs and behaviors toward students impact students' academic performance and behavior (Erchul & Martens, 1997). For example, it has been reported that negative teacher attitudes toward students generally emerge in the first few weeks of classes and that these attitudes tend to remain stable *even after students display consistent improvement in behavior* (Safran & Safran, 1985). Consequently, school social workers, in their role as consultants, can help teachers become more aware of these harmful behaviors and attitudes as well as point out any efforts that students may be making to improve their behavior.

Perhaps the most important reason that consultation is becoming an increasingly important role for school social workers is that the current pull-out student service delivery model, consisting of traditional one-on-one or small group counseling, does not reflect the ecological perspective. According to the ecological perspective, student problems are viewed as emanating from student-environment mismatches rather than internal child deficits (Rathvon, 1999). Given this view, it is important to address problems in the environment where the behavior occurs. Rather than pulling students out or labeling them, school districts across the United States are implementing school-based intervention assistance programs (IAPs) or teacher assistance teams (TATs) that provide consultative services to teachers to assist students with academic or behavioral problems (Rathvon, 1999). School social workers are key members of these school-based IAPs and TATs.

Why Teachers Seek Consultation

Teachers may seek the assistance of a school social worker as a consultant for several reasons. The primary reason is lack of knowledge, skills, or both (Erchul & Martens, 1997). For example, many teachers are overwhelmed in their attempts to work with students who demand constant attention and fail to complete class assignments. Teachers may not understand why certain behavior problems are taking place in their classroom (as illustrated in the case vignette at the beginning of this chapter). School social workers, in the role of consultant, can provide teachers with a number of reasons for students' misbehavior (see Table 9.1), including the teacher's failure to reward appropriate behaviors or positively reinforce undesirable behaviors. In addition to seeking help with classroom behavior problems, teachers may seek information about child abuse reporting laws or community resources and school social workers are able to provide teachers with answers to these questions. Another reason teachers may seek a consultant is a need for attention, support, approval, or a "pat on the back." Still another reason is a lack of objectivity (Erchul & Martens, 1997), which can reveal itself in several ways. For example, a teacher may be too close to a problem to be able to deal with it effectively, or a teacher may have taken on a rescuer role by doing more for a student than is necessary in a given situation.

Table 9.1   Why Classroom Behavior Problems Occur

- The child has not learned a more appropriate behavior that leads to the same consequences.
- More appropriate behaviors are ignored.
- More appropriate behaviors lead to undesired consequences.
- The problem behavior is followed by desired sensory, edible, tangible, social, or activity consequences.
- The problem behavior allows the child to stop or avoid undesired situations.
- The problem behavior occurs when it is likely to be reinforced.
- The problem behavior occurs when it is initiated by other individuals.
- The problem behavior occurs because the child observed someone else doing it.

Source: From *School Consultation: Conceptual and Empirical Bases of Practice* (p. 122), by W. P. Erchul and B. K. Martens, 1997, New York: Plenum Press. Copyright 1997 by Plenum Press. Reprinted with permission.

Defining Characteristics of Consultation in Schools

Several characteristics define consultation in a school setting. Friend and Cook (1992) and Erchul and Martens (1997) have delineated several characteristics that are central to successful consultation:

1. *Consultation is triadic and indirect.* The consultant (e.g., school social worker) and the consultee (an individual teacher or administrator) together design services that the consultee provides to the client (e.g., student or group of students). The school social worker's relationship to the student in a consultative relationship is indirect; students are not direct participants but are beneficiaries of this process.

2. *Consultation is voluntary.* The consultant and consultee are free to enter into or terminate the relationship at any time. The consultation process can be implemented only as long as the consultant's and consultee's participation is voluntary.

3. *All interactions between the consultant and consultee are to be held in confidence* unless the consultant believes that someone will be harmed if this silence is maintained.

4. *Consultation typically involves an expert relationship.* While their relationship is nonhierarchical, the primary reason for this relationship is that the consultee has a problem that requires the expertise of the consultant.

5. *Consultation is a problem-solving process with steps or stages.* These steps include establishing a working relationship (e.g., "Can we work together?"), identifying the problem (e.g., "What is the problem?"), planning and intervening (e.g., "What can you do to address the problem?"), evaluating the intervention (e.g., "Did the intervention work?"), and terminating the consultation.

6. *Participants in consultative interactions have shared but differentiated responsibilities and accountability.* As consultants, school

social workers must offer assistance that is responsive to the consultee's needs while the consultee is responsible for seriously considering the assistance being offered. However, the consultee is always free to reject whatever the consultant offers.

7. *Consultation has a dual purpose—to help the consultee with a current professional problem and to equip the consultee with added insights and skills that will permit him or her to deal effectively with similar future problems without the consultant's assistance.* Through the consultation process, school social workers empower teachers to become better problem solvers in addressing present as well as future problems.

To help ensure that teachers will be receptive to the consultation process, Erchul and Martens (1997) presented a series of steps that can be taken by consultants to help facilitate the consultation process in schools (see Table 9.2). As shown in the

Table 9.2   Steps to Facilitate the Consultation Process

- Listen attentively to teacher frustrations with classroom problems.
- Provide a "sounding board" for teacher ideas.
- Compliment teacher actions when successful.
- Offer encouragement when teacher efforts are less than successful.
- Instruct teachers in how to assess classroom problems in a sympathetic manner.
- Help identify and, whenever possible, take an active role in recruiting additional resources or seeking alternative solutions that may be available elsewhere in the school.
- Help teachers help themselves, as in peer coaching.
- Make school-based consultation available to a greater number of consultees.
- Inform teachers of the best available treatment technologies.
- Guide teachers through the problem-solving process of consultation.
- Assist teachers in treatment implementation and evaluation.
- Help teachers make assessment information relevant for intervention.

Source: School Consultation: Conceptual and Empirical Bases of Practice (p. 148), by W. P. Erchul and B. K. Martens, 1997, New York: Plenum Press. Copyright 1997 by Plenum Press. Reprinted with permission.

table, many of these steps involve giving teachers a "pat on the back," recognizing them for the efforts they are making in their classrooms as well as being a sounding board for teachers who need to ventilate and problem solve. Another critical step for consultants is to provide teachers with the best available treatments such as those described later in this chapter.

Rathvon (1999) offered two points to keep in mind before initiating the consultation process. First, consultation will usually result in teachers taking on responsibilities or demands beyond their already-substantial workload. Therefore, teachers will be much more likely to use interventions that are relatively simple to implement and require little time and few material resources. Second, no intervention works equally well with every student, with every teacher, or in every situation. Therefore, the selection of interventions should be a collaborative exercise between consultant and teacher or, in the case of intervention assistance teams, among team members and referring teachers.

Pitfalls to Avoid in Consultative Relationships

Before entering into consultive relationships with teachers and administrators, school social workers should be aware of several pitfalls. Teachers, administrators, or both could have hidden agendas in seeking a consultant. Erchul and Martens (1997) offered a number of pitfalls to avoid. For example, rather than seeking help in problem solving, a teacher may really want the consultant to take his or her side in a conflict with a student, a school administrator, or with another teacher. Or a teacher may seek a consultant but is unwilling to change first because he or she believes that students should initiate all changes. Or a teacher may want help with a personal problem rather than a professional problem. Another pitfall to be aware of is a building principal who, under the guise of consultation, may really want the school social worker to spy on a teacher and report back to him or her about that teacher's performance. (See the Pitfalls in Consultative Relationships: A Case Vignette box.) If a

Pitfalls in Consultative Relationships: A Case Vignette

You are a school social worker at Pineview School. One day Ms. Jones, the principal at Pineview, approaches you and explains that she has some concerns about a particular teacher at the school. Ms. Jones has been told that this teacher is making emotionally abusive statements (e.g., "You are so stupid!"; "You are such a poor excuse for a student") to several students in her classroom but has no direct evidence that these statements were made. Ms. Jones asks you to go into this teacher's classroom to observe her actions on several different occasions under the pretense of observing a student in her class. How would you respond to Ms. Jones? What ethical dilemmas are involved in this situation? How would you go about resolving these dilemmas?

school social worker suspects that there is a hidden agenda, he or she needs to ensure that the teacher or administrator understands what consultation is and isn't before proceeding. Essentially, the school social worker needs to make sure that everyone involved understands that consultation focuses on work-related problems rather than personal problems and that the consultant has no administrative responsibility for or formal authority over the consultee (Erchul & Martens, 1997).

School Teams and Effective Collaboration

In some schools, a student identified as at risk for substance abuse, truancy, and dropout may be assigned to three different interventions carried out independently. To avoid this duplication, fragmentation, and piecemeal delivery of programs and services, schools have increasingly turned to a group of professionals who work as a team in addressing the multiplicity of problems impacting students and their families. Cohesive school teams help to maximize the impact and results of interventions ("Framing New Directions," 2001). As mentioned earlier, school social workers are key members of school-based intervention assistance programs (IAPs) and teacher assistance teams (TATs). As a member of these teams, school social workers serve as consultants to teachers who need assistance with students who have learning problems, behavior problems/disorders, or both. School social workers are also integral members of another form of school team multidisciplinary teams. These teams implement evaluation and placement procedures for children suspected of having disabilities. As members of these teams, school social workers conduct social assessments and mobilize a variety of services for students with disabilities, both in and outside the school, to help attain individualized educational program (IEP) goals (see Chapter 6).

The effectiveness of any school team depends on the extent to which its respective team members (e.g., school social workers, school psychologists, school counselors, and other specialists) are able to collaborate. Friend and Cook (1992) have described a number of essential components of effective collaboration. Team members must perceive and believe they are part of a team. Team members must trust each other, uphold confidentiality, and have a mutual respect for each other. The contributions of each team member must be valued, and there must be a sense of interdependence and parity among all participants. Team members must be able to share their resources and share accountability for outcomes.

While effective collaboration may appear to be relatively easy to achieve, it is much more difficult to accomplish in actual practice. Collaboration has been aptly described as an "unnatural act between nonconsenting adults" (Dryfoos, 1994). To achieve effective collaboration on any school team, a number of institutional, professional, and interpersonal barriers must be overcome. Hooper-Briar and Lawson (1996) have discussed a number of these barriers:

- Lack of physical space in schools for all student service professionals.
- The itinerant status of school social workers and school psychologists.
- Professional job descriptions that do not specify or support collaborative activities.
- One or more school team members perceiving other team members as less qualified.
- Lack of trust and defending one's own "turf."
- Differing conceptual orientations and professional values and ethics among various professional groups.
- Lack of flexibility and resistance to change.
- Lack of leadership.

These barriers suggest that true collaboration is difficult work and requires a substantial commitment of time, energy, and patience from each team member. Rather than focusing on who gets credit for the program, true collaboration requires a professional commitment on the part of every team member to remain focused on providing the most effective interventions and programs for students with learning or behavioral problems. Collaboration also requires a need for changes in preservice preparation, certification, and continuing professional development for school social workers as well as other student service professionals ("Framing New Directions," 2001). See Chapter 10 for a detailed discussion of the importance of school-community collaborations in meeting the needs of large numbers of disadvantaged, at-risk students.

Strategies and Programs Designed to Prevent Classroom Behavior Problems

When a teacher refers an individual student because of a learning or behavior problem, consultants often discover that the referred student's problematic behavior extends beyond the referred student because student misbehavior is often "embedded in the ineffective organizational, instructional, or behavioral management strategies in the classroom" (Rathvon, 1999). As a result, school social workers in the role of consultants (like Linda in the case vignette) can assist teachers in selecting and implementing effective strategies or programs that will help them decrease off-task, disruptive behavior by changing ineffective organizational, instructional, or behavioral management strategies in the classroom. A number of empirically supported programs that address these ineffective organizational and classroom management strategies have been successful in minimizing or preventing classroom behavior problems. The programs that follow are designed for implemention by regular classroom teachers, often with the ongoing support of consultants. For a partial listing of contacts for these programs, see Table 9.3.

Table 9.3   **Partial Listing of Contacts for Programs Shown to Be Successful in Minimizing or Preventing Classroom Behavior Problems**

The Good Behavior Game	*Consistency Management and Cooperative Discipline*
Sheppard G. Kellam, PhD	H. Jerome Freiberg, Project Director
Prevention Research Center	Telephone: (713) 743-8663
Department of Mental Hygiene	Fax: (713) 743-8664
Johns Hopkins University—	E-mail: CMCD@uh.edu
School of Hygiene and Public Health	www.coe.uh.edu/~freiberg/cm
Mason F. Lord Building, Suite 500	
Francis Scott Key Medical Center	
4940 Eastern Avenue	
Baltimore, MD 21224	
Telephone: (410) 550-3445	
Fax: (410) 550-3461	
E-Mail:	
skellam@welchlink.welch.jhu.edu	
www.bpp.jhu.edu	

Good Behavior Game (GBG)

The *Good Behavior Game* (GBG) is one of the best-known behavioral intervention programs in the literature (Rathvon, 1999). According to Greenberg et al. (2000) and the U.S. Departments of Education and Justice (1999), GBG is a classroom team-based program for first graders that is designed to reduce early aggressive behaviors. At the beginning of the game, the teacher assigns the children to one of three heterogeneous teams. Students work in teams in such a way that each student is responsible to the rest of the group. During the GBG period, teams are penalized points whenever a member engages in verbal disruption or physical disruption, leaves his or her seat without permission, or otherwise does not comply. At the same time, teams of classmates who do not exhibit inappropriate behavior are rewarded with stickers or longer recesses. GBG is conducted three times per week for 10-minute periods and increases until it reaches a maximum of three hours. An evaluation found that students in the classes that use the GBG displayed significantly less aggressive and shy behavior than students in a comparison group (Howard, Flora, & Griffen, 1999). For example, middle school boys who had exhibited aggressive behavior in the first grade and participated in GBG were less likely to engage in aggressive behavior (U.S. Departments of Education and Justice, 1999). During a nine-month follow-up, teachers reported a 10 percent reduction in aggressive behavior, and peers reported a 19 percent reduction. These reductions were maintained in middle school for boys who had displayed aggressive behavior in first grade (U.S. Departments of Education and Justice, 1999). See the Good Behavior Game box on pages 181–182 for a detailed description of this exemplary program.

Consistency Management and Cooperative Discipline

Consistency Management and Cooperative Discipline (CMCD) is a schoolwide program designed to improve discipline in inner-city schools. The Center for the Study of Violence Prevention at the

The Good Behavior Game (GBG)

The purpose of the *Good Behavior Game* (GBG) is to reduce disruptive classroom behavior using a team competition strategy.

The game is played in the following manner:

The teacher selects an instructional period during which students are especially disruptive and unproductive. The intervention is introduced by telling students that they will be playing a game to help everyone get more out of the subject during which the game will be played. The teacher explains the criterion for the maximum number of demerits permitted to earn the reward and rewards for the winning team(s), such as wearing victory tags for the rest of the day, extra recess, lining up for lunch, or extra computer time. If both teams win, possible rewards include viewing a videotape, 15 minutes of free time, homework passes, or a special art project at the end of the day. The teacher divides the class into two teams, making sure that disruptive students are divided between the teams. Teams may select names because this fosters team spirit. The teacher displays a chart or a section of the chalkboard visible to all students with "Team 1" and "Team 2" (or the names of the teams) written on it. The teacher then reviews the classroom rules at the beginning of the game and records a demerit beside the team name each time any member of a team breaks a rule (e.g., verbal disruption, physical disruption, leaving his or her seat without permission, or other noncompliance). The teacher tallies demerits at the end of the instructional period and declares the team with the fewer number of demerits as the winner. If neither team exceeds the predetermined limit, both teams are winners. Teachers are encouraged to gradually lower the limit for the demerits or extend the period during which the game is played. Critical components in reducing disruptive behavior appear to be the assignment of consequences, the criteria set for winning, and the division of students into teams. Direct feedback alone, that is, placing marks on the chalkboard for breaking class rules, does not affect behavior.

(continued)

Occasionally, chronically disruptive students will declare that they do not want to play the game and will deliberately violate the rules. If this occurs, the teacher should explain that it is not fair to penalize an entire team because one member will not control himself or herself. Create a third team consisting of the problem students and add a negative contingency such as remaining five minutes after school or deducting five minutes of recess for each marked scored over the criterion. GBG is conducted three times per week for a 10-minute period and increases until it reaches a maximum of three hours. GBG has been successfully implemented in regular elementary grade classrooms for emotionally disturbed adolescents.

Sources: From *Preventing mental disorders in school-age children: A review of the effectiveness of prevention programs,* by M. T. Greenberg, C. Domitrovich, and B. Bumbarger, 2000, University Park: Pennsylvania State University, College of Health and Human Development, Prevention Research Center for the Promotion of Human Development; *1999 Annual Report on School Safety,* by U.S. Departments of Education and Justice, 1999, retrieved June 22, 2001 from http://www.ed.gov/PDFDocs/InterimAR.pdf; *Effective school interventions: Strategies for enhancing academic achievement and social competence* (pp. 360–364), by N. Rathvon, 1999, New York: Guilford Press; "Good behavior game: Effects of individual contingencies for group consequences on disruptive behavior in a classroom," by H. H. Barrish, M. Saunder, and M. M. Wolf, 1969, *Journal of Applied Behavior Analysis, 2,* 119–124; and "Use and analysis of the 'good behavior game' to reduce disruptive behavior," by V. W. Harris and J. A. Sherman, 1973, *Journal of Applied Behavior Analysis, 6,* 405–417. Reprinted with permission.

University of Colorado reviewed 116 programs in the year 2000 and CMCD was one of only four U.S. programs that met their rigorous evaluation criteria. A core component of CMCD is creating classrooms in which teachers and students work collaboratively to set rules for classroom management and transform teacher-centered classrooms into person-centered classrooms (Fashola & Slavin, 1998). In person-centered classrooms, all students are provided with the opportunity to become an integral part of the management of the classroom. Classroom rules are developed collaboratively by the teacher and students; and rewards for positive behavior, rather than punishment for negative behavior, is emphasized in these classrooms. Students, as well as teachers, are responsible for classroom rules; and it is assumed that their involvement would reduce behavior problems because students would be less likely to break their own rules (Fashola & Slavin, 1998). CMCD has been evaluated primarily with African American and Latino students in inner-city Houston schools. A five-year evaluation comparing five CMCD schools with five matched control schools found significant positive effects on standardized achievement tests, especially for students who remained in the program for six years (Freiberg, Stein, & Huang, 1995).

Behavioral Consultation to Reduce Violence/Vandalism

According to G. R. Mayer, Butterworth, Nafpaktitus, and Sulzer-Azaroff (1983), *Behavioral Consultation to Reduce Violence/Vandalism* is a 20-hour series of workshops that trains teams of school personnel applied behavioral analysis techniques (i.e., identification of antecedent conditions and consequences of the problem behavior) to reduce the intensity, duration, or frequency of the problematic behavior in the lunchroom, on the playground, and in the classroom. Teachers participate on a school team with student service professionals to plan and implement programs that teach students alternative behaviors to disruption and vandalism. An evaluation of the *Behavioral Consultation to Reduce Violence/Vandalism* program indicated that rates of disruptive student behavior and vandalism costs declined in significantly more treatment schools than control schools between the beginning and end of the school year (G. R. Mayer et al., 1983).

Effective Classroom Management

According to Gottfredson (2001), *Effective Classroom Management* (ECM) is an in-service training course for teachers focusing on the teaching of communication skills (e.g., "I-messages," clarifying responses, and reflecting feelings), problem-solving skills (e.g., brainstorming, evaluating alternative solutions, and developing an action plan), and self-esteem enhancement techniques for use in their classrooms (Gottfredson, 2001, p. 119). Studies evaluating the impact of ECM training found intermittent significant effects on measures of correlates of problem behaviors (Gottfredson, 2001). For example, ECM boys had lower alcohol involvement than control boys and ECM girls had lower marijuana involvement than control girls (Moskowitz, Malvin, Schaeffer, & Schaps 1984).

In their role as consultants, school social workers can assist teachers in implementing these empirically supported programs. In addition to assisting teachers with classroom behavior problems, there are times when school social workers are called to consult with teachers to assist in schoolwide crisis events such as a student's suicide, death of a teacher, and school shootings. Pitcher and Poland's book (1992) includes a chapter on how student service professionals, including school social workers, can provide crisis intervention consultation in schools.

Summary

Consultation is becoming an increasingly important role for school social workers. In the role of consultant, school social workers can support classroom teachers in the teaching-learning process and be more effective and efficient in meeting the needs of large numbers of students who respond poorly to traditional instructional and behavioral management methods. School social workers serve as consultants either individually or as team members of school-based intervention assistance programs (IAPs) or Teacher Assistance Teams (TAT). Because of a number of pitfalls, it is essential that the school social worker communicate to teachers and administrators an understanding of what consultation is and what it isn't before becoming engaged in a consultative relationship. To avoid duplication, fragmentation, and piecemeal delivery of programs and services, schools have increasingly turned to teams of professionals who collaborate to address the multiplicity of problems impacting students and their families. While these school teams help to maximize the impact and results of interventions, truly collaborative teams must overcome a number of institutional, professional, and interpersonal barriers.

Because a referred student's problematic behavior is often embedded in an ineffective organizational, instructional, or behavioral management system that impacts many or all the students in that classroom, the school social worker in the role of consultant must often assist the teacher in selecting and implementing empirically supported strategies and programs that impact entire classrooms. A number of programs, such as the *Good Behavior Program,* have been shown to be successful in increasing student attention and learning and decreasing off-task, disruptive behavior.

Questions for Discussion

1. Why is consultation becoming an increasingly important role for school social workers?
2. Identify and briefly describe the defining characteristics of consultation in schools.
3. For what reasons do teachers seek school social workers for consultation?
4. What steps can be taken by school social workers to help teachers be more receptive to consultation?
5. What is the name of the exemplary classroom, team-based, behavioral intervention program for first graders designed to reduce early aggressive behaviors?

Refer to the case study at the beginning of this chapter:

1. What factors might be contributing to Mrs. Cooper's difficulty in relating to her class?
2. How might Linda help Mrs. Cooper identify and build on her strengths?

3. If several students had approached the school social worker with complaints about Mrs. Cooper's teaching style, how might the school social worker have responded?

Additional Resources

- Gazin, A. (1999). Keeping them on the edge of their seats. *Instructor, 1*(109), 28–30. This article provides an overview of how teachers can maintain control in the classroom yet still give students the freedom to explore. Gazin argues that the key to maintaining control in the classroom is to keep students fully involved in the decision-making process of rules, being clear about behavior policies, and addressing different learning styles. Gazin also believes that when teachers are excited about what they are teaching, students will also become excited about learning.
- National Information Center for Children and Youth with Disabilities. (1999). Interventions for Chronic Behavior Problems: NICHCY Research Brief. Washington, DC: www.nichcy.org/pubs/research/rb1txt.htm
- The National Education Service is one of the nation's leading publishers of research-based resources for practitioners who are interested in creating environments where all children can succeed. For a complete list of resources, visit their Web site: www.nesonline.com

Involving Parents and the Community in Restructuring Schools

In this chapter, we discuss:

- New perspectives on the role of school social workers.
- Challenges in building school-community collaborations.
- Increasing parental connectedness with schools.
- Proven and promising school-community collaborations and initiatives.

10

Chapter

Mr. James had just started a new job as school social worker in an urban school. According to a student survey taken the previous year, drug usage was disproportionately high in this community. Mr. James wanted to take some steps to begin to address this problem but was told by one of his principals that parents in this community were particularly "hard to reach." The principal based this conclusion on the fact that the previous school social worker organized a Parents' Night focusing on drug abuse and sent out more than a thousand invitations, and only two parents showed up, in spite of the fact that food was provided. The principal was extremely disappointed but felt that it was worth trying again because of the valuable information offered. Mr. James decided to plan another Parents' Night and to make a special effort to involve Hispanic parents because 20 percent of the population in this community are Hispanic.

In times of limited resources for education, health, and social services, collaboration is essential. (Lim & Adelman, 1999)

Introduction

Nearly four million children live in troubled or economically disadvantaged inner-city neighborhoods (U.S. General Accounting Office [GAO], 2000). Most have chronic health problems and may not receive regular medical exams, they do not participate in cultural or recreational activities, they do not have access to mentors and role models, and they engage in high-risk behaviors (GAO, 2000). Schools with large numbers of disadvantaged, at-risk students often struggle to both educate their students and prepare them for further education or a career (GAO, 2000). There is no single solution or "magic bullet" to improving the educational success of at-risk children who reside in disadvantaged communities. However, schools are increasingly turning to collaborations and partnerships with parents, local businesses, universities, medical and religious centers, foundations, and other community-based organizations in an effort to meet the multiplicity of needs of at-risk students and their families.

This chapter discusses new perspectives on the role of school social workers in bringing about systemic school reform through school-community collaborations. It discusses challenges in building school-community collaborations and the unique challenges awaiting school social workers in their efforts to increase parental connectedness with schools, particularly with ethnically diverse and poor parents. This chapter concludes with a description of several proven or promising school-community collaborations and initiatives.

New Perspectives on the Roles of School Social Workers

The UCLA School Mental Health Project recently published a report that highlights overcoming barriers to student learning through systemic school restructuring and reform by reframing the roles and functions of school counselors, psychologists, and social workers. According to this report, school social workers, school psychologists, and school counselors have been largely marginalized in educational reform efforts. While they continue to be needed to provide student-focused interventions, these groups of student service professionals have yet to emerge as key participants in designing and implementing systemic changes in schools and in neighborhoods surrounding schools ("Framing New Directions," 2001). To provide the type of integrated and comprehensive approaches necessary to deal with the complex concerns confronting schools, school social workers and other student service professionals must advocate the development and implementation of school-community initiatives.

One mechanism for enlarging the role of school social workers to include facilitating and enhancing this coordination and collaboration of resources in schools and communities is the *resource coordinating team*. Members of *resource coordinating teams* include school social workers, school psychologists, school counselors, nurses, dropout counselors, health educators, special education staff, after-school program staff, bilingual and Title I program coordinators, safe and drug-free schools staff, as well as school administrators, regular classroom teachers, noncertified staff, and parents ("Framing New Directions," 2001). While intervention assistance programs (IAPs) and teacher assistance teams (TATs) focus on specific cases, *resource coordinating teams* are responsible for systemic issues related to the delivery of services ("Framing New Directions," 2001). For example, these teams are responsible for enhancing service delivery systems and procedures for effectively managing programs, and exploring ways to organize and expand resources in the school district and community ("Framing New Directions," 2001).

Challenges in Building School-Community Collaborations

It has been found that community participation, especially by parents, is positively correlated with academic achievement, attendance rates, and school accountability (Abrams &

Taylor-Gibbs, 2000). In building school-community collaborations, school social workers must recognize that the "range of resources in a community is much greater than the service agencies and community-based organizations that often are invited to the table. While the most important resource in a community is the families that reside there, other community resources include businesses, libraries, parks, youth, religious and civic groups, and any facility that can be used for recreation, learning, enrichment, and support" ("Framing New Directions," 2001, p. 4).

The need for school social workers to take a leadership role in developing and implementing school-community collaboration initiatives is greatest in ethnically diverse and low-income schools and neighborhoods. A number of cultural barriers and differences in social class often impede the development of cooperative relationships between school staff, parents, and other community members (Abrams & Taylor-Gibbs, 2000). These impediments include language barriers of immigrant families and concentrations of poverty in neighborhoods that limit access to cultural institutions, libraries, and recreational activities ("Strong families: Strong schools," 1994). Other barriers include a long history of negative relationships, mistrust, and misunderstandings between urban parents and school staff. Many urban parents are skeptical of public education because of their own negative experiences or because of a sense of unfulfilled promises and unrealistic expectations of them as parents (Hampton, Mumford, & Bond, 1998). Low-income urban parents stay away from their child's public school because they see no role for themselves, they feel they have little to offer academically because of their own poor school performance, they find schools to be unapproachable, or they may be intimidated by school administrators and teachers (Davies, 1994).

Some of these parental perceptions of school personnel may be accurate in that administrators and teachers often disregard low-income parents' input as misguided or ignorant (Comer, 1980; Winters, 1993). Despite all the rhetoric about parental involvement, school officials are highly resistant to input from certain outsiders and are ambivalent about establishing partnerships, in general, with members of the community. This reluctance or ambivalence may be because some parents' ideas about school reform are often very different from those of school personnel (Fantini, Gittell, & Magat, 1970; Henry, 1996). For example, whereas school personnel may be interested in only "tinkering at the edges," community members may be interested in making significant structural changes in schools (Sarason, 1971). Since school staff have not treated parents as true partners in making important decisions, retaining parents (especially ethnically diverse and low-income parents) as active and equal decision makers is probably the most difficult type of participation to achieve (Abrams & Taylor-Gibbs, 2000).

Examples of conflicts between school personnel and ethnically diverse urban parents are vividly depicted in an article by Abrams and Taylor-Gibbs (2000) that explores the relationships between school staff and community members as they work together to implement a full-service school in an ethnically diverse urban elementary school. In their article, Abrams and Taylor-Gibbs reported that many low-income parents and parents of color complained that this particular school principal's attitude was condescending and often prejudiced and, in response, these parents adopted an oppositional stance toward the principal's leadership. This constant conflict between parents and school staff played out in a number of ways. For example, during planning meetings, community members would often argue with the principal or express anger toward the principal's leadership style and interactions and blame and criticize teachers for their methods of instruction. Meetings were often spent dealing with conflicting opinions. As the underlying tone of meetings became more and more confrontational, it became harder for the groups to move forward or proceed with their tasks. Some school staff quit attending planning meetings altogether because they felt so dissatisfied with the process. The lack of shared experiences between various groups of parents exacerbated the communication barriers that already existed between parents of different socioeconomic backgrounds and racial groups.

These barriers, impediments, and conflicts are inevitable in attempting to establish collaborative relationships between ethnically diverse parents and schools. Like Mr. James in the case vignette at the beginning of this chapter, school social workers will be asked to help the school to develop ways to increase parental involvement in schools. School social workers, with their mediation skills and expertise in handling group conflict, can be very helpful in assisting groups of ethnically and economically diverse parents on one side and school staff on the other side face up to and work through this school-community divide.

Increasing Parental Connectedness with Schools

School social workers can play a substantial role in engaging and empowering ethnically diverse and poor parents. However, this parental "connectedness" goes beyond classroom visits, bringing refreshments to class parties, or selling items for a school fundraising event. For ethnically diverse and poor parents, it involves a shift from parents being passive recipients of services to taking on responsible and meaningful roles in schools. These efforts will also require school social workers to shift from a "deficit approach" to an "empowerment, family strengths approach" to practice. For example, in an empowerment, family strengths approach to practice, barriers to parental engagement do not necessarily result from a parent's "unwillingness to change" or lack of motivation but rather from a variety of factors including the parent's history of negative experiences with schools, lack of sensitivity by the workers, or community obstacles such as violence (McKay, Tolan, Kohner, & Montaini, 1994). Since many low-income parents care as much about their child's school success as middle-class parents (Davies, 1994), school social workers can empower low-income parents by building on this strength. However, before attempting to gain the trust of poor and ethnically diverse parents and making efforts to engage them in a mutually respectful relationship, school social workers must examine their own attitudes and expectations toward poor and ethnically diverse parents as well as their overall sensitivity to diversity issues (Dupper & Poertner, 1997).

Proven and Promising School-Community Collaborations and Initiatives

A number of innovative school-community collaborations and initiatives have been developed and evaluated. Contact information for several of the programs discussed in this section is listed in Table 10.1. The *School of the 21st Century* (21C), the *Comer-Zigler*

Table 10.1   **Exemplary School-Community Collaborations and Initiatives**

School of the 21st Century (21C) and Comer-Zigler (CoZi) Initiative
School of the 21st Century Office
Yale University
Telephone: (203) 432-9944
www.yale.edu/21c

Foshay Learning Center and Elizabeth Learning Center
www.urbanlearning.com

The Families and Schools Together (FAST) Program
Family Service America
11700 West Lake Park Drive
Milwaukee, WI 53224-3099
Telephone: (800) 221-3726

Communities in Schools, Inc. (CIS)
1199 North Fairfax
Suite 300
Alexandria, VA 22314-1436
Telephone: (703) 519-8999
Fax: (703) 519-7213
www.cisnet.org

Initiative (CoZi), *Families and Schools Together* (FAST), and *Project FAST* are four exemplary programs that meaningfully involve and support parents in schools.

School of the 21st Century (21C)

The *School of the 21st Century* (21C), also known as family re-source centers in some areas of the country, is a school-based or school-linked child care and family support program that pro-motes the optimal growth and development of children ages 0 to 12 (Yale University Bush Center in Child Development and Social Policy, n.d.). These 21C schools are linked to community resources to create an environment that values children (Yale University Bush Center in Child Development and Social Pol-icy, n.d.). See the School of the 21st Century box on page 195 for a description of this exemplary program.

Comer-Zigler (CoZi) Initiative

CoZi is a combination of Dr. Zigler's 21C model and Dr. Comer's *School Development Program* (SDP; described in detail in Chapter 7). According to information contained in Yale University Bush Center in Child Development and Social Policy (n.d.), the CoZi model offers a set of comprehensive family support services linked to the school through a child-centered, collaborative decision-making structure. The importance of parents as active partners in the school is recognized and encouraged. By com-bining the SDP goals of creating a strong school community and actively involving parents in every aspect of the school program (e.g., volunteers, decision makers, learners, partners in home school learning) with the 21C goals of starting early with young children and their parents, the CoZi model creates schools where children's development is at the center of all planning and decision making. Evaluations of CoZi programs in schools in Norfolk, Virginia, and Bridgeport, Connecticut, have been positive.

School of the 21st Century (21C)

Established by Dr. Edward Zigler at Yale University in 1987, the 21C model transforms the school into a year-round, multiservice center providing services from early morning to early evening. One of the unique strengths of the 21C model is that its services are available to all families in a community regardless of income or family circumstances through the use of sliding fee scales and other innovative funding strategies. Core components of 21C schools are designed to be flexible and adaptable to the needs and resources of a given community. These core components include all-day, year-round child care for preschoolers; before-school, after-school, and vacation care for school-age children; information and referral service for families; networks and training for community child care providers; and health education and services (Yale University Bush Center in Child Development and Social Policy, n.d.). Since the 21C model was piloted in Independence, Missouri, in 1988, more than 1200 schools in 17 states have implemented the program. Both Connecticut and Kentucky have launched statewide initiatives based on the model. The Bush Center in Child Development and Social Policy at Yale University provides leadership and technical assistance to 21C schools. The 21C model has proven equally successful in urban, rural, and suburban areas, as well as affluent, middle-class, and impoverished communities with benefits for students (e.g., high scores in math and reading), parents (e.g., experiencing less stress, missing fewer days of work), and school (e.g., substantial reductions in school vandalism, increased parental involvement, changes in teaching practices).

Source: Excerpted from "School of the 21st Century (21C)," by Yale University, Bush Center in Child Development and Social Policy, n.d., retrieved from www.yale.edu/21c

Families and Schools Together (FAST)

The *Families and Schools Together* (FAST) Program "systematically reaches out to entire families and organizes multifamily groups to increase parent involvement with at-risk youth. FAST has been especially successful at involving low-income, stressed, and isolated parents"(McDonald & Frey, 1999, p. 1). The overall goal of the FAST program is "to intervene early to help at-risk youth succeed in the community, at home, and in school and thus avoid problems including adolescent delinquency, violence, addiction, and dropping out of school. The FAST process utilizes the existing strengths of families, schools, and communities in creative partnerships" (McDonald & Frey, 1999, p. 2). Since its development in 1988 by social worker Lynn McDonald, FAST has been implemented in more than 450 schools in 31 states and five countries and has won numerous national awards as a research-based, family-strengthening, family-supporting, collaborative, prevention/early intervention program (McDonald & Frey, 1999). FAST has also been identified as one of six culturally competent education programs by the American Institutes for Research (AIR; 1998). FAST has been continuously evaluated at each new site with the FAST Process and Outcome Evaluation Package and is systematically replicated with certified FAST team trainers by four states and two national organizations (McDonald & Billingham, 1998). An evaluation of the FAST program among Wisconsin families has shown statistically significant improvements in children's classroom and home behaviors, family closeness, and parental involvement in school and a reduction in social isolation (McDonald & Sayger, 1998). A thorough description of the program may be found in McDonald and Frey's (1999) work.

Project FAST (Families Are Students and Teachers)

Project FAST redefines the school as the extended family for students and their parents (Hampton et al., 1998). According to Hampton et al., teachers and parents have continuous year-round contact for three years from kindergarten through second grade in Project FAST. That is, students entering kindergarten remain with each other and the same teacher through the end of second grade. In this way, students return to a classroom where they are aware of the teacher's expectations, and the teacher begins with an informed view of each child's abilities and personality as well as some knowledge of the child's home situation. This long-term, three-year relationship allows parents to collaborate with the teacher on ways to promote achievement and interest in school. These relationships are further strengthened throughout this three-year period by the establishment of parent workshops, which are held monthly. Parent workshops are scheduled in the early evening at a time convenient for parents. In planning and conducting parent workshops, Project FAST teachers emphasize four areas:

1. The knowledge and tools parents need to reinforce instruction.
2. The skills parents need to create a home environment that facilitates achievement.
3. The development of children's self-concept.
4. Discussions to enhance basic parenting skills.

As Project FAST teachers become increasingly viewed as the extended family, parents become more receptive to information/ discussions about effective parenting. Students also participate in annual summer enrichment camps. Early results of Project FAST are impressive. A four-year study involving five kindergarten classrooms in East Cleveland, Ohio (a 99 percent African American community in which 69 percent of the students come from single-parent households and 49 percent are members of families living at or below the poverty line), concluded that when parents were involved with this process, student achievement (reading, language, mathematics) and parental commitment to education far surpassed that of students and parents who remained in more traditional school settings.

Most school-community collaborations offer supportive services at or near schools. These services include medical, dental, and eye-care services; mental health services (often provided by social workers); career counseling, tutoring, mentoring; organized recreational or arts activities; child care and parenting classes; and teen programs. The goal of these collaborations is to bring services that children need into the school so that all children are emotionally, socially, and physically prepared to learn and achieve and teachers are free to teach. This *full-service school* model, also referred to as *school linked services, coordinated services, wraparound services, one-stop shopping,* and *community schools,* transforms schools into community hubs for services, activities, and supports rather than solely a place for academic instruction (Cahill, Perry, Wright, & Rice, 1993; "Framing New Directions," 2001; GAO, 2000). The *full service school* model requires extensive community and parent participation to ensure that services best meet the needs of students and families and to fully integrate services into the academic program (Dryfoos, 1994). The *Children's Aid Society Community School* and *Communities in Schools* (CIS) are two exemplary full-service school models.

Children's Aid Society Community School

The *Children's Aid Society Community School,* located in New York City, is a full-service, community school that combines academics with a complete range of child and family services. According to James (1999), students select an academy on entering the school and generally stay with the same group of students, teachers, and staff through their middle school years (grades five through eight). Students enter one of four academies:

1. *Expressive Arts,* where students put on seasonal performances and special cultural events throughout the year.
2. *Math, Science, and Technology,* where students sponsor programs that encourage other students to use science and technology to spur their creativity.

3. *Community Service,* where students undertake community projects such as tutoring younger students, and organize the school's annual book fair and community garden.

4. *Business Studies,* where students engage in entrepreneurial activities, which include a school store, and sponsorship of the annual career day.

A formal three-year evaluation of the Children's Aid Society Community School reported that student attendance rates had improved, parents were more involved, students were receiving more health care, and the school environment was reported to be more friendly. It was also reported that the percentage of students who tested at their grade level was almost twice as high for math and three times as high for reading when compared to the percentages for similar populations (American Youth Policy Forum, 1999).

Communities in Schools (CIS)

Communities in Schools (CIS) brings together businesses and public and private agencies in communities (e.g., welfare and health professionals, employment counselors, social workers, recreation leaders, the clergy, and members of community groups) and places them in the schools (Cantelon & LeBoeuf, 1997). According to Cantelon and LeBoeuf, CIS programs are designed to provide at-risk youth with the basics that every child needs and deserves—a personal one-on-one relationship with a caring adult, a safe place to learn and grow, a marketable skill to use upon graduation, and a chance to give back to peers and the community. One study, based on a sample of 659 students, found that 70 percent of students with high absenteeism prior to participation in CIS improved their attendance and 60 percent with initially low grades improved their grades. Moreover, a majority of students expressed high levels of satisfaction with the program (Cantelon & LeBoeuf, 1997). Qualities of strong CIS community programs are listed in Table 10.2.

Table 10.2   Qualities of Strong CIS Community Programs

Case studies of ten CIS programs describe examples of collaborative partnerships, strategic planning effective management practices, case management, employment training, substance abuse prevention, mental health services, crime and violence prevention, and parental involvement. Lessons learned from the study of these programs are as follows:

- Community support and multiple sources of funds are critical to the success of community programs.
- Early and continued strong private sector involvement with the active involvement of CIS program staff members in community efforts is important for generating continued support and awareness.
- An involved and trained board is important for raising resources to support the program.
- A strong, periodic strategic planning process including determining the program's expansion strategy, focus, and criteria for both site selection and students involvement supports development of program strategies closely related to needed services.
- Strong top-down support from the school district and/or principal enables CIS to be more than an "add on" social service program and promotes schoolwide reforms.
- Good working relationships with the schools established by surveying staff opinions, serving on school management teams, and providing training and assistance for teachers assigned to work with CIS help ensure that the program operates smoothly.
- Integration of services achieved through formal agreements that stipulate roles, responsibilities, and working conditions is a key factor to program success.
- Joint selection and evaluation of staff repositioned or assigned to CIS through agreements by schools and service agencies to strengthen the program's partnerships.
- Strong oversight and accountability maintained through a comprehensive records and reporting system allow directors to plan and implement program improvements and to demonstrate effectiveness to stakeholders.
- Ongoing case management is particularly important to successful service coordination in locations where high levels of community and/or family disorganization exist.

Source: Reprinted from *Keeping Young People in School: Community Programs that Work,* 1997, Washington DC: U.S. Department of Justice, Office of Justice Programs, Office of Juvenile Justice and Delinquency Prevention, Juvenile Justice Bulletin. This document is in the public domain.

One of the primary purposes of school-community collaborations is to improve the academic achievement of students. According to the U.S. GAO (2000), there are a number of innovative ways this can be accomplished including offering students special opportunities if they improve or maintain good grades and exhibit positive student behavior; developing partnerships with local colleges and universities to enhance their school's academic programs; providing career readiness skills such as resume writing and interviewing; and providing smaller and more personalized school-within-a-school career academies that focus on career-oriented course work and experience. Another important purpose of school-community collaborations is to expose and connect disadvantaged students to geographical areas that extend beyond their neighborhoods (GAO, 2000). The Foshay Learning Center and Elizabeth Learning Center are two exemplary programs that incorporate a career academy model.

Foshay Learning Center and Elizabeth Learning Center

The *Foshay Learning Center* and the *Elizabeth Learning Center*, both located in Los Angeles, use the full career academy approach. According to the U.S. GAO (2000), all students in grades 10 through 12 participate in a career academy as part of their academic program, and local businesses and agencies provide work experience through internships and job shadowing. The Foshay Learning Center offers health, finance, and information technology academies; and the Elizabeth Learning Center has health and information technology programs. Both academies attempt to provide graduates with the skills and knowledge that prepare them for one of three options:

1. Enroll in a university and pursue an advanced degree in the selected academy focus.
2. Enroll in a technical or vocational school and pursue a career in the selected academy focus.
3. Obtain an entry-level job in the selected academy focus.

Both of these career academies have been shown to be effective in improving attendance rates and graduation rates. For example, the Foshay Learning Center reported that the average daily attendance rate was between 90 and 94 percent compared to about 80 percent in 1990. At the Elizabeth Learning Center, the graduation rate for students entering sixth grade was 98 percent, and for those entering ninth grade, it was 100 percent compared to a graduation rate of about 50 percent in a neighboring school with no school-community initiative (GAO, 2000).

Several key principles are essential for establishing and maintaining effective school-community collaborations (see Table 10.3). These key principles should guide the actions of school social workers in their efforts to create and maintain successful school-community collaborations. For example, school social workers must consider the fact that most school staff will be unprepared for this paradigm shift, and both school staff and parents must be adequately prepared beforehand. Moreover, the limits of power sharing must be discussed, and roles and responsibilities must be clarified at the beginning of the planning process. Another key principle is that programs and interventions should be tailored to community needs and resources and change as community conditions change. Perhaps most importantly, school social workers must be patient because institutional change is a slow and gradual process.

Summary

There is no "magic bullet" to improve the educational success of at-risk children who reside in troubled or economically disadvantaged inner-city neighborhoods. Therefore, schools are increasingly turning to collaborations and partnerships with parents and other resources in the community. Some new perspectives on the role of school social workers in bringing about systemic school reform through school-community collaborations are needed. Major challenges await school social workers in building school-community collaborations, including language

Table 10.3   **Key Principles in Establishing and Maintaining Effective School-Community Collaborations**

- It is important to recognize that the collaboration model is relatively new and most school staff are unprepared for this paradigm shift.
- School staff must be offered time and training to accept community members' new role in the school. Without adequate preparation, community members will continue to feel their outsider or subordinate status in the school milieu, particularly those parents from low-income and/or ethnic minority communities.
- Parent participation should be highly valued and encouraged.
- Parents, students, community members and organizations, and other stakeholders play an active role in guiding policy and practices through entities such as advisory committees and governance councils.
- The challenge of collaboration must be recognized. Participants must understand and acknowledge the depth of the cultural and class inequalities that alienate community members from the institution of the public school. These common understandings might pave the way for mutual accommodation and compromise from the onset of the collaboration process.
- Since leadership and power sharing are central arenas of struggle, the limits of power sharing must be discussed and roles and responsibilities must be clarified at the beginning of the planning process in meetings between the two groups.
- Rather than blaming each other for poor school achievement, school staff must be able to view elements of the school itself as barriers to academic success, and community members must be able to see that public schools in low-income communities are part of the cycle of neighborhood disadvantage, often mirroring the class, race, and gender inequalities found in the larger society.
- Specific and reasonable goals should be set. Holding on to the vision of the full-service school with specific goals and objectives will keep both school staff and community members involved in their committee work and in the planning process itself.
- Services and activities should be tailored to community needs and resources and have the flexibility to change as community conditions change.
- Working toward institutional changes is generally a slow and gradual process; time and patience are essential.

Source: Adapted from "Planning for School Change," by L. S. Abrams and G. J. Taylor Gibbs, 2000, *Urban Education, 35,* pp. 79–103; *At-Risk Youth,* by U.S. General Accounting Office, 2000, October.

barriers of immigrant families, a long history of negative relationships, mistrust, and misunderstandings between urban
parents and school staff and the ambivalence of school staff in
establishing partnerships with members of the community.
School social workers can play a substantial role in engaging
and empowering ethnically diverse and poor parents. However, these efforts will require a shift from a deficit approach
to an empowerment, family strengths approach to practice. To
make this shift, school social workers must examine their own
attitudes and expectations toward poor and ethnically diverse
parents, as well as their sensitivity to diversity issues. A number of innovative school-community collaborations and initiatives meaningfully involve parents and offer a complete range
of child and family services at the school site, making schools
the community hub for services, activities, and supports rather
than solely a place for academic instruction. The School of the
21st Century (21C) is one of several innovative exemplary
programs. While a number of challenges exist, a significant
opportunity awaits school social workers to play a key role in
this emerging school-community collaboration movement.

Questions for Discussion

1. What are some of the reasons that low-income and ethnically diverse parents may be reluctant to become involved
   in public schools?
2. Why are educators often hesitant to establish partnerships
   with members of the community?
3. How can school social workers empower parents, especially low-income and culturally diverse parents?
4. Identify several key principles necessary for establishing and
   maintaining effective school-community collaborations.
5. The School of the 21st Century (21C) was identified as an
   exemplary program that meaningfully involves parents in
   schools. Briefly describe the 21C model and the potential

roles that school social workers can assume in implementing the 21C model.

Refer to the case study at the beginning of this chapter:

1. What factors might be contributing to this lack of parental involvement in general and in the Hispanic community specifically?

2. Is a Parents' Night the most effective way to involve Hispanic parents? Why or why not?

3. In what other ways might this school social worker increase parental involvement in the Hispanic community?

Additional Resources

- The mission of the *Coalition for Community Schools* is to strengthen and sustain community-school partnerships with the goal of improving student learning and building stronger communities.
  Telephone: (202) 822-8405
  E-mail: ccs@iel.org
  www.communityschools.org
- The mission of the *National Center for Schools and Communities* is to improve the education of children in poverty by initiating and sustaining joint action by universities, schools, community-based organizations, and families. National Center for Schools and Communities, Carolyn Denham, PhD, Director, Fordham University, 113 W. 60th Street, Suite 704, New York, NY 10023.
  Telephone: (212) 636-6699
  FAX: (212) 636-6033
- *Schools as Centers of Community: A citizen's guide for planning and design* is available at: www.ed.gov/inits/construction/ctty-centers.html
- The mission of the *Center for Research on the Education of Students Placed at Risk* (CRESPAR) is to conduct research, development, evaluation, and dissemination needed to transform schooling for students placed at risk. The work of the Center is guided by three central themes: ensuring the success of all students at key developmental points, building on students' personal and cultural assets, and scaling up effective programs.
  www.ed.gov/offices/OERI/At-Risk/howhop1.html

EVALUATING SCHOOL SOCIAL WORK PRACTICE

Traditionally, social workers have relied upon the practice wisdom of colleagues and supervisors, anecdotal information, impressions, clinical experience and judgment, and theoretical orientation in assessing client change. While these informal methods may have been helpful in the past, this age of increased public scrutiny and accountability demands that school social workers use more scientific methods in assessing change at the client level as well as at the systems level. "Hard data" is necessary to justify the expenditure of public tax dollars on school social work services and avoid possible cutbacks in times of retrenchment.

Unfortunately, few social workers are comfortable with or adequately prepared to design and carry out scientific evaluations of their practice. Why is this the case? There appear to be several reasons. Some believe that social work practice is an art rather than a science and, therefore, too complex to be evaluated appropriately. Another reason is that some social workers do not want to discover that their theoretical approach or therapy, which may have involved extensive training, may be ineffective. Perhaps most importantly, many social work students and practitioners feel that research is too difficult and time consuming, and they fail to appreciate the link between social work practice and research—that both involve systematic, problem-solving steps, and the setting of concrete goals.

The chapters in this section are intended to dispel some of these misconceptions and equip school social workers with some beginning knowledge and skills in how to design and evaluate student-focused (Chapter 11) and system-focused (Chapter 12) interventions using empirically based methods and measures. This more scientific approach to practice evaluation is often referred to as *empirically based, empirically supported,* or *research-based* practice. Each chapter includes a summary of currently available assessment instruments/tests/measures that can be used by school social workers to evaluate the effectiveness of their student- and system-focused interventions. In addition, Chapter 12 contains guidelines for successfully planning, implementing, and evaluating new programs based on *Comprehensive Quality Programming* (CQP) steps.

Evaluating Student-Focused Interventions

In this chapter, we discuss:

- *Process versus outcome evaluations.*

- *Categories of measures to evaluate student-focused interventions.*

- *Research designs.*

- *Using single-system designs and classical group designs in evaluating the effectiveness of student-focused interventions.*

11

Chapter

When Pam began work as a school social worker, the idea of evaluating her practice seemed daunting. She didn't think she would have time to collect or analyze data. However, as Pam prepared to facilitate an eight-session anger management group for five high school girls, she recognized the importance of monitoring their progress. Pam asked each group member to complete the Children's Perceived Self-Control Scale (CPSC) for three consecutive weeks prior to the beginning of the group to establish a baseline and then asked them to complete the scale at the beginning of each group for the following eight weeks. Because this scale contained only ten questions, it took the girls just a few minutes to complete them each time. Pam also gathered data for two school archival measures—number of disciplinary referrals and classroom conduct grades. These, too, were easy measures to obtain. Pam, using an A-B design, graphed these data so that each girl could visually inspect the graph and see her own progress over time. Pam believed that seeing these positive changes in the form of a graph would be rewarding and motivating. By gathering the archival data in the weeks following the completion of the group sessions, Pam could assess if changes were maintained over time.

Research must also be a part of the job and not left to academicians. The credibility of pupil services professionals' roles within the school partly depends on the ability to document that services make a difference to students and their families and to the achievement of the school system's goals. (Gibelman, 1993, p. 48)

Introduction

In this age of increasing accountability, school social workers must be able to empirically demonstrate that their interventions contribute to or result in improved outcomes in those areas highly valued by school board members, school administrators, and the general public (Dibble, 1999). This chapter focuses on measures and methods available to school social workers to assess, using scientific procedures, whether their *student-focused* interventions have contributed to or resulted in improved outcomes. It also discusses the differences between process and outcome evaluation, categories of scientific measures available to school social workers to evaluate their student-focused interventions, research designs that can be used by school social workers to evaluate their student-focused interventions, and an illustration of how school social work interventions were evaluated using an A-B single-system design and a classical group design.

Process versus Outcome Evaluations

Many school social work practitioners and supervisors confuse process evaluation with outcome evaluation. For example, in evaluating the performance of a school social worker, many supervisors limit their questions to what the worker *did*, such as "How many home visits did this worker make this month?" or "How much time and effort did this worker spend carrying out his or her interventions this month?" While these questions are important, they focus solely on process rather than outcomes. On the other hand, outcome evaluation focuses on questions such as "Did the school social worker's intervention reduce the student's problem behavior, increase attendance, improve grades, or a combination of these?" Outcome evaluation answers whether the school social work intervention resulted in any "tangible positive changes" (Dibble, 1999, p. 7). It is no longer sufficient to limit evaluations to what the school social worker did (process evaluation); it is becoming increasingly important for school social workers to use systematic, objective procedures for determining whether the client improved and, with more rigorous research designs, if the worker's interventions were responsible for that improvement (outcome evaluation). Conducting systematic and objective outcome evaluations of student-focused interventions is the focus of this chapter.

Categories of Measures to Evaluate Student-Focused Interventions

While a number of modalities for assessing client change have been discussed elsewhere (see Radin, 1988), this discussion focuses on four major categories of measures available to school social workers that readily lend themselves to single-system research designs. These are standardized questionnaires, school archival data, individualized rating scales (IRS), and behavioral measures.

1. *Standardized questionnaires* are reliable and valid ways of repeatedly measuring targets identified for intervention (Bloom, Fischer, & Orme, 1999). Table 11.1 contains a partial list of standardized questionnaires that can be used as outcome measures in evaluating student-focused interventions. As shown in the table, each outcome measure is clearly linked to school performance (both externalizing and internalizing behaviors) and associated with social work interventions (Dibble, 1999). For example, outcome

Table 11.1   **Standardized Questionnaires to Evaluate Student-Focused Interventions**

Conners Teacher Rating Scale-39 (CTRS-39) is a 39-item behavioral rating scale for teachers to assess patterns of behavior in children between the ages of 3 and 12. The CTRS-39 includes the following seven subscales: hyperactivity, conduct problem, emotional indulgent, anxious passive, asocial, daydream-attention problems, and hyperactivity index.

Aggression Scale is designed to measure the frequency of self-reported aggressive behaviors (e.g., hitting, name-calling, threatening) of sixth, seventh, and eighth graders. More information about this scale can be found in Orpinas, P. (1993). *Skills training and social influence for violence prevention in middle schools: A curriculum evaluation.* Doctoral Dissertation. Houston: University of Texas Health Science Center at Houston. Dissertation Abstracts International, 94-01778.

Self-Control Rating Scale (SCRS) is a 33-item instrument designed to measure a child's degree of self-control from grade four and up. This instrument can be used to assess changes in self-control due to treatment. The publisher is Dr. Phillip Kendall, Department of Psychology, Temple University, 478 Weiss Hall, Philadelphia, PA 19122.

Children's Perceived Self-Control Scale (CPSC) measures interpersonal self-control, personal self-control, and self-evaluation. The author has also published a similar form for teacher's assessment of a child's self-control. The publisher is Laura Humphrey, PhD, Department of Psychiatry, Northwestern University Medical School, 320 E. Huron, Chicago, IL 60611.

Children's Depression Inventory (CDI) is a self-report instrument that asks the child to choose the best of three sentences. It is designed to be used with children from 8 to 17 years of age. The CDI is able to distinguish depressed from nondepressed children and youth and is sensitive to treatment effects.

Piers-Harris Children's Self Concept Scale (The Way I Feel About Myself) is a self-report inventory for use with children in grades 4 to 12 that contains the following subscales: behavior, intellectual and school status, physical appearance and attributes, anxiety, popularity, and happiness and satisfaction. It can be used as a general screening device or as a measure of treatment outcome. The publisher is Western Psychological Services, Publishers and Distributors, 12031 Wilshire Boulevard, Los Angeles, CA 90025-1251. (800) 648-8857. E-mail: custsv@wpspublish.com

Anxiety Scales for Children and Adults (ASCA) determines the presence and intensity of anxiety in adults and school-age children and can be used as a clinical outcome measure. The publisher is Pro-Ed, Inc., 8700 Shoal Creek Blvd., Austin, TX 78757-6897. E-mail: rspencer@proedinc.com

(continued)

Table 11.1 *(Continued)*

ADD-H: Comprehensive Teacher's Rating Scale, Second Edition (ACTeRS) is a short, concise teacher rating scale designed to be a practical tool for the diagnosis and treatment monitoring of attention deficit disorder. The publisher is Metri Tech, Inc., 4106 Fieldstone Rd., P.O. Box 6479, Champaign, IL 61826-6479. (800) 747-4868. E-mail: mtinfo@metritech.com

Assertiveness Scale for Adolescents (ASA) is designed to measure assertiveness of adolescents (grades 6 through 12) in specific situations. The ASA can be used to identify personal problem areas and as a research tool to measure changes in assertiveness. The publisher is Department of Educational Psychology, University of Western Ontario, Ontario, Canada N6G 1G7.

Children's Loneliness Questionnaire (CLQ) is designed to measure children's feelings of loneliness, feelings of social adequacy versus inadequacy, and subjective estimations of peer status (with eight filler items to relax the subject). The publisher is Dr. Steven Asher, University of Illinois at Urbana-Champaign, Bureau of Educational Research, 1310 South Sixth Street, Champaign, IL 61820.

measures include assessment of changes in aggression, self-control, depression, self-concept, anxiety, monitoring of attention deficit disorder with hyperactivity (ADHD) symptoms, assertiveness, and loneliness. Since Pam, in the case vignette at the beginning of the chapter, wanted to monitor changes in girls' self-control, she selected the Children's Perceived Self Control Scale (CPSC), which measures interpersonal self-control, personal self-control, and self evaluation. Several standardized questionnaires (e.g., Conners Teacher Rating Scale-39 and Piers-Harris Children's Self Concept Scale) have been widely used in published research studies. Several excellent resources on standardized questionnaires, scales, tests, and measures useful to school social workers are listed in the Additional Resources section at the end of this chapter.

2. *School archival measures* can be readily obtained by school social workers in evaluating their student-focused interventions. These measures are data collected by schools that are kept for purposes not related to school social work

interventions. This is an important category of measures because archival measures are unobtrusive and nonreactive; that is, they can be used without the knowledge of the student being measured, and they do not directly impact the behavior of the student (Bloom et al., 1999). In addition, this is an important category of measures because it includes outcomes that school board members, school administrators, and the general public are most interested in—academic achievement, attendance, and student behavior. See Table 11.2 for a list of readily available and easily obtainable school archival measures that can be used to evaluate student-focused interventions. Some of these archival measures are found in students' report cards (e.g., unexcused absences/tardies, grades and grade point averages, conduct grades, and classroom work habits) while other archival measures are maintained in students' disciplinary files at the school (e.g., written referrals for student misbehavior, in- and out-of-school suspensions, detentions). Pam, in the case vignette, was able to obtain the archival measures she used as outcome measures from each girl's disciplinary folder (i.e., number of disciplinary referrals) and from each girl's classroom teacher (i.e., classroom conduct grades) on a weekly basis. Because of the relative ease with which these archival measures can be obtained, their nonreactivity as measures, and their importance as outcome measures in the educational setting, school social workers should always include at least one or

Table 11.2   **School Archival Data to Assess the Impact of Student-Focused Interventions**

▪ Unexcused absences/tardies.	▪ Grades and grade point averages.
▪ Written referrals for student misbehavior.	▪ Classroom conduct grades.
▪ In- and out-of-school suspensions.	▪ Classroom work habits.
▪ Detentions.	▪ Standardized test scores.

Source: Adapted from *Outcome Evaluation of School Social Work Services*, by N. Dibble, 1999, Madison: Wisconsin Department of Public Instruction.

two archival measures as part of their measurement "package." The School Archival Records Search (SARS) provides a profile of a student's status on 11 archival measures. A description of the SARS can be found at the end of this chapter under Additional Resources.

3. *Individualized rating scales* (IRS) are practical scales that are constructed for a particular client to measure the intensity or severity of his or her internal thoughts and feelings by using numbers, words, or pictures that represent anchors along a continuum (Bloom et al., 1999). IRSs are especially useful if no standardized questionnaire is available to measure the target problem or if the client is not old enough to complete a standardized questionnaire. See the box and Figure 11.1 for an illustration of how an IRS might be used with a six-year-old student.

Illustration of How an IRS Could Be Used with a Six-Year-Old Student

Helen, a school social worker, is interested in assessing changes in Jeff's severity of feelings of anger toward another student named Tom. Rather than using words as "anchor points" along a continuum, the school social worker could construct an IRS by drawing a number of facial expressions corresponding to a continuum of points that range from 1 to 5. A somewhat happy face could be drawn on the anchor point corresponding to the number 1. A very angry face could be drawn as the other anchor point corresponding to the number 5. Three more faces could then be drawn showing a growing severity of anger that correspond to the numbers 2 to 4. Helen will ask Jeff to rate the intensity of his feelings of anger toward Tom by looking at the IRS and circling the number that corresponds to the facial expression that best describes his feelings of anger toward Tom. An example of how this IRS might be drawn is shown in Figure 11.1.

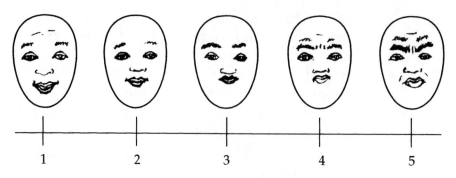

<u>Figure 11.1</u>

Example of an Individual Rating Scale for a Young Child.

4. *Behavioral measures* are the fourth category of measures readily available to school social workers. Behavioral measures include both overt and covert behaviors. A student's overt behavior can be observed directly and recorded by school social workers, parents/guardians, and teachers. A student's covert behavior can be recorded by having a student observe and record his or her own behavior through a process called self monitoring (Bloom et al., 1999).

It is important for school social workers to keep in mind several guidelines in selecting measures. It is important to develop an overall measurement package. A *measurement package* uses multiple measures from multiple sources to increase the chances that positive programmatic outcomes will be detected and measured. In developing a measurement package for an individual student, it is always advisable to assess change in a student's behavior by collecting teacher and parental reports of change, as well as a student self-report or self-monitoring measure and archival data. It is also important to develop a measurement package in which the potential weaknesses of certain measures are offset by other measures in the overall package (e.g., reactive measures are offset by nonreactive measures; Bloom et al., 1999). Because behavioral measures are the most direct and valid measure of a target problem, they should be selected as part of an overall measurement package whenever possible (Bloom et al., 1999). School social workers should also decide on a time frame for collecting these data. Some data can be collected on a daily basis (e.g., school archival data and student self-monitoring data), while other data can be collected only on a weekly basis (e.g., standardized questionnaires).

Research Designs

After a school social worker has collected data using one or more of the measures previously discussed, he or she is ready to assess the effectiveness of student-focused interventions using either single-system designs or group research designs. The term *single-system research designs* (SSRDs) "refers to a set of empirical procedures used to observe changes in an identified target [or problem] that is measured repeatedly over time" (Bloom et al., 1999, p. 5). SSRDs are valuable tools for school social workers for a number of reasons as outlined by Bloom et al.:

1. SSRDs are designed to answer the outcome evaluation questions "Have changes occurred in the target problem?" and "Was this particular intervention responsible for observed changes?"
2. They are relatively easy to use and understand.
3. They are flexible, client-focused, and are usable by practitioners adhering to any practice theory in almost any practice situation.

While a number of SSRDs are available to school social workers, the A-B design is considered the "workhorse" of practice evaluation (Bloom et al., 1999). By visually analyzing the data, the A-B design can clearly reveal whether there has been a change in target problems between baseline and intervention phases. The A-B design provides ongoing feedback to the school social worker and client about whether to continue a given intervention, modify it, or change to another intervention (Bloom et al., 1999). The box and Figure 11.2 illustrate how a school social worker, Helen, used an A-B design to evaluate the effectiveness of Interpersonal Cognitive Problem Solving (ICPS), an exemplary 12-week interpersonal cognitive problem-solving program described in Chapter 3 of this book.

A-B Design Used to Evaluate Effectiveness of Interpersonal Cognitive Problem Solving

Consider the case of Helen and Jeff. Helen wants to know if Jeff's severity of feelings of anger toward Tom has changed during the intervention phase of treatment. Using data from the IRS described in the previous box, Helen constructs a graph using the Microsoft EXCEL program. As shown in Figure 11.2, there was a slightly upward trend to the data during the baseline phase. While the severity of anger decreased slightly at week 2, an upward trend can be seen in weeks 3 and 4. In week 5, Jeff participated in *Interpersonal Cognitive Problem Solving* (ICPS), an exemplary 12-week interpersonal cognitive problem-solving program. Jeff's severity of anger rises slightly at week 6 and continues into week 7 but then begins to trend downward at week 8 and levels off through week 10. A distinctly downward trend begins at week 11 to the end of the ICPS program at week 16. Comparing the trends in data between the baseline phase and intervention phase, it appears that the severity of Jeff's self-reported anger toward Tom decreased in a clinically significant way during the intervention phase. To assess the maintenance of this decrease in anger over time, Helen contacted Jeff about a month later and asked him to complete the IRS one more time. As shown in Figure 11.2, Jeff's severity of anger remained at 1 at week 20, indicating that Jeff's decrease in anger was maintained four weeks after the conclusion of the ICPS program.

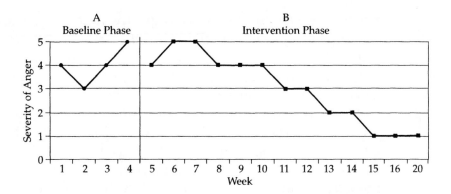

Figure 11.2

Jeff's Severity of Feelings of Anger toward Tom.

As shown in Figure 11.2, the A-B design is useful in assessing whether any change occurred between the baseline and intervention phases. The primary drawback of the A-B design is that the school social worker cannot determine whether the intervention *caused* the observed change. More sophisticated SSRDs (e.g., A-B-A design) are necessary to determine these causal links (Bloom et al., 1999). For example, in an A-B-A design, the school social worker examines whether the introduction of the intervention results in changes in the target behavior. In this design, the data between the first baseline and the intervention are compared, and the data between the intervention and the second baseline are compared. A causal link between the intervention and observed changes can be established if the target behavior returns to first baseline levels during the second baseline phase (Bloom et al., 1999). For more detailed information about SSRDs, see Bloom et al. (1999).

In addition to SSRDs, group research designs can be used to determine the effectiveness of student-focused interventions. While it is beyond the scope of this chapter to describe each of these group research designs in detail as well as the relative strengths and limitations of each particular group design, it is important to distinguish between quasi-experimental research designs and experimental research designs. *Quasi-experimental research designs* use comparison groups that are not formed by random assignment while *experimental research designs* use groups that are formed by randomly assigning students to either the treatment group or the control group (which does not receive treatment; Flannery, 1998). While random assignment of students to treatment and control conditions may not be possible in many real-world situations, random assignment of two equally deserving groups of students provides the strongest empirical evidence that the intervention caused observed differences in outcomes (Flannery, 1998). For more detailed information about group designs, see Mark (1996).

Using Single-System Designs and Classical Group Designs in Evaluating the Effectiveness of Student-Focused Interventions

An illustration of how a school social worker can apply SSRDs in evaluating student-focused interventions is found in an article by Franklin, Biever, Moore, Clemons, and Scamardo (2001). They evaluated the effectiveness of five to ten sessions of solution-focused therapy, using A-B single-system designs, with children who were referred with learning disabilities and classroom behavior problems. A visual analysis of data from Conners Teacher Rating Scales (CTRS-39) indicated that solution-focused therapy was followed by observable positive changes on one or more subscales of the CTRS-39 for five of the seven children involved in the study. Based on these findings, the authors concluded that solution-focused therapy shows promise for helping special education students with academic difficulties and classroom behavior problems. This article contains a number of figures that illustrate how data from a repeated measure (in this case data from the CTRS-39) can be graphed and visually analyzed to assess changes over time using an A-B design across students.

Several articles illustrate how a school social worker can apply a group design to evaluate student-focused interventions. In an initial study, Dupper and Krishef (1993) tested the effectiveness of a school-based social-cognitive skills training program (highlighted in Chapter 3) with 35 middle school students with school behavior problems in a Florida school district. Students who met the selection criteria were randomly assigned to the treatment group (school survival group) or the control group (no intervention) using a pretest-posttest control group design. Scores from the Nowicki-Strickland Locus of Control Scale (N-SLCS) and the Teachers Self-Control Rating Scale (TSCRS) were used to assess students' cognitive and behavioral changes before and after the treatment program. Findings from this initial experiment supported the short-term effectiveness of this group treatment program. In a follow-up study, Dupper (1998) further developed and tested the school survival group with a larger sample (84) of middle/junior high school students with school behavior problems. In this follow-up study, several group leaders were trained to conduct school survival groups throughout several Illinois school districts. Again, all students who met the selection criteria were randomly assigned to either treatment groups (school survival groups) or attention-only control groups and administered the Nowicki-Strickland Locus of Control Scale (N-SLCS) at pretest, posttest, and one-month follow-up. Dupper found that students who participated in this skills training program reported a shift from a more external to a more internal locus of control as measured by the N-SLCS and that this shift was maintained one month after treatment. This finding is important because a shift to a more internal locus of control has been shown to be positively correlated with school success in other studies.

Summary

School social workers must demonstrate, using hard data, that their interventions lead to improvement in students' grades, attendance, behavior, and other educational outcomes. Process evaluation focuses on what the worker did, while outcome evaluation focuses on whether the school social work intervention resulted in any tangible positive changes. Four major categories of measures are available to school social workers that readily lend themselves to single-system research designs: standardized questionnaires, school archival data, individualized rating scales, and behavioral measures. It is important to develop an overall measurement package and to decide on a time frame for collecting data. Because they are the most direct and valid measure of a target problem, behavioral measures should be selected as part of an overall measurement package whenever possible. Single-system research designs (SSRDs) are valuable tools for school social workers in evaluating whether changes have occurred in the target problem (e.g., A-B design) or if an intervention was responsible for observed changes (e.g., A-B-A design). Group research designs can also be used to determine the effectiveness of student-focused interventions. Quasi-experimental research designs use comparison groups that are not formed by random assignment while experimental research designs use groups that are formed by randomly assigning students to either the treatment group or the control group (which does not receive treatment).

Questions for Discussion

1. Why are school social workers often reluctant to evaluate the effectiveness of their interventions?

2. How does process evaluation differ from outcome evaluation?

3. Identify and briefly describe the four major categories of measures available to school social workers that readily lend themselves to single-system research designs.

4. What is the most direct and valid measure of a target behavior?

5. What two types of research designs can be used by school social workers to determine the effectiveness of student-focused interventions?

Refer to the case study at the beginning of this chapter:

1. Pam selected a standardized scale and two school archival measures for her measurement package. Discuss the strengths and limitations of her measurement package.

2. What other outcome measures could Pam have selected to assess the effectiveness of the anger management group? Discuss their appropriateness as outcome measures in this particular case.

Additional Resources

- *The School Archival Records Search* (SARS) provides the school professional with a profile of a student's status on 11 archival variables (i.e., number of schools attended, days absent, low achievement, grades retained, in-school referrals, current IEP, non-regular placement, Chapter I, referrals out, negative narrative comments, and discipline contacts). The SARS is available from Sopris West, 1140 Boston Avenue, P.O. Box 1809, Longmont, CO 80501-1809.

- The *WALMYR Assessment Scales* (WAS; Hudson & Faul, 1998) is a set of standardized scales designed to monitor and evaluate the extent, degree, or intensity of a client's problem through repeated administrations of the same questionnaire to a client. None of the WAS scales should be completed by persons under the age of 12 years. Examples of WAS scales that may be of use to school social workers include: Generalized Contentment Scale, Index of Self Esteem, Index of Clinical Stress, Clinical Anxiety Scale, Index of Alcohol Involvement, Index of Drug Involvement, Index of Peer Relations, Index of Homophobia, Index of Family Relations, Child's Attitude toward Mother, Child's Attitude toward Father, Index of Brother Relations, Index of Sister Relations, Child's Behavior Rating Scale, and Index of Sexual Harassment. Information on how to obtain WAS scales and a scoring manual for WAS scales can be obtained by contacting: WALMYR Assessment Scales (WAS), WALMYR Publishing Co., P.O. Box 12217, Tallahassee, FL 32317-2217.
  Telephone: (850) 383-0045
  Fax: (850) 383-0970
  www.walmyr.com

- *Tests in Print* (TIP), published by the Buros Institute for Mental Measurements, Lincoln, Nebraska, is an encyclopedia of information on every published and commercially available test in psychology and achievement.

- The *Mental Measurements Yearbook* (MMY), published by the Buros Institute for Mental Measurements, Lincoln, Nebraska, contains descriptive information about tests and one or more reviews of the test by qualified psychologists.
- *Tests*, published by Pro-Ed, Inc., Austin, Texas, is an encyclopedia containing information on thousands of testing instruments in psychology, education, and business.
- *Test Critiques*, a companion to *Tests*, contains supplemental psychometric information such as reliability, validity, and norm development. *Test Critiques* is published by Pro-Ed, Inc., Austin, Texas.
- Additional scales and tests may be located through a literature search using PsycINFO, Psychological Abstracts, the print counterpart to PsycINFO, or PsycLIT, the CD-ROM version of PsycINFO. PsycINFO, Psychological Abstracts, and PsycLIT provide abstracts for each article.
- *Measures for clinical practice: A sourcebook (Volume 1: Couples, families, and children, 3rd ed.)* by Kevin Corcoran and Joel Fischer (published by Free Press; ISBN: 0-684-84830-9). describes the essentials of measurement and presents the most up-to-date rapid assessment instruments (RAIs) that have been developed to measure change for almost any problem.
- *Handbook of tests and measurement in education and the social sciences* by Paula E. Lester and Lloyd K. Bishop is another anthology of instruments designed for education and the social sciences.This book may be ordered by calling:
Telephone: (800) 233-9936

Evaluating System-Focused
Interventions

In this chapter, we discuss:

- Measures to assess system-focused interventions.
- Guidelines for successfully planning, implementing, and evaluating new programs.
- Comprehensive quality programming (CQP) steps.

12

Chapter

Mary is a school social worker in a medium-sized school district. She is very concerned about the problem of substance abuse among youth in this community. In speaking to several of her colleagues about her concerns, she learns that the Drug Abuse Resistance Education (DARE) program, despite a lack of empirical support, has been implemented for a number of years in this school district and is strongly supported by the majority of members of the local school board. Mary is committed to implementing a program that works in reducing substance abuse among youth. Mary knows that she will inevitably encounter strong resistance in trying to implement a new and different approach to substance abuse prevention in this particular community. To have any chance of success, Mary needs to be very thoughtful and deliberate in planning, implementing, and evaluating a new programmatic approach to reducing substance abuse among youth in this community.

As change agents, school social workers can expand their role beyond provision of direct services to become team leaders, advocates, and capacity builders at macro levels of practice in school systems." (Lim & Adelman, 1999)

Introduction

According to the National Association of Social Workers (NASW) Code of Ethics, a fundamental aspect of school social work practice is targeting detrimental conditions in schools, families, neighborhoods, and communities. Many programs, in addition to changing individuals, seek to make changes in those systems surrounding children and youth. Some programs are entirely focused on making system-level changes. However, assessing the impact of such system-focused programs/interventions has been difficult. This is largely because outcome measures have historically been person-focused rather than system-focused. Fortunately, over the past decade, a growing number of standardized scales have been developed to measure the extent to which changes have occurred in those systems that exert the greatest impact on children and youth, namely schools, families, and neighborhoods/communities.

This chapter discusses a number of standardized measures that are readily available to school social workers who want to assess the impact of programs/interventions on schools, families, and neighborhoods/communities. The chapter then presents a series of guidelines and steps for successfully planning, implementing, and evaluating new programs/interventions with a particular focus on the eight steps of comprehensive quality programming (CQP).

Measures to Assess System-Focused Interventions

Several outcome measures are available to assess changes in schools, families, and neighborhoods/communities. Some of these measures are similar to those discussed in Chapter 11. The critical difference is the *unit of attention*. In Chapter 11, the focus is on evaluating *student-focused* interventions where the individual student is the unit of attention and the data are gathered and reported at the individual level. In this chapter, the units of attention are system-level variables including classrooms, schools, families, neighborhoods, communities, or a combination of these. All data are gathered and reported at the level of that particular system-level variable. *It is essential that the unit of attention remain consistent throughout the data collection, data analysis, and reporting of findings.*

A number of standardized questionnaires are readily available for use as outcome measures to evaluate system-level changes. Table 12.1 describes several standardized questionnaires that assess changes in families, schools, classrooms, and neighborhoods/communities. As shown in this table, standardized scales have been developed to assess changes using a large number of system-level variables, including family cohesion (CYDS Family Assessment Scale), family bonding and communication (Individual Protective Factor Index), the organizational health of a school (Organizational Health Inventory), the social climates of classrooms (Classroom Environment Scale), children's exposure to violence in the home or neighborhood (Survey of Children's Exposure to Community Violence), residents' sense of belonging in their neighborhood and sharing the same values as their neighbors (Neighborhood Cohesion), and residents' attitudes toward their neighborhood (Neighborhood Satisfaction). These measures provide a reliable and valid means for school social workers to assess changes at these various system levels.

In addition to standardized questionnaires, archival data can be used to assess the impact of school-level programs/interventions. Table 12.2 lists a some archival data that can be used to assess changes in the level of school violence (e.g., costs to repair vandalism, property destruction, law enforcement referrals, conduct ratings on students' report cards, and referrals for misbehavior/learning problems) as well as changes in a school's discipline procedures (e.g., detentions, number of students placed in in-school suspension, out-of-school suspension rates, expulsion rates). In addition to school archival data, an extensive amount of archival data are available at the community level to assess the impact of programs/interventions. Examples of community-level archival

Table 12.1   **Standardized Questionnaires Used to Evaluate Family, School, Classroom, and Neighborhood/Community Interventions**

CYDS Family Assessment Scale measures family adaptability, cohesion, religious values, and somatization tendencies. Scale is completed by primary caretaking parent and older siblings usually 13 years of age and older. More information about this scale can be found in Tolan, P. H. & Gorman-Smith, D. (1991). *The Chicago stress and coping interview.* Champaign, IL: University of Illinois. Unpublished manuscript.

Individual Protective Factor Index measures family bonding and communication. Its target group is low-income students in grades 7 through 11. More information about this scale can be found in Phillips, J. and Springer, F. (1992). *Extended national youth sports program: 1991–1992 evaluation highlights.* Report prepared for the National Collegiate Athletic Association. Sacramento, CA: EMT Associates.

Organizational Health Inventory (OHI) measures the health of schools along seven dimensions of teacher-teacher, teacher-student, and teacher-administrator interactions. This scale includes one indicator of health at the institutional level (i.e., institutional integrity), four measures of health of the managerial system (i.e., principal influence, consideration, initiating structure, and resource support), and two measures of health at the technical level (i.e., morale and academic emphasis). More information about this scale and its development can be found in Hoy, W. K. and Feldman, J. A. (1987). Organizational health: The concept and its measure. *Journal of Research and Development in Education, 20,* 30–38.

Classroom Environment Scale (CES) measures the social climates of middle and high school classrooms. It focuses on the measurement and description of teacher-student and student-student relationships and the type of organizational structure of a classroom. More information about this scale can be found in Moos, R. H. and Trickett, E. J. (1974). *Classroom environment scale: Manual.* Palo Alto, CA: Consulting Psychologists Press, Inc.

The Effective School Battery (ESB) assesses the climates of secondary schools. The ESB can be used to identify a school's strengths and weaknesses, to develop improvement plans, and to evaluate improvement projects. Detailed information about this scale can be found in *The Effective School Battery: User's Manual* (1999) that can be obtained by contacting Gottfredson Associates, Inc., 3239 B Corporate Court, Ellicott City, MD 21042, (410) 461-5530.

School Victimization Scale measures exposure to violence and victimization in the home and at school. This scale is designed for use with adolescents and young adults. More information about this scale can be found in Spellman, M. (1992).

Posttraumatic stress disorder in abusive employment situations. New York: Yeshiva University. Unpublished dissertation.

(continued)

Table 12.1   *(Continued)*

Survey of Children's Exposure to Community Violence measures frequency of exposure (through sight and sound) to violence in one's home and neighborhood. This scale is designed to be used by African American males ages 12 to 16. More information about this scale can be found in Richters, J. E. and Martinez, P. (1990). *Things I have seen and heard: A structured interview for assessing young children's violence exposure.* Rockville, MD: National Institute of Mental Health.

Stressful Urban Life Events Scale compiles an inventory of stressful life events over the past year (e.g., poor grades, family illness or death, robbery). This scale is designed for use with children in grades two through five. More information about this scale can be found in Attar, B. K., Guerra, N. G., and Tolan, P. H. (1994). Neighborhood disadvantage, stressful life events, and adjustment in urban elementary-school children. Special issue: Impact of poverty on children, youth, and families. *Journal of Clinical Child Psychology, 23,* 391–400.

Neighborhood/Block Conditions measures residents' perceptions of neighborhood conditions (e.g., severity of problems, sense of safety). This scale is designed for use by urban residents age 18 and older. More information about this scale can be found in Perkins, D. D., Florin, P. L., Rich, R. C., Wandersman, A., and Chavis, D. M. (1990). Participation and the social environment of residential blocks: Crime and community context. *American Journal of Community Psychology, 18,* 83–115.

Neighborhood Cohesion measures the extent to which residents feel a sense of belonging in the neighborhood and share the same values as their neighbors. This scale is designed for use by urban residents age 18 and older. More information about this scale can be found in Perkins, D. D., Florin, P. L., Rich, R. C., Wandersman, A., and Chavis, D. M. (1990). Participation and the social environment of residential blocks: Crime and community context. *American Journal of Community Psychology, 18,* 83–115.

Neighborhood Satisfaction measures residents' attitudes toward their neighborhood (e.g., good place to live). This scale is designed for use by urban residents age 18 and older. More information about this scale can be found in Perkins, D. D., Florin, P. L., Rich, R. C., Wandersman, A., and Chavis, D. M. (1990). Participation and the social environment of residential blocks: Crime and community context. *American Journal of Community Psychology, 18,* 83–115.

Neighborhood/Community Action measures perceived likelihood that the resident or a neighbor will intervene when presented with a problem in the neighborhood (e.g., break up a fight, stop drug selling). This scale is designed for use by urban residents age 18 and older. More information about this scale can be found in Perkins, D. D., Florin, P. L., Rich, R. C., Wandersman, A., and Chavis, D. M. (1990). Participation and the social environment of residential blocks: Crime and community context. *American Journal of Community Psychology, 18,* 83–115.

Table 12.2   **Archival Data to Assess the Impact of Programs/Interventions at the School Level**

- Schoolwide attendance rates.
- Truancy/tardiness rates.
- School enrollment.
- Grades and grade point averages.
- Standardized test scores.
- Conduct ratings on students' report cards.
- Referrals for misbehavior/learning problems.
- Detentions.
- Number of students placed in in-school suspension (ISS).
- Out-of-school suspension rates.
- Expulsion rates.
- Retentions.
- Number of students considered to be "at-risk."
- Graduation rates.
- Dropout rates.
- Number of students taking college board exams.
- Number of students continuing with postsecondary education.
- Number of students receiving awards.
- Weapons violations.
- Visits to the nurse's office for treatment of injury.
- Costs to repair vandalism and property destruction.
- Results of student and teacher attitude surveys.
- Abuse and neglect referrals.
- School age parents.
- Student mobility.
- Law enforcement referrals.
- 504 students.
- Special education referrals/placements/dismissals.
- Parents attending conferences and meetings.
- Students receiving free and reduced lunch.
- Extracurricular violations.
- Students involved in extracurricular activities.

Source: Adapted from *Outcome Evaluation of School Social Work Services*, by N. Dibble, 1999, Madison: Wisconsin Department of Public Instruction; *School Violence*, by D. J. Flannery, 1998, New York: Columbia University. ERIC Document Reproduction Service No. ED417244; and "Evaluation of School-Linked Services," by D. S. Gomby and C. S. Larson, 1992, *Future of Children, 2*, pp. 68–84; Center for Mental Health in Schools at UCLA, 2000.

data can be found in Table 12.3, including rates of teen pregnancy, sexually transmitted diseases, child abuse and neglect, youth suicide, youth substance abuse, and homelessness among children and youth. This data can be used by school social workers as outcome measures in assessing the impact of a particular program/intervention at the community level. A number of other criteria and indicators (see Table 12.4) can be used by school social workers to assess the impact of programs/interventions at the school and community level. While some of these indicators are easily measured (e.g., counting the number of stories covered by the local media, teachers' and students' perceptions of school safety and school climate), others indicators (e.g., coordination and collaboration between school and community) are more difficult to operationalize and measure.

A major challenge awaiting school social workers is the development of a measurement package that assesses change in

Table 12.3   **Archival Data to Assess the Impact of Programs/Interventions at the Community Level**

- Arrests/citations/probation violations.
- The nature and types of contacts that students from a particular school have with police.
- Communitywide rates of teen pregnancy.
- Communitywide rates of sexually transmitted diseases.
- Communitywide rates of child abuse and neglect.
- Communitywide rates of youth suicide.
- Communitywide rates of youth unemployment and readiness for adult employment.
- Communitywide rates of youth substance abuse.
- Communitywide rates of homelessness among children and youth.
- Family preservation and youth foster care placements.
- Amount of funding for children's programs.

Source: Adapted from *Outcome Evaluation of School Social Work Services,* by N. Dibble, 1999, Madison: Wisconsin Department of Public Instruction; *School Violence,* by D. J. Flannery, 1998, New York: Columbia University. ERIC Document Reproduction Service No. ED417244; and "Evaluation of School-Linked Services," by D. S. Gomby and C. S. Larson, 1992, *Future of Children, 2,* pp. 68–84; Center for Mental Health in Schools at UCLA, 2000.

Table 12.4   **Criteria and Indicators to Assess the Impact of an Intervention on Families, Schools, and Communities**

- Quality of parent-child interactions.
- Processes by which families learn about available programs and services and access those they need.
- Utilization of services.
- Parental satisfaction with school and community programs.
- Bilingual ability and literacy of parents.
- Parental attitudes toward school.
- Parental involvement and participation in school.
- Family access to special assistance.
- Teachers' and students' perceptions of school safety.
- Teachers' and students' perceptions of psychological sense of community.
- Students' perceptions of school climate.
- Students' perceptions of the extent to which curriculum is stimulating and innovative.
- School administrators' expectations, attitudes, and behaviors.
- Number of services/programs at school site.
- The degree to which school staff work collaboratively.
- Community participation in school activities.
- Coordination and collaboration between school and community.
- Extent of school-community collaborations.
- Media coverage of school program/intervention/initiative (e.g., number of stories).
- Quality of services and programs as measured by systems for requesting, accessing, and managing assistance for students and families (including overcoming inappropriate barriers to confidentiality).
- Extent of community advocacy for children and families (e.g., amount of funding for children's programs).
- Establishment of a long-term financial base.

Source: Adapted from *Outcome Evaluation of School Social Work Services*, by N. Dibble, 1999, Madison: Wisconsin Department of Public Instruction; *School Violence*, by D. J. Flannery, 1998, New York: Columbia University. ERIC Document Reproduction Service No. ED417244; and "Evaluation of School-Linked Services," by D. S. Gomby and C. S. Larson, 1992, *Future of Children, 2*, pp. 68–84; Center for Mental Health in Schools at UCLA, 2000.

classrooms, schools, families, neighborhoods, or communities in a reliable and valid manner. Flannery (1998) discussed several steps to guide this process:

1. *Collect outcome data before the intervention is implemented.* This information provides the school with a baseline from which

change can later be determined. For example, schoolwide attendance rates from the year prior to the implementation of a new program can be used as one baseline.

2. *An assessment of a comparison group of students (or classrooms or schools) not exposed to the intervention should be conducted.* Having a comparison group, preferably very similar to the one receiving the intervention program, allows the school to rule out a number of plausible alternative explanations for any observed changes. A comparison group also allows a determination of the effectiveness of an intervention by comparing the data from the group receiving the intervention with the same data from the group not receiving the intervention.

3. *Classrooms or schools should be randomly assigned to treatment groups or controls.* As stated in Chapter 11, random assignment provides the strongest evidence that the intervention program itself caused any observed differences. Random assignment at the classroom and school level is much easier to accomplish in the real world than random assignment of individuals.

A variety of research designs are used to establish experiments. Several books that discuss experimental research designs in depth are listed in the Additional Resources section at the end of this chapter.

Guidelines for Successfully Planning, Implementing, and Evaluating New Programs

A number of exemplary interventions and programs have been identified and discussed throughout this book, and school social workers have been encouraged to implement and evaluate these empirically supported interventions and programs. However, the implementation of new programs in schools involves more planning than you might envision because it entails change as well as resistance to that change. In his book, *The Culture of the*

School and the Problem of Change, Sarason wrote " . . . man's desire
to change is more than matched by his ingenuity in avoiding
change, even when the desire to change is powered by strong
pain, anxiety and grief" (1971, p. 121). This strong resistance to
change was evident in Chapter 2 of this book in the discussion
of the 20-60-20 theory of school change. The obstructors were
identified as that group of school staff who actively attempt to
undermine any attempts to make changes in school policy, programs, or procedures. The following discussion augments and
builds on that discussion.

For change to be productive, it must be planned (Everson,
1995). Like Mary in the case vignette at the beginning of this
chapter, school social workers must spend a considerable
amount of time and effort anticipating the inevitable resistance
they will encounter and how they will attempt to successfully
work through that resistance. For example, school social workers should anticipate how they will respond to school administrators in trying to implement a new program after one has
failed, or how to effectively address the concerns of school administrators who want to make programmatic changes too
quickly or give up on a new program too soon. In essence, how
do school social workers set up a new program to ensure its
greatest probability for success? Mary will encounter resistance
from school board members who see no need to change approaches, despite the fact that the current, popular approach
has not been proven effective.

Everson (1995), Everhart and Wandersman (2000), and
Fullan (1990) have suggested several guidelines for managing
productive, planned change:

1. Ensure that the planned changes match the areas that need
   changing, thus having the best chances for success.

2. Change efforts should not just be talked about but action
   must be taken early in the process. School social workers
   can't wait for everyone to get on board and experience a
   complete buy-in before taking action because ownership of
   a new program grows over time.

3. Educators must feel involved and supported as they try out a new program. School social workers should reach out and involve administrators, teachers, parents, and other community members early in the process.

4. Since a person's beliefs and practices must change to produce successful results, it is important to acknowledge and reinforce the changes that occur along the way.

A systematic approach for managing productive, planned change efforts is important. comprehensive quality programming (CQP) is one such approach.

Comprehensive Quality Programming (CQP)

Comprehensive quality programming (CQP) consists of eight sequential steps designed to increase the probability of success of new programs in schools (Everhart & Wandersman, 2000; Wandersman et al., 1998). While CQP requires additional time and effort, "the benefits of demonstrating program effectiveness to ensure continued funding and provide quality programs far outweigh such costs. In most cases, using CQP to improve programs does not add much additional work to program evaluation; rather it increases the usefulness of the data that is already being collected" (Wandersman et al., 1998, p. 18). The following discussion of the eight steps comprising CQP have been adapted from the Wandersman et al. study.

1. *Why is the program/intervention needed?* Needs assessments are often conducted to determine the extent to which a need exists for a program being considered in a given school and community. Needs assessments should include the identification of strengths, assets, and resources in the community and school and elicit input from as many members of the community and school as possible. Surveys, census data, and focus groups are methods used to conduct needs assessments (Ginsberg, 2001).

2. *How does the program/intervention use scientific knowledge regarding "what works"?* Some of the empirically supported interventions and programs discussed throughout this book are student-focused, some combine student-focused with system-focused components, while others are entirely system-focused. In selecting a program/intervention, school social workers should focus on those programs/interventions that have been shown to work best for a particular problem for a particular population. Besides being empirically supported, interventions and programs should be developmentally and culturally relevant. In the case vignette, Mary will argue that the DARE program should be replaced by the Life Skills Training program (discussed in Chapter 7) since the Life Skills Training program has been shown to be effective in reducing the prevalence rate for use of alcohol, tobacco, and marijuana among program participants and has been recognized as a program that works by the Centers for Disease Control and Prevention, the American Medical Association, and the American Psychological Association.

3. *How will this program/intervention fit in with other programs or interventions already being offered?* Key questions include: Will the proposed program or intervention enhance, interfere with, or be unrelated to existing programs? Is it duplicative? It is important that school social workers examine what programs and interventions currently exist in a particular school or school district and be prepared to give specific answers to these questions.

4. How *will this program/intervention be carried out?* A program implementation plan must be developed. Outlining how a program will be implemented includes (a) determining specific steps to carry out the program; (b) identifying the roles and responsibilities of teachers and other school personnel, stakeholders, and evaluators and any other persons responsible for carrying out these steps; and (c) a time line for this plan, including dates of program implementation.

5. How *well was the program/intervention carried out?* This step focuses on process evaluation, which determines whether

the program was carried out as designed. Process evaluation explores what was actually done and what was learned from implementing a program. Was it implemented as planned? Was all of the program delivered? What went right and what went wrong? It is as important to understand how a program was implemented as it is to know the program outcomes (Ginsberg, 2001).

6. *How well did the program/intervention work?* Outcome evaluation is concerned with measuring the short-term as well as long-term effects of a program. Did it achieve its goals and desired outcomes? Were there any unanticipated consequences? This step provides school social workers with empirical evidence to determine if their efforts are leading to positive changes and allows funders to decide if their investment is worthwhile. To measure program outcomes, broad and ambitious program goals need to be operationalized into concrete and measurable outcomes (see Tables 12.1, 12.2, and 12.3). Another important outcome is a measure of the overall level of client satisfaction with program services referred to as *satisfaction studies*. Satisfaction studies may also be used to identify serious program problems, such as an incompetent staff member (Ginsberg, 2001). In addition to determining the beneficial results that result from a program, funders want to determine the costs associated with a program. This procedure is referred to as a *cost-benefit analysis*. For example, group counseling is often seen as preferable to individual counseling, using a cost-benefit analysis.

7. *What can be done to improve the program/intervention the next time it is implemented?* Program evaluation is a feedback mechanism that provides opportunities for refinements and improvements for future planning and implementation. For example, program components that worked well should be included in the future, and components that did not work should not be included.

8. *If the program was (or parts of it were) found to be effective, what can be done to continue or institutionalize this program/*

intervention? This is a largely neglected question. Even when programs are successful, they often do not continue due to lack of funding, staff turnover, or loss of momentum. In addition to implementing and evaluating new programs, school social workers must explore ways to ensure that successful school programs and interventions are maintained. This step entails long-range planning.

A model school adjustment program (MSAP) that targeted potential dropouts in grades 6 through 8 used several CQP steps. The coordinator performed a needs assessment to document the need for the program in middle school (as opposed to high school), garnered substantial community support for the MSAP, reviewed the literature to determine which interventions were empirically supported, and developed the MSAP based on these interventions. He organized and maintained an MSAP community task force to oversee the program and was involved in evaluating the MSAP and presenting findings to the school board. See Dupper (1993) for a detailed discussion of the planning and implementation of the MSAP.

Summary

A fundamental aspect of school social work practice is targeting detrimental conditions in schools, families, neighborhoods, and communities. Over the past decade, a growing number of standardized scales have been developed to measure the extent to which changes have occurred in those systems that exert the greatest impact on children and youth, namely schools, families, and neighborhoods/communities. A number of standardized questionnaires, as well as school and community archival measures, are readily available for use as outcome measures to evaluate system-level changes. Standardized scales have been developed to measure the extent to which changes have occurred in a number of larger systems including the culture or climate of the classroom or in the organizational health of the school, parental discipline practices or family cohesion, affordable housing, and exposure to violence. School-level archival data such as attendance rates, standardized test scores, number of students placed in in-school suspension (ISS), and costs to repair vandalism and property destruction can also be used to assess the impact of school-level interventions. Archival data found at the community level such as the nature and types of contacts that students from a particular school have with police, communitywide rates of teen pregnancy, and communitywide rates of child abuse and neglect can also be used to assess the impact of interventions targeting communities. To assess change in classrooms, schools, families, neighborhoods, or communities in a reliable and valid manner, it is important to collect outcome data before the intervention is implemented, conduct an assessment of a comparison group of students (or classrooms or schools) not exposed to the intervention, and assign classrooms or schools to treatment groups or controls.

The implementation of new programs in schools involves much planning because it entails change as well as resistance to that change. School social workers must be able to anticipate how this resistance will manifest itself and how this resistance will be handled. School social workers must be able to set up new programs to ensure its greatest probability of success. This involves a systematic approach for managing productive, planned change. Comprehensive quality programming (CQP) is one such systematic approach.

Questions for Discussion

1. How do system-focused evaluations differ from student-focused evaluations?

2. Several outcome measures to assess changes in schools, families, and neighborhoods/communities are discussed in this chapter. Identify at least one outcome measure for each of these system levels.

3. How does a school social worker set up a new program to ensure its greatest probability for success?

4. What is the name of the systematic approach used to plan, implement, and evaluate school-based prevention and intervention programs?

5. What methods are used to conduct needs assessments?

Refer to the case study at the beginning of this chapter:

1. How might Mary overcome this inevitable resistance to a new substance abuse prevention program in this particular community?

2. What community support would be important?

3. Discuss how Mary might implement the steps of comprehensive quality programming (CQP) to help ensure the success of a new program.

Additional Resources

- The Sage series entitled *Program Evaluation Kit* provides practical and detailed instructions on how to evaluate a program. Of particular note for school social workers are the following books from this series: Morris, L. L., Fitz-Gibbon, C. T., & Lindheim, E. (1987). *How to measure performance and use tests.* Thousand Oaks, CA: Sage; and Stecher, B. M., & Davis, W. A. (1987). *How to focus an evaluation.* Thousand Oaks, CA: Sage.

- Detailed information on experimental designs may be found in: Rubin, A., & Babbie, E. R. (2001). *Research methods for social work* (4th ed.). Belmont, CA: Wadsworth; or Campbell, D. T., & Stanley, J. C. (1963). *Experimental and quasi-experimental designs for research.* Boston: Houghton Mifflin.

- *Measurements in prevention: A manual on selecting and using instruments to evaluate prevention programs.* (1993). Washington, DC: U.S. Department of Health and Human Services, Public Health Service, Substance Abuse and Mental Health Services Administration, Center for Substance Abuse Prevention, 5600 Fishers Lane, Rockwall II, Rockville, MD 20857.

- Freiberg, H. J. (Ed.). (1999). *School climate: Measuring, improving and sustaining healthy learning environments.* Philadelphia: Falmer Press.

"School Survival Group" Curriculum*

Session One

*Introduction to Group, Purpose, Rules, and
Introductory Activity*

The group leader welcomes all the group members and states:

> All of you are in this group because you have been experiencing problems getting along with teachers, administrators, or other students in school. Some of you may have already been suspended as a result of your behavior. Some of you may hate school and may want to drop out of school as soon as you can. Some of you are on your way to being labeled a "troublemaker" or "loser" by the school.

---

*John Kackley is the original author of the "School Survival Group."
David Dupper has made several revisions to the original curriculum.

The leader states the purpose:

> The purpose of this group is to help you survive in school. Most of you have learned behaviors that continue to get you into trouble in school. This group is designed to help you look at those attitudes and behaviors and figure out if there are any other ways to handle situations in school that won't get you into trouble. My purpose in leading this group is to help you be successful in school. I believe that most of you want to be successful, but you may not know how to handle situations that cause you difficulty.

The leader explains that this group will meet for the next 10 weeks during one class period per week. Group members will be excused from class but are responsible for getting back with their teachers to make up any work missed. It is again stressed that this group requires a personal commitment from each group member to attend each group session and participate in group activities. All group members who attend all group sessions will be invited to a "group pizza party" following the last group session. If any group member is reluctant to make a commitment to attend all group sessions, the leader should encourage that student to try out the group for a few sessions and make his or her decision at that time.

The leader next discusses five group rules. The leader states:

> I have done a number of these groups in the past and I have found that the following five rules help the group run smoothly. When group members follow these five rules, the group is more helpful; and students really have a chance to share their concerns and frustrations and learn ways to handle school situations more productively.

The leader discusses each rule and the rationale for each rule:

Rule 1. Be on time to all group sessions. Since this group will meet for only one class period per week, it is important to start on time. Some students may be having difficulty getting to their classes on time and this is a behavior that needs to be worked on and reinforced in this group.

Rule 2. Only one person talks at a time. Many of us never have the chance to share our thoughts and feelings without being interrupted or "put down" by others. In addition, some of us may talk out without thinking in class and that gets us into trouble. It is important that everyone has a chance to talk in this group but that will happen only if all group members agree to this rule. If you have something to say, please wait until the person who is talking has finished talking.

Rule 3. Everybody listens. Most people don't know how to listen. Most people think about what they want to say rather than listening to what another person is saying. Some students may be having difficulty in school because they do not listen to their teachers. One of the most important skills we can learn in life is how to listen to others well and without interrupting them.

Rule 4. No "put-downs" or "cuts." Provide examples of put-downs such as "That was a stupid thing to say," "Boy, are you dumb," and ask group members for other examples. We all have become pretty good at giving and receiving put-downs in our society. What effect do put-downs have on people? Even if they are meant in fun, put-downs hurt people, and sometimes this hurt turns into anger and that turns into a verbal or physical fight. Put-downs will not be allowed in this group because they hurt people. This group is designed to be a place where members can speak without the fear of being attacked by others. Group members are also asked to not put themselves down. People will sometimes say things like "I'm so stupid" or "If I had a brain in my head . . ." but these statements are not helpful. Group members should help the leader in stopping putdowns that occur during the group by pointing out which rule is being broken.

Rule 5. What is said in the group stays in the group. Confidentiality is important if group members are to feel free to discuss their concerns with each other and the group leader. The leader will not share anything that is said in the group except for the following: If a group member shares something that is against the law or indicates that he or she is planning to do something that is harmful to either himself or herself or to others, the group leader is required by law to share this information. The leader will discuss any situation that must be shared outside the group with that group member individually before any action is taken. Group members may share their feelings and thoughts about a number of issues in the group and this information will not be shared outside the group.

After sharing all the group rules, the leader asks the group members if the rules seem to make sense and if there are any questions about why we have certain rules. The leader asks if any additional rules are needed to help the group run smoothly. The leader states that he or she will need the help and cooperation of all group members, making sure that everyone follows these rules each week.

The group leader next introduces an activity designed to help group members get to know one another better and to "break the ice." Each group member is asked to take out a sheet of paper and do the following: "List three things you are good at doing and that make you feel proud of yourself." The leader waits for everyone to complete this, then directs: "Next, list three words or phrases that describe you, not your height and weight, but words that describe what kind of person you are." The leader also participates in this activity. The activity concludes with all group members having a chance to share what is on paper with the other group members.

The leader concludes the group with a positive statement about how well the group members did today, thanking them for their cooperation, and stating that he or she is looking forward to seeing everyone next week.

Session Two

Five Goals to Adolescent Behavior
(Walton, 1980)

The leader begins by reviewing the five group rules. The leader next asks each group member to share the best thing that happened to them in school since the last group session. The leader begins by sharing something positive that happened to him or her, and other group members are encouraged to share. The leader states that each group session will begin by asking this question and therefore group members are asked to make sure that at least one good thing happens to them in school so that they will have something to share at the beginning of each group.

The leader next asks the question:

Why do some students have difficulty getting along with teachers and other authority figures in school? Today, we are going to discuss the reason we all behave in certain ways. All of us do things to meet certain needs that we have. What are some of these basic needs, beyond food, shelter, and clothing?

The first need we all have is to get attention. Why do we need attention? How does it feel when someone pays attention to us? We all need attention because we know we exist if someone is paying attention to us. If no one ever notices us, no matter what we do, we begin to feel like we don't exist. We all need attention but some of us don't know how to get it in a positive way and negative attention is better than no attention at all. Unfortunately, some of us have learned how to get only negative attention (e.g., being the "class clown," being hyperactive, bizarre dress) rather than positive attention. Later in this group, we discuss ways to get positive attention rather than negative attention.

The second need we all have is the need for power. We need to feel that we have a say in what happens to us. Many of you may not feel you have much of an opportunity to exert your power in school (or at home). At your age, adults are always telling you what to do and you have little or no say in things that happen to you. This need for power is behind most of the problems between teenagers and adults. The adults want power over teens and the teens fight back because they want power, also. One of the most important things to remember in this group is that teens always lose in power struggles with adults. For example, who loses if you tell off a teacher? Who loses if you make an obscene gesture at the assistant principal because of some discipline? Students always lose. You cannot give a teacher a disciplinary referral for his or her misbehavior in class, but your teacher can give you one. You cannot suspend the principal, but he can suspend you. One of the things we will discuss later in this group is how to not lose when you are in a power struggle with an adult.

The third need that motivates behavior is the desire for revenge. People who feel hurt by life will strike back at others in an attempt to get even. Some people may resort to violence and destructive behavior in their efforts to get revenge. Remember that people who act this way are hurting very deeply inside and revenge is the way they have learned to deal with their hurt feelings. During this group, we will discuss more productive ways of dealing with hurt.

The fourth need that motivates some of our behavior is the need to be left alone. Some of us intentionally quit easily or avoid trying to do something altogether for fear that we may fail. This fear of failing school may lead us to start skipping school and dropping out of school at the first opportunity. Our thought is that if we don't try, teachers and parents will give up on us and leave us alone. One of the goals of this group is to help you have more confidence in yourself and what you are able to do to survive in school.

The fifth need many of us have is the need for excitement. Many of us are turned off by routine and become bored easily. Many teens believe that school is *sooooo* boring! And the way we deal with our boredom is by daydreaming, skipping school, doing alcohol or drugs, or anything that provides excitement. I hope that this group will help you to problem solve ways to beat the boredom and routine of school.

The leader asks if anyone has questions or comments on these needs that motivate much of student misbehavior in school. The leader asks for group members to state which of these needs he or she is attempting to meet and what the behavior is that he or she engages in to meet this need at school. The leader then asks group members to discuss the consequences of each action if a student is caught in the act during the school day. The leader needs to stress that having attention and power, dealing with hurt, having more self-confidence, and having more excitement are worthwhile goals. What is essential is learning how to achieve these goals in ways that do not bring about negative consequences to us in school.

The leader concludes the group with each group member being asked to complete the following statement: "Today in group, I learned . . ."

Session Three

The Transactional Analysis (TA) Concept of Scripts
(James & Jongeward, 1977)

The leader again begins this session with a round-robin sharing of statements about "the best thing that happened to me in school since last week's group." The leader asks if any group

member can remember what was discussed last week. Group
members are asked to state the five goals of adolescent behavior
and why we discussed them as part of a school survival group.
The leader asks if anyone has any questions or concerns.

The leader states that today's group will focus on an important concept called *life scripts*. The leader asks:

> What is a script? When an actor reads from his script,
> he or she plays that particular role. Just like actors, all
> of us have a life script that influences how we feel
> about ourselves and how we behave in certain situa-
> tions. How do we get our life script? It begins when
> we were babies. If our parents or guardians comforted
> us when we were upset (held us, whispered to us
> softly) and took care of our physical and emotional
> needs, we felt safe and secure and felt good about our-
> selves. However, if our parents or guardians yelled at
> us, didn't pay attention to us when we needed help,
> maybe even hit us, we felt very afraid and insecure as
> we grew up. The way we feel about ourselves today
> has a lot to do with how our parents and others very
> close to us treated us when we were growing up.

The leader writes on the blackboard as he or she talks.

> Basically, there are three types of life scripts—win-
> ners, losers, and spinners. Winners are people who feel
> good about themselves; they know their strengths as
> well as their limitations (We all can't be good at every-
> thing); they accept responsibility for their actions
> (They don't blame others for what happens to them);
> they are honest and straightforward with people (They
> don't manipulate or play games with people). Winners
> had parents who told them "You will be successful at
> whatever you do," "You have a good head on you
> shoulder," "You are very creative and talented." On
> the other hand, losers are people who feel insecure

about themselves; they give up on things very easily because they lack self-confidence; they blame others for what happens to them (it's never their fault); they manipulate and play a lot of head games with others. People who feel and act like losers had parents who told them things like "You will never make it; why do you even try," "You will end up in jail just like your uncle Joe," "You never do anything right," "You were a mistake; we wish we never had you." The third type of life script is a spinner. A spinner will put out a lot of energy but doesn't seem to get anywhere (just like a car with tires stuck in the mud). A spinner just hangs out without any real direction or goals.

The leader goes on to point out that our life scripts influence the way we think and act. In school, students with a winner script do well because they do what is expected of them. It is important to remember that winners in school receive a lot of support and encouragement from their parents or guardians. Students with a loser script in school may play the role of the class clown, the class idiot, the class troublemaker, or a combination of these. Students with loser scripts in school have trouble getting along with authority figures and other peers, and have a difficult time learning. Students with spinner scripts in school just hang out and are really not very involved in what happens in school. Spinners are bored and disinterested in school.

The leader concludes with a discussion of how to change our life scripts if we are unhappy with them. It is stressed that although a student may see himself or herself as having a loser script, he or she can change his script and, by doing so, change how others respond to him or her. A loser script can be torn up completely or can be altered so that more appropriate behavior takes place and more positive attitudes are developed. It is stressed that it is very hard to change a loser script into a winner script because other people (friends, teachers, parents) are so used to the old script that they may resist the student's attempts at changing his or her script. There may be a lot of pressure from classmates and some teachers and some administrators to continue in the old behavior, because that is what they are used to and what they expect. It is emphasized that one of the major purposes of this group is to help group members change their script if they are unhappy with it. In this group, members can think through a number of new behaviors and the consequences of those behaviors. They can try on new behaviors to see how it feels to respond in different ways and receive support and feedback from other group members. It is very difficult, if not impossible, to change our life script unless we receive support and encouragement from others. The leader emphasizes that students are in charge of their own lives, can change their life scripts and, by doing so, can have a great deal of influence over how other people in school treat them.

The leader asks group members about their school scripts. Do they see themselves as winners, losers, or spinners? How do they feel about their school script? What changes would they like to make in their school script? The leader concludes the group with each group member being asked to complete the following statement: "Today in group, I learned . . ."

Session Four

The Transactional Analysis Concept of Ego States
(James & Jongeward, 1977)

The leader again begins this session with a round-robin sharing of statements about "the best thing that happened to me in school since the last group." If group members find it difficult to share positive things about school, the leader needs to remind them that they are responsible for making positive things happen in school (e.g., having a good or bad week is largely dependent on each student's response to certain situations). How students behave toward adults will impact how adults behave toward students. For example, if they got to class on time, or did all their homework, or spoke nicely to their teacher as they left the classroom, they may receive a kind response in return. If students wait for teachers or other school authorities "to make the first move," they may be waiting a long time to share positive things about their week in school.

The leader reviews last week's discussion of scripts by asking group members to state the three types of life scripts we can have. The leader then asks how we get our life scripts and how to change our scripts if we are unhappy with them.

The leader then moves on to this week's topic: ego states. The leader asks:

> How many of you have ever been in a conversation with someone and things end up in a misunderstanding, hurt feelings, or even a fight? Today, and during the next few group sessions, we are going to discuss several tools that will help you analyze what happens when you are trying to communicate with someone or someone is trying to communicate with you and things go wrong. I am going to begin today by discussing the concept of *ego states* [The leader draws three large circles on the blackboard or easel and writes as he or she discusses each ego state.] All of us have three ego states in us—the parent, the adult, and the child. When I say the word *parent,* what words come to your mind? What do parents say and how do they act?

The leader waits for responses and then begins to write key words and phrases about the parent ego state. The leader continues:

> The parent ego state is made up of two types of parents, the punitive parent and the nurturing parent. The punitive parent is that part of people that tells us we are no good, stupid, and will never amount to anything. The punitive parent is the part of all of us that is authoritarian and that produces guilt and anger in

others. When we hear others say things like "you never," "you better," "you ought to"; when others point a finger at us, or hover over us, or push their weight around in any manner, they are coming from their punitive parent. Do any of you know anybody in school who comes from his or her punitive parent ego state? What do they do and say? Do any of you ever act toward others in this way? The second part of the parent ego state is the nurturing parent. This is the part of people that is helpful, kind, and considerate. These are people who encourage us and help us to do our best. Do any of you know anyone in school who comes from their nurturing parent ego state? What do they do and say? Do any of you ever act in this way toward others?

The next ego state we are going to discuss is the child ego state. What words describe a child? It is that part of us that is selfish, affectionate, playful, whining, and manipulative. Similar to the parent ego state, the child ego state is made up of three parts: the natural child, the adaptive child, and the rebellious child. The natural child is the part of us that behaves as if we were a small child. The natural child is that part of us that is spontaneous, creative, and fun-loving. Our natural child is extremely self-centered; it is that part of us that does what we want when we want to do it and there is no one around telling us to stop acting that way. The adaptive child is that part of us that does pretty much what adults want him or her to do or say. It is that part of us that does what is expected of us. It is the compliant part of us. Students who are in their adaptive child state sit back and are very quiet in class. The last part of the child ego state is the rebellious child. The rebellious child is that part of us that has been hurt by adults and fights back. Most anything that an adult in a position of authority says or does is wrong to a rebellious child. Students operating out of their rebellious child are usually very disruptive in the classroom, do not bring their materials, talk back to the teacher, and are always trying to get negative attention. Do any of you know anyone who operates out of their rebellious child state in school? Can any of you identify what need the rebellious child is trying to meet in school? The need for power. What happens when a rebellious child and a punitive parent confront each other in a classroom?

The leader provides a number of classroom examples to illustrate how a punitive parent teacher and a rebellious child student "hook" each other and engage in a power confrontation where the rebellious child student ends up in the principal's office with a disciplinary referral or possibly even suspended. It is pointed out that the rebellious child ego state will usually get us into trouble in school with authority figures.

The leader concludes today's discussion of ego states with the adult ego state. The adult ego state is that part of us (although some of us use it very infrequently) that is unemotional and analytical. It is like a human computer part of us. The adult ego state helps us to stop and think through all of our alternatives before we decide to act. The leader emphasizes the importance of the adult ago state by stating, "Whenever we feel angry, hurt, confused, or upset in any way, we should turn to our adult ego state, which helps us to stop and think before we speak or act."

The leader concludes the group by asking group members to complete "What I learned today in group. . ." The leader asks group members to be aware of the ego states they find themselves and others using throughout the week.

Session Five

Games Students and Teachers Play in School
(Ernst, 1972)

The leader again begins by asking group members to share "the best thing that happened to me this past week in school." Have each group member identify which ego state he or she was in when these good things happened during the week in school. The leader reviews the transactional analysis (TA) concept of ego states. Special emphasis is placed on how teacher behavior can trigger student behavior in unproductive ways for the student (e.g., the "hooking" that occurs when a punitive parent teacher confronts a rebellious child student). The leader asks group members if any of them found themselves operating out of the rebellious child ego state during the week in school and, if so, to share the specific situation with the rest of the group members. [It may be helpful for the leader and the student to role-play the situation and to diagram the transaction on the blackboard.] The leader demonstrates the use of the adult ego state ("think it through before I act") in specific school situations by modeling both verbal and nonverbal behaviors for the group members. It is stressed that the adult ego state can help us to solve problems more effectively and change our life scripts by changing the way we react in certain school situations.

The leader next turns to the TA concept of "games." The leader states:

> Remember when we discussed the "loser script" and we stated that people who have the "loser script" try to manipulate others a lot and play a lot of games with other people. Well, today we are going to discuss a few of these games that are played a lot in school among groups of students and between students and teachers.

The leader writes on the blackboard as he or she discusses each game. The leader begins the discussion of games with "ain't it awful." This is a game that students play a lot with each other when they sit around and talk about how rotten the teachers are, how stupid the teachers are, how mean the teachers are, how unfair the teachers are, and generally how rotten school is. Although the game of "ain't it awful" is easy to play and is actually a lot of fun, nothing happens to change the situation. All students do is sit around and complain and nothing changes for them in school. No alternative solutions are discussed, students just complain and don't take any responsibility for their own behavior. It should be mentioned that a lot of adults play this game also.

The next game that students often play in school is "stupid." The game of "stupid" is very easy to play when students are confronted by teachers. For example, a teacher says to a student, "Why don't you . . . .," "Why didn't you . . . .," "When will you . . . .," and so on, and all the student has to say is "I don't know," or "I don't know how to do it," or shrugs a shoulder. This is a way for the student to refuse to take responsibility for his or her behavior. The student is trying to convince the teacher that he or she is so stupid that nothing can be expected of him or her and that the teacher has to take responsibility for him or her while the student goes on doing the same "stupid" things in school. However, the student usually resents the teacher for taking responsibility. When we play the game of "stupid," we disappoint others, but more important, we disappoint ourselves.

Another game that is played in school is "yes, but . . ." This game is played whenever a student approaches an adult and says "I have a problem, but I don't know what to do about it" and the adult responds with a number of suggestions concerning what the student may do to solve the problem. The student then says something like, "Yes, but if I do that . . . ." or "Yes, but I've already tried doing that and it doesn't work." The adult may offer a number of other suggestions and the student continues to cite a number of reasons why those suggestions won't work. As you can see, this interaction becomes a vicious circle because it is extremely frustrating for the adult offering help and it permits the student to avoid taking personal responsibility for his or her actions.

The fourth game is a very common game played in schools. It is called "uproar." "Uproar" is typically started in the classroom by a student's failure to get there on time, bring appropriate materials, make an effort to do the required work, or refusal to sit down and be quiet. It starts off very innocently, with the teacher just asking the student why he or she is late. "Uproar" gets played when the student chooses to respond to the teacher in his or her rebellious child ego state and says something like, "Why are you always picking on me" or "I'm not doing anything, leave me alone." A rebellious child response will hook the teacher's punitive parent and the teacher and student continue to exchange words back and forth. Teacher and students take sides and a mini-war has begun. Before it is over, the entire classroom is in an uproar. This game is frequently played by students who are bored in class. It is an attempt by students to meet their needs for attention or excitement (negative attention is better than no attention at all). It is a game that is also played by students who are experiencing difficulty doing the classwork; it is a lot easier to be known as the class clown or trouble-maker than as a stupid kid who cannot do the classwork.

If time permits, the leader role-plays a number of these games with group members for further illustration. The leader will ask the group members if any of these games are familiar to them and if there are any other games played in school that involve students and teachers or students and administrators.

The leader concludes the discussion of "games" by discussing the consequences of game-playing for teachers and administrators. It must be emphasized that students may end up in the office or suspended from school as a consequence of too much game playing, particularly "uproar." The consequences for adults is very different. Adults in school will continue to do their job and receive their paycheck whether the student is there or not there. In fact, some teachers and administrators will be happy to be rid of difficult students. In essence, students lose when they play certain games and act in disruptive ways in school. When students are disruptive, they provide adults in the school with an excuse to get rid of them. When students act appropriately in school, the student is in control of the situation rather than the teacher or administrator.

The leader says:

Over the next week I want all of you to do an activity that will help you to stop and think before you act. I want all of you to take out a sheet of paper and write the following:

1. What my teacher said or did.
2. How my teacher make me feel when she did or said this.

Skip several more inches and write:

3. What I felt like saying or doing as a result of these feelings.

Skip a few more inches and write:

4. What I actually said or did.

The leader continues, "I want you to answer these four questions after you have had an interaction with a teacher that upset you. Bring this sheet with your answers to group next week. Any questions about what I want you to do?"
The leader concludes the group with "What I learned today in group . . ."

Session Six

Overview of the Problem-Solving Process

Have each student share "the best thing that happened to me this past week in school." Have group members share their activity from last week. The leader states that the next few group sessions will be spent trying to help group members resolve specific school-related problems. The leader begins by making the statement:

> Certain groups of students get into trouble at school, not because they don't have the intelligence to do well, but because they have learned to react to others in ways that get them into trouble at school. Knowing how to act and react to others is learned, we are not

born with that knowledge. If we see people around us "losing their cool" all the time by yelling and striking out at others, we will learn from them that yelling and hitting is how we deal with people when we are angry at them. However, to survive in school, yelling and hitting are not okay because they are not tolerated and students who "lose their cool" and play "games" in school receive negative consequences for their actions. To survive in school and "play the game right," you must learn how to control your anger and frustration by using the tools we have discussed so far in group.

The leader reviews the TA concepts significance for understanding student-teacher, student-administrator, as well as student-student conflict in school.

One of the most important things we can learn is how to stop and think before we act. How a student chooses to respond to an adult (e.g., both verbal and nonverbal behaviors) will largely determine what happens to the student. We need to practice and learn how to be in control of our feelings rather than having our feelings control us. If we act on how we feel at that moment, we will usually get into trouble. Remember that all feelings are okay; it's what we do with our feelings that makes all the difference in what happens to us. For example, it's okay to be angry with someone at school, but it's not okay to hit them or tell them off because we are the ones who will suffer adverse consequences. If we truly want to be winners, we must learn how to use our adult ego state to solve problems.

The leader models several specific ways of using the adult ego state in the school setting. Emphasis is placed on the distinction between what a person wants to do and what a person actually does after weighing a number of possible actions. The adult ego state allows us to stop and think before we act and

Figure A.1

Problem-Solving Flow Chart.

Name: _____ **Date:** _____

Step 1: What's the problem?

Step 2: Who's got the problem?

Step 3: What happens if the problem goes on?

Step 4: How did you get into this mess?

Step 5: Who can get you out of it?

Step 6: What can you do to solve the problem? (List everything you can think of.)

Step 7: Order your list into the most and least attractive solutions.

Step 8: Tell what will happen if you use each solution.

Step 9: Predict if you can really carry out each solution.

Step 10: Pick the best solution. Say why you chose it and when you will use it.

weigh the various consequences of our actions. Discuss the importance of the problem-solving process and the fact that "everyone has choices about how he or she will react in any situation."

The leader discusses the problem-solving process by giving the students the Problem-Solving Flow Chart (see Figure A.1)." The leader emphasizes how these steps can help students stay out of conflicts with teachers and other persons in authority (e.g., how to use your adult ego state and not get hooked into your rebellious child state).

The leader asks for group members to volunteer specific school-related problems and talks them through how they would go about solving that particular problem using these steps. This activity is done for at least two different school-related problems. The leader then asks group members to use this same problem-solving process to help them solve real problems they are having in school. Each group member is asked to fill out the problem-solving sheet through step 9 and bring it to next week's group session. The leader concludes the group with "What I learned today in group . . .

Session Seven

Application of the Problem-Solving Process to
Specific School Situations

Have each student share "the best thing that happened to me this past week in school." Share each group member's problem-solving sheets from the previous week. Continue to discuss specific school situations that are causing students difficulty. These may include:

- How to approach persons in authority in school.
- How to ask for help from a teacher in an appropriate manner.
- How to say no to peers.
- How to deal with anger.

After several school problems have been listed, ask students to brainstorm a number of ways they could handle each of these problems under a column titled Choices. Role-play a number of these situations, emphasizing the number of possible responses (i.e., choices) available to students and how their responses will largely determine what will happen to them (e.g., what a teacher will say or do).

Have each student complete the problem-solving sheet through to step 10. For next week's group, each group member will actually try out his or her specific solution and be prepared to discuss what happened.

Session Eight

Discussion of Specific School Survival Skills and Self-Monitoring Checklist

As usual, the leader begins the session with "the best thing that happened to me this past week in school." The leader points out that each group member made good things happen by choosing to act in certain ways. Good things in school don't just happen, students make them happen by their actions.

The leader allows each group member the opportunity to share his or her problem-solving process from the previous week in a round-robin fashion. If a group member is successful in carrying out the entire process, the leader praises the student for the effort recognizing how difficult it must have been to carry out this process and how proud that group member must be to actually have done it. If a group member is not able to carry out the entire problem-solving process, he or she is praised for attempting to do what he or she was able to do. The group leader then asks the group member what problems he or she is experiencing in carrying out this process. Other group members are encouraged to assist in offering solutions and providing feedback.

The leader then proceeds with a discussion of specific school survival skills by stating:

> Up to this point in our group, we have discussed a number of reasons that students get into trouble (e.g., loser script, responding from their rebellious child ego state), and we have discussed how to begin to stop and think before we act or say something that will get us into more trouble (i.e., problem-solving steps).
>
> Today, I want to discuss specific things you can do in your classrooms that may help you to be more successful in school and begin to change your school script. Do you think that it is possible to change the way a teacher or other authority figure acts toward you? Can you influence the actions or thoughts of

your teachers by what you say or do? I want to challenge each of you to do an experiment and see what happens. First, I want to list a number of school survival skills on the blackboard. These are specific behaviors that will help you to stay out of trouble in school. [Leader writes on blackboard.] Can anyone name one specific behavior that would keep you out of trouble in school? What is expected of you in school? What are some behaviors that come out of your adapted child ego state?

The leader makes sure that the following behaviors are among those listed on the blackboard:

- Ready to work in class.
- In seat and quiet before the tardy bell rings.
- Work on class assignments without talking.
- Raise your hand if you want help from your teacher.
- Do what your teacher asks without talking back or pouting or whining.

The leader asks for several group members to role-play and practice each of these behaviors in the group so that they don't seem so strange when they try them out in the classroom.

The leader asks group members to complete the statement "Today in group, I learned . . ." The leader then hands out a School Survival Checklist (see Figure A.2) so that each student can check each time he or she does a specific behavior on the checklist. Each member is asked to also make a mental note of how the teacher responds to his or her behavior.

Session Nine

Continued Discussion of School Survival Skills and
Self-Monitoring Checklist

As before, the leader begins the session with "the best thing that happened to me this past week in school." The leader then asks

Figure A.2

School Survival Skills Checklist.

Place a checkmark next to each school survival skill each time you perform that behavior.

School Survival Skills	Checkmarks
1. Ready to work in class.	_____
2. In seat and quiet before the tardy bell rings.	_____
3. Work on class assignments without talking.	_____
4. Raise your hand if you want help from the teacher.	_____
5. Do what your teacher asks without talking back or pouting or whining.	_____

Other school survival skills:

6. _____   _____

_____   _____

7. _____   _____

_____   _____

8. _____   _____

_____   _____

each group member to share the specific behaviors that they tried out during the past week and how many marks they placed beside each behavior. They are then asked to share how it felt to carry out these behaviors and how the teacher responded to them (i.e., How did their actions influence the behavior of their teacher?). The leader points out that some group members may find it extremely difficulty to try out these new behaviors but that it will get easier the more they do them in class. Any new behavior is hard to do at first and that the only way to learn new behaviors is through practice and more practice. The leader asks group members to remember how difficult it was for them when they were first learning how to ride a bike and that the only way they learned how to do it was through practice. The leader states: "Surviving in school requires that you learn certain skills and behaviors that may be very difficult at first but through practice become easier to do."

The leader tells the group that each group member can learn to stay out of trouble in school and that one of the ways to do that is to think before you act and keep practicing the skills discussed in the group. The leader concludes this session by asking group members to complete the statement "Over the past nine weeks, the most important thing I learned in this group was . . ." "The thing we discussed in group that helped me the most was . . ."

Session Ten

Concluding Activity

The leader begins the final group session with the statement:

> All of us in this group have done a lot of work and changed a lot over the past nine weeks. Today, we are going to have the opportunity to share these positive changes with each other. This activity is called the *care chair.* Each of us will have the opportunity to give and receive positive feedback. Each person will have the opportunity to be the focus person. When a group member is the focus person, he or she cannot say anything: All he or she can do is listen while the rest of the group shares at least one positive change they have seen in that person over the course of the group. For example, a group member may say, "I noticed that you are able to keep your cool a lot more now than you used to." The important thing in this activity is to share only positive changes you have observed in each group member. If you have nothing positive to say,

please do not say anything to that particular group member.

After everyone has had the opportunity to participate in the activity, the leader discusses the importance of continuing to use the skills learned in this group. The leader encourages group members to help each other around school (even after the group ends) and provide support and encouragement in helping each other to continue to change their scripts from loser or spinner to a winner script (e.g., identify social support systems and personal rewards for changing one's behavior). The leader concludes by asking each group member to share two things in a round-robin fashion: first, the most important thing each group member learned about himself or herself over the course of the group; and second, the names of one or more support people who will provide ongoing support and encouragement to each group member after the group ends.

References

Aber, J. L., Brown, J. L., Chaudry, N., Jones, S. M., & Samples, F. (1996). The evaluation of the resolving conflict creatively program: An overview. *American Journal of Preventive Medicine, 12,* 82–90.

Abrams, L. S., & Taylor-Gibbs, G. J. (2000). Planning for school change: School-community collaboration in a full-service elementary school. *Urban Education, 35,* 79–103.

Achenbach, T. M. (1979). The child behavior profile: An empirically based system for assessing children's behavioral problems and competencies. *International Journal of Mental Health, 7,* 24–42.

Achenbach, T. M. (1982). *Developmental psychopathology.* New York: Wiley.

Achenbach, T. M. (1996). The Child Behavior Checklist (CBCL) and related instruments. In L. I. Sederer & B. Dickey (Eds.), *Outcomes assessment in clinical practice* (pp. 97–99). Baltimore: Williams & Wilkins.

Achenbach, T. M., & Edelbrock, C. S. (1981). Behavioral problems and competencies reported by parents of normal and disturbed children aged four through sixteen. *Monographs of the Society for Research in Child Development, 46,* 1–82.

Alan Guttmacher Institute. (1999). *Facts in brief: Teen sex and pregnancy.* Retrieved March 10, 2000, from www.agi-usa.org/pubs/fb_teen_sex.html

Allen-Meares, P., Washington, R. O., & Welsh, B. L. (Eds.). (2000). *Social work services in schools.* Needham Heights, MA: Allyn & Bacon.

Alpert-Gillis, L. J., Pedro-Carroll, J. L., & Cowen, E. L. (1989). The Children of Divorce Intervention Program: Development, implementation, and evaluation of a program for young children. *Journal of Consulting and Clinical Psychology, 57,* 583–589.

Altshuler, S. J. (1997). A reveille for school social workers: Children in foster care need our help! *Social Work in Education, 19,* 121–127.

American Association of University Women. (1993). *Hostile hallways: The AAUW survey on sexual harassment in America's schools.* Washington, DC: Author.

American Institutes for Research. (1998). *Families and Schools Together (FAST).* Retrieved July 26, 2001, from www.air-dc.org/index.htm

American Psychiatric Association. (1987). *Diagnostic and statistical manual of mental disorders,* (3rd ed., rev.). Washington, DC: Author.

American Youth Policy Forum. (1999). *More things that do make a difference for youth: A compendium of youth programs and practices* (Vol. 2, pp. 15–17). Washington, DC: Author.

America's children: Key national indicators of well-being 2000. (2000). Federal Interagency Forum on Child and Family Statistics. Retrieved April 17, 2001, from childstats.gov

Angold, A., & Costello, E. J. (1993). Depressive comorbidity in children and adolescents: Empirical, theoretical, and methodological issues. *American Journal of Psychiatry, 150,* 1779–1791.

Annie E. Casey Foundation. (1998). *When teens have sex: Issues and trends.* Baltimore: Author.

Annie E. Casey Foundation. (2000). *Kids count data book: State profiles of child well-being.* Baltimore: Author.

Apter, S. J., & Propper, C. A. (1986). Ecological perspectives on youth violence. In S. J. Apter & A. P. Goldstein (Eds.), *Youth violence: Programs and prospects* (pp. 140–159). Oxford, England: Pergamon Press.

Arnette, J. L., & Walsleben, M. C. (1998). *Combating fear and restoring safety in schools.* Washington, DC: U.S. Department of Justice, Office of Juvenile Justice and Delinquency Prevention.

Arnold, E. M., Smith, T. E., Harrison, D. F., & Springer, D. W. (1999). The effects of an abstinence-based sex education program on middle school students' knowledge and beliefs. *Research on Social Work Practice, 9,* 10–24.

Asher, S. R., Parkhurst, J. T., Hymel, S., & Williams, G. A. (1990). Peer rejection and loneliness in childhood. In S. R. Asher & J. D. Coie (Eds.), *Peer rejection in childhood* (pp. 253–273). New York: Cambridge University Press.

Ayasse, R. H. (1995). Addressing the needs of foster children: The Foster Youth Services Program. *Social Work in Education, 17,* 207–216.

Baker v. Owen, 395 F. Supp. 294 (M.D.N.C. 1975).

Barker, R. L. (1987). *The social work dictionary.* Washington, DC: NASW Press.

Barrish, H. H., Saunder, M., & Wolf, M. M. (1969). Good behavior game: Effects of individual contingencies for group consequences on disruptive behavior in a classroom. *Journal of Applied Behavior Analysis, 2,* 119–124.

Bassuk, E. (1990). Who are the homeless families?: Characteristics of sheltered mothers and children. *Community Mental Health Journal, 26,* 434–435.

Batsche, G. M., & Knoff, H. M. (1994). Bullies and their victims: Understanding a pervasive problem in the schools. *School Psychology Review, 23,* 165–174.

Bennett, C. (1990). *Comprehensive multicultural education.* Boston: Allyn & Bacon.

Berne, L., & Huberman, B. (Eds.). (1999). *European approaches to adolescent sexual behavior and responsibility.* Washington, DC: Advocates for Youth.

Beswick, R. (1990). *Racism in America's schools.* Eugene, OR: ERIC Clearinghouse on Educational Management. (ERIC Digest No. ED320196).

Birmaher, B., Brent, D. A., & Benson, R. S. (1998). Summary of the practice parameters for the assessment and treatment of children and adolescents with depressive disorders. *Journal of the American Academy of Child and Adolescent Psychiatry, 37,* 1234–1238.

Birmaher, B., Ryan, N. D., Williamson, D. E., Brent, D. A., Kaufman, J., Dahl, R. E., et al. (1996). Childhood and adolescent depression: A review of the past 10 years. Part I. *Journal of the American Academy of Child and Adolescent Psychiatry, 35,* 1427–1439.

Bloom, M., Fischer, J., & Orme, J. G. (1999). *Evaluating practice: Guidelines for the accountable professional* (3rd ed.). Needham Heights, MA: Allyn & Bacon.

Bosworth, K. (1997). *Drug abuse prevention: School-based strategies that work.* Washington, DC: ERIC Clearinghouse on Teaching and Teacher Education. (ERIC Document Reproduction Service No. ED409316)

Bracey, G. W. (1992). Technology, falling SAT scores, and the transformation of consciousness. *Technos, 1,* 8–11.

Brent, D. A., Holder, D., Kolko, D., Birmaher, B., Baugher, M., Roth, C., et al. (1997). A clinical psychotherapy trial for adolescent depression comparing cognitive, family, and supportive therapy. *Archives of General Psychiatry, 54*, 877–885.

Brindis, C. (1999). Building for the future: Adolescent pregnancy prevention. *Journal of the American Medical Women's Association, 54*, 129–132.

Brophy, J. (1986). Teacher influences of student achievement. *American Psychologist, 41*, 1069–1077.

Brophy, J. (1995). *Elementary teachers' perceptions of and reported strategies for coping with twelve types of problem students.* East Lansing: Michigan State University, Institute for Research on Teaching. (ERIC Document Reproduction Service No. ED389390)

Brophy, J. (1996). *Working with shy or withdrawn students.* Urbana, IL: ERIC Clearinghouse on Elementary and Early Childhood Education. (ERIC Document Reproduction Service No. ED402070)

Brower, A. M., & Nurius, P. S. (1993). *Social cognition and individual change: Current theory and counseling guidelines.* Newbury Park, CA: Sage.

Brown v. Board of Education, Topeka, KS, 347 U.S. 483 (1954).

Bryk, A. S., & Thum, Y. M. (1989). The effects of high school organization on dropping out: An exploratory investigation. *American Educational Research Journal, 26*, 353–383.

Bullock, J. R. (1998). *Loneliness in young children.* Urbana, IL: ERIC Clearinghouse on Elementary and Early Childhood Education. (ERIC Document Reproduction Service No. ED419624)

Burnette, J. (1999). *Critical behaviors and strategies for teaching culturally diverse students.* Reston, VA: ERIC Clearinghouse on Disabilities and Gifted Education. (ERIC Document Reproduction Service No. ED435147)

Burrell, S., & Warboys, L. (2000). *Special education and the juvenile justice system.* Washington, DC: U.S. Department of Justice, Office of Juvenile Justice and Delinquency Prevention.

Cahill, M., Perry, J., Wright, M., & Rice, A. (1993). *A documentation report on the New York City beacons initiative.* New York: Youth Development Institute.

Callahan, C. (1992). *1991–92 Evaluation report for the mental health schools project.* Chicago: Mental Health Association of Illinois.

Campbell, M., Armenteros, J. L., Malone, R. P., Adams, P. B., Eisenberg, Z. W., & Overall, J. E. (1997). Neuroleptic-related dyskinesias in autistic children: A prospective, longitudinal study. *Journal of the American Academy of Child and Adolescent Psychiatry, 36*, 835–843.

Cantelon, S., & LeBoeuf, D. (1997). *Keeping young people in school: Community programs that work.* Washington, DC: U.S. Department of Justice, Office of Juvenile Justice and Delinquency Prevention.

Catalano, R. F., Loeber, R., & McKinney, K. C. (1999). *School and community interventions to prevent serious and violent offending.* Washington, DC: U.S. Department of Justice, Office of Juvenile Justice and Delinquency Prevention.

Catterall, J. S. (1985). *On the social costs of dropping out of school.* Stanford, CA: Stanford University Education Policy Institute. (ERIC Document Reproduction Service No. ED271837)

Cellini, H. R., Schwartz, B. K., & Readio, S. (1993). *Child sexual abuse: An administrator's nightmare.* Malibu, CA: Pepperdine University's National School Safety Center.

Center for Mental Health in Schools at UCLA. (2000). *An introductory packet on evaluation and accountability: Getting credit for all you do.* Los Angeles, CA: Author.

Center for Mental Health Services. (n.d.). *Major depression in children and adolescents.* Retrieved December, 5, 2001, from www.mentalhealth.org/publications/allpubs/CA-0011/default.asp

Chandler, K., Nolin, M. J., & Davies, E. (1995). *Student strategies to avoid harm at school* (National Center for Education Statistics 95-203). Rockville, MD: Westat.

Chavkin, N. F. (Ed.). (1993). *Families and schools in a pluralistic society.* Albany: State University of New York Press.

Chittooran, M. M. (2000). *Conflict resolution and peer mediation: A guide for educators* [Communique]. Bethesda, MD: National Association of School Psychologists.

Civil Rights Act of 1964, 42 U.S.C. § 1983.

Civil Rights Project. (2000). *Opportunities suspended: The devastating consequences of zero tolerance and school discipline policies.* Retrieved May 15, 2001, from Harvard University Web site: www.law.harvard.edu/civilrights/conferences/zero/zt_report2.html

Cohn, D., & Cohen, S. (2001, August 6). Census sees vast change in language and employment: More people work at home, more speak little English. *The Washington Post,* p. A1.

Comer, J. (1980). *School power.* New York: Free Press.

Committee for Children. (n.d.). *Second Step: A violence prevention program.* Retrieved April 17, 2000, from www.cfchildren.org/violence.htm

Constable, R. (1999). The Individualized Education Program and the IFSP: Content, process and the social worker's role. In R. Constable, S. McDonald, & J. P. Flynn (Eds.), *School social work: Practice, research, and policy perspectives* (4th ed., pp. 289–306). Chicago: Lyceum Books.

Corbin, J. N. (2001). Assessing school violence: Using the framework of group psychotherapy to explore the impact of the School Development Program on school violence. *Smith College Studies in Social Work, 71,* 243–258.

Cornell, D. G. (1999). *What works in youth violence prevention.* Virginia Youth Violence Project. Retrieved February 24, 2000, from http://curry.edschool.virginia.edu/curry/centers/youthvio/subpages/current/special/truewhatworks.html

Costin, L. (1978). *Social work services in schools: Historical perspectives and current directions* (National Association of Social Workers, Continuing Education Series No. 8). Washington, DC: NASW Press.

Cowan, D. (2000). *Identifying ADD/ADHD in the classroom.* The ADD/ADHD Information Library. Retrieved October 9, 2000, from www.newsideas.net/0000503.htm

Cowen, E. L., Hightower, A. D., Pedro-Carroll, J. L., Work, W. C., Wyman, P. A., & Haffey, W. G. (1996). *School-based prevention for children at risk: The Primary Mental Health Project.* Washington, DC: American Psychological Association.

Crowe, A. H. (1998). *Drug identification and testing in the juvenile justice system: Summary.* Washington, DC: U.S. Department of Justice, Office of Juvenile Justice and Delinquency Prevention.

DADS of Tennessee, Inc. (2000). *Children need their dads, responsible fatherhood: The research.* Retrieved November 27, 2000, from www.tndads.org/tcorf.htm

Davies, D. (1994). IRE's international league of schools reaches out to hard-to-reach parents. *Family Resource Coalition Report, 13,* 9–10.

Davis v. Monroe County Board of Education 120 S. Ct. 1390 (1999).

DeJong, W. (1994, Spring). School-based violence prevention: From the peaceable school to the peaceable neighborhood. *Forum, 25.*

DeJong, W. (1999). *Building the peace: The Resolving Conflict Creatively Program.* Washington, DC: National Institute of Justice.

DeKalb, J. (1999). *Student truancy.* Eugene, OR: ERIC Clearinghouse on Educational Management. (ERIC Document Reproduction Service No. ED429334)

DeRidder, L. M. (1990). How suspension and expulsion contribute to dropping out. *Education Digest, 56,* 44–47.

Deutsch, M., Mitchell, V., Zhang, Q., Khattri, N., Tepavac, L., Weitzman, E. A., et al. (1992). *The effects of training in cooperative learning and conflict resolution in an alternative high school.* New York: Columbia University.

Dibble, N. (1999). *Outcome evaluation of school social work services.* Madison: Wisconsin Department of Public Instruction.

Donovan, D. (2000). An alternative approach to ADHD. *Harvard Mental Health Letter, 16,* 11–15.

Dryfoos, J. G. (1994). *Full-service: A revolution in health and social services for children, youth, and families.* San Francisco: Jossey-Bass.

Dryfoos, J. G. (1996). Full-service schools. *Educational Leadership, 53,* 18–23.

Dunlap, G., & Bunton-Pierce, M. K. (1999). *Autism and autism spectrum disorder (ASD).* Reston, VA: ERIC Clearinghouse on Disabilities and Gifted Education. (ERIC Document Reproduction Service No. ED436068)

Dunlap, G., & Fox, L. (1999). *Teaching students with autism.* Reston, VA: ERIC Clearinghouse on Disabilities and Gifted Education. (ERIC Document Reproduction Service No. ED435148)

Dupper, D. R. (1993). School-community collaboration: A description of a model program designed to prevent school dropouts. *School Social Work Journal, 18,* 32–39.

Dupper, D. R. (1994a). Reducing out-of-school suspensions: A survey of attitudes and barriers. *Social Work in Education, 16,* 115–123.

Dupper, D. R. (1994b, Spring). School dropouts or "pushouts"? Suspensions and at-risk youth. *UIUC School of Social Work Newsletter, 7(1).*

Dupper, D. R. (1998). An alternative to suspension for middle school youths with behavior problems: Findings from a "school survival" group. *Research on Social Work Practice, 8,* 354–366.

Dupper, D. R., & Bosch, L. A. (1996). Reasons for school suspensions: An examination of data from one school district and recommendations for reducing suspensions. *Journal for a Just and Caring Education, 2,* 140–150.

Dupper, D. R., & Halter, A. P. (1994). Barriers in educating children from homeless shelters: Perspectives of school and shelter staff. *Social Work in Education, 16,* 39–45.

Dupper, D. R., & Krishef, C. H. (1993). School-based social-cognitive skills training for middle school students with school behavior problems. *Children and Youth Services Review, 15,* 133–145.

Dupper, D. R., & Meyer-Adams, N. (2002). Low-level violence: A neglected aspect of school culture. *Urban Education, 37,* 350–364.

Dupper, D. R., & Poertner, J. (1997). Public schools and the revitalization center of impoverished communities: School-linked, family resource centers. *Social Work, 42,* 415–422.

Eddowes, E., & Hranits, J. (1989). Educating children of the homeless. *Children Education, 65,* 197–200.

Education Amendments of 1972, 20 U.S.C.A.

Education for All Handicapped Children Amendments, 1986, Pub. L. No. 99-457.

Education for All Handicapped Children Act, 1975, Pub. L. No. 94-142, 20 U.S.C. 1400–1485, 34 CFR-300.

Ekstrand, M., Siegel, D., & Krasnovsky, F, et al. (1994). *A school-based, peer-led AIDS prevention program delays the onset of sexual behaviors among adolescents.* Presented at the Second International Conference on Biopsychosocial Aspects of HIV Infection, Brighton, England.

Elementary and Secondary Education Act, 1994, Pub. L. No. 103-382.

Elia, J. P. (1993). Homophobia in the high school: A problem in need of a resolution. *High School Journal, 77*, 177–185.

Ellickson, P. L., & Bell, R. M. (1990). Drug prevention in junior high: A multi-site longitudinal test. *Science, 247*, 1299–1305.

Elliott, D. S. (1998). *Prevention programs that work for youth.* Boulder: University of Colorado, Center for the Study and Prevention of Violence.

Epstein, M. H. (1999). Development and validation of a scale to assess the emotional and behavioral strengths of children and adolescents. *Remedial and Special Education, 20*, 258–262.

Erchul, W. P., & Martens, B. K. (1997). *School consultation: Conceptual and empirical bases of practice.* New York: Plenum Press.

Ernst, K. (1972). *Games students play (and what to do about them).* Millbrae, CA: Celestial Arts.

Everhart, K., & Wandersman, A. (2000). Applying comprehensive quality programming and empowerment evaluation to reduce implementation barriers. *Journal of Educational and Psychological Consultation, 11*, 177–191.

Everson, S. T. (1995). Selecting school improvement programs. In J. H. Block, S. T. Everson, & T. R. Guskey (Eds.), *School improvement programs: A handbook for educational leaders* (pp. 433–452). New York: Scholastic.

Family Education Rights and Privacy Act of 1974, Pub. L. No. 93-385.

Fantini, M., Gittell, M., & Magat, R. (1970). *Community control and the urban school.* New York: Praeger.

Fashola, O., & Slavin, R. E. (1998). School-wide reform models: What works? *Phi Delta Kappan, 79*, 370–379.

Felner, R. D., Brand, S., Adan, A. M., Mulhall, P. F., Flowers, N., Sartain, B., et al. (1993). Restructuring the ecology of the school as an approach to prevention during school transitions: Longitudinal follow-ups and extensions of the School Transitional Environment Project (STEP). *Prevention in Human Services, 10*, 103–136.

Felner, R. D., Ginter, M., & Primavera, J. (1982). Primary prevention during school transitions: Social support and environmental structure. *American Journal of Community Psychology, 10*, 277–290.

Field, M. L., & Aebersold, J. (1990). Cultural attitude toward reading: Implications for teachers of ESL/bilingual readers. *Journal of Reading, 33*, 406–410.

First, J. M. (1988). Immigrant students in U.S. public schools: Challenges with solutions. *Phi Delta Kappan, 70*, 205–210.

First, J. M., Kellog, J. B., Almeida, C. A., & Gray, R. (1991). *The good common school: Making the vision work for all children.* Boston: National Coalition of Advocates for Students.

Flannery, D. J. (1998). *School violence: Risk, preventive intervention, and policy.* New York: Columbia University, Teachers College, Institute for Urban and Minority Education. ERIC Clearinghouse on Urban Education. (ERIC Document Reproduction Service No. ED417244)

Framing new directions for school counselors, psychologists, and social workers. (2001, March). Los Angeles: UCLA Center for Mental Health Services in Schools.

Franklin, C., Biever, J., Moore, K. Clemons, D., & Scamardo, M. (2001). The effectiveness of solution-focused therapy with children in a school setting. *Research on Social Work Practice, 11,* 411–434.

Freeman, E. M. (1995). School social work overview. In R. L. Edwards (Ed.), *Encyclopedia of social work* (19th ed., Vol. 3, pp. 2087–2099). Washington, DC: NASW Press.

Freiberg, H. J., & Stein, T. A. (1999). Measuring, improving and sustaining healthy learning environments. In H. J. Freiberg (Ed.), *School climate: Measuring, improving and sustaining healthy learning environments* (pp. 11–29). London: Falmer Press.

Freiberg, H. J., Stein, T. A., & Huang, S. H. (1995). Effects of a classroom management intervention on student achievement in inner-city elementary schools. *Educational Research and Evaluation, 1,* 36–66.

Friend, M., & Cook, L. (1992). *Applications of collaboration in special services* (pp. 16–33). White Plains, NY: Longman.

Frost, J. J., & Forrest, J. D. (1995). Understanding the impact of effective teenage pregnancy prevention programs. *Family Planning Perspectives, 26,* 188–195.

Fullan, M. G. (1990). *Management of change: An implementation perspective.* Paper presented at School Year 2020 Conference, Oxford, England.

Furlong, M. J., Chung, A., Bates, M., & Morrison, R. L. (1995). Who are the victims of school violence? A comparison of student non-victims and multi-victims. *Education and Treatment of Children, 18,* 282–298.

Gandara, P. (1989). Those children are ours: Moving toward community. *Equity and Choice, 5,* 5–12.

Garbarino, J., Dubrow, N., Kostelny, K., & Pardo, C. (1992). *Children in danger: Coping with the consequences of community violence.* San Francisco: Jossey-Bass.

Garry, E. (1996, October). *Truancy: First step to a lifetime of problems.* Washington, DC: U.S. Department of Justice, Officeof Juvenile Justice and Delinquency Prevention.

Gaustad, J. (1992, November). Tutoring for at-risk students. *Oregon School Study Council Bulletin, 36*(3).

Gay, Lesbian and Straight Education Network. (1999). *GLSEN's national school climate survey: Lesbian, gay, bisexual, and transgendered and their experiences in school.* Retrieved April 5, 2000, from www.glsen.org/pages/sections/news/natlnews/1999/sep/survey

Gerdtz, J. (2000). Evaluating behavioral treatment of disruptive classroom behaviors of an adolescent with autism. *Research on Social Work Practice, 10,* 98–110.

Germain, C. B. (1999). An ecological perspective on social work in schools. In R. Constable, S. McDonald, & J. P. Flynn (Eds.), *School social work: Practice, research, and policy perspectives* (4th ed., pp. 33–44). Chicago: Lyceum Books.

Gfroerer, J. (1997). *Preliminary results from the 1996 National Household Survey on Drug Abuse.* Rockville, MD: U.S. Department of Health and Human Services, Substance Abuse and Mental Health Services Administration, Office of Applied Studies.

Gibelman, M. (1993). School social workers, counselors, and psychologists in collaboration: A shared agenda. *Social Work in Education, 15,* 45–53.

Ginsberg, L. H. (2001). *Social work evaluation: Principles and methods.* Needham Heights, MA: Allyn & Bacon.

Glenn, C. L. (1989). Just schools for minority children. *Phi Delta Kappan, 70,* 777–779.

Glennon, B., & Weisz, J. R. (1978). An observational approach to the reassessment of anxiety in young children. *Journal of Consulting and Clinical Psychology, 46,* 1246–1257.

Goals 2000: Educate America Act 1994, Pub. L. No. 103-227.

Gomby, D. S., & Larson, C. S. (1992). Evaluation of school-linked services. *Future of Children, 2,* 68–84.

Gorman, A. (2000, September 11). Schools step up effort to protect gay students. *Los Angeles Times,* p. 1.

Goss v. Lopez, 419 U.S. 565, 95 S.Ct. 729 (1975).

Gottfredson, D. C. (1997). School-based crime prevention. In L. W. Sherman, D. C. Gottfredson, D. MacKenzie, J. Ech, P. Reuter, & S. Bushway (Eds.), *Preventing crime: What works, what doesn't, what's promising.* A report to the United States Congress, prepared for the National Institute of Justice by Department of Criminology and Criminal Justice, University of Maryland, College Park. Retrieved May 10, 2001, from http://www.ncjrs.org/works/index.html

Gottfredson, D. C. (2001). *Schools and delinquency.* Cambridge, MA: Cambridge University Press.

Goyette, C. H., Conners, C. K., & Ulrich, R. F. (1978). Normative data on the revised Conners' Parent and Teacher Rating Scales. *Journal of Abnormal Child Psychology, 6,* 221–236.

Greenberg, M. T., Domitrovich, C., & Bumbarger, B. (2000). *Preventing mental disorders in school-age children: A review of the effectiveness of prevention programs.* University Park: Pennsylvania State University, College of Health and Human Development, Prevention Research Center for the Promotion of Human Development.

Greenberg, M. T., & Kusche, C. A. (1997). *Improving children's emotion regulation and social competence: The effects of the PATHS curriculum.* Paper presented at meeting of Society for Research in Child Development, Washington, DC.

Greenberg, M. T., Kusche, C. A., Cook, E. T., & Quamma, J. P. (1995). Promoting emotional competence in school-aged deaf children: The effects of the PATHS curriculum. *Development and Psychopathology, 7,* 117–136.

Griller-Clark, H. (2001). *Transition services for youth in the juvenile justice system. Focal Point.* A national bulletin on family support and children's mental health. Retrieved March 10, 2001, from www.edjj.org

Grossman, D. C., Neckerman, H. J., Koepsell, T. D., Liu, P., Asher, K. N., Beland, K., et al. (1997). Effectiveness of a violence prevention curriculum among children in elementary school. *Journal of the American Medical Association, 277,* 1605–1611.

Grossman, J., & Garry, E. (1997). *Mentoring: A proven delinquency prevention strategy.* Washington, DC: U.S. Department of Justice, Office of Juvenile Justice and Delinquency Prevention.

Gun Free Schools Act, 1994, Pub. L. No. 89-10.

Gutkin, T. B., & Conoley, J. C. (1990). Reconceptualizing school psychology from a service delivery perspective: Implications for practice, training, and research. *Journal of School Psychology, 28,* 203–223.

Hahn, A. (1987). Reaching out to America's dropouts: What to do? *Phi Delta Kappan, 69,* 256–263.

Hamilton, M. L., & Richardson, V. (1995). Effects of the culture in two schools on the process and outcomes of staff development. *Elementary School Journal, 95,* 367–385.

Hammack, F. M. (1986). Large school systems' dropout reports: An analysis of definitions, procedures, and findings. *Teachers College Record, 87,* 324–341.

Hampton, F. M., Mumford, D. A., & Bond, L. (1998). Parent involvement in inner-city schools: The Project FAST extended family approach to success. *Urban Education, 33,* 410–427.

Hare, I., & Rome, S. H. (1999). The changing social, political and economic context of school social work. In R. Constable, S. McDonald, & J. P. Flynn (Eds.), *School social work: Practice, research, and policy perspectives* (4th ed., pp. 97–123). Chicago: Lyceum Books.

Harrington, R., Rutter, M., & Weissman, M. M. (1997). Psychiatric disorders in the relatives of depressed probands. I: Comparison of prepubertal, adolescent and early adult onset cases. *Journal of Affective Disorders, 42,* 9–22.

Harris, V. W., & Sherman, J. A. (1973). Use and analysis of the "good behavior game" to reduce disrupted classroom behavior. *Journal of Applied Behavior Analysis, 6,* 405–417.

Hart, E. L., & Parmeter, S. H. (1992). Writing in the margins: A lesbian and gay inclusive course. In C. M. Hurlbert & S. Totten (Eds.), *Social issues in the English classroom* (pp. 154-173). Urbana, IL: National Council of Teachers of English. (ERIC Document Reproduction Service No. ED349574)

Hartocollis, A. (2001, March 22). *Not-so-simple reasons for dropout rate. The New York Times, New York Times on the Web.* Retrieved from www.nytimes.com/2001/

Hawkins-Stafford Elementary and Secondary School Improvement Amendments of 1988, Pub. L. No. 100-297.

Hawkins, J. D., Von Cleve, E., & Catalano, R. F. (1991). Reducing early childhood aggression: Results of a primary prevention program. *Journal of the American Academy of Child and Adolescent Psychiatry, 30,* 208–217.

Hawkins, J. D., & Weis, J. G. (1985). The social development model: An integrated approach to delinquency prevention. *Journal of Primary Prevention, 6,* 73–97.

Hazler, R. J. (1994). Bullying breeds violence: You can stop it. *Learning, 22,* 38–41.

Henggeler, S. W. (1997, May). *Treating serious anti-social behavior in youth: The MST approach.* Washington, DC: U.S. Department of Justice, Office of Juvenile Justice and Delinquency Prevention.

Henggeler, S. W., Schoenwald, S. K., Borduin, C. M., Rowland, M. D., & Cunningham, P. B. (1998). *Multisystemic treatment of antisocial behavior in children and adolescents.* New York: Guilford Press.

Henry, M. (1996). *Parent-school collaboration: Feminist organizational structures and school leadership.* Albany: State University of New York.

Herrera, C. (1999). *School-based mentoring: A first look into its potential.* Philadelphia: Public/Private Ventures.

Hoagwood, K., & Erwin, H. D. (1997). Effectiveness of school-based mental health services for children: A 10-year research review. *Journal of Child and Family Studies, 6,* 435–451.

Hodges, K. (1993). Structures interview for assessing children. *Journal of Child Psychology and Psychiatry, 34,* 49–68.

Honig, A. (1987). The shy child. *Young Children, 42,* 54–64.

Hooper-Briar, K., & Lawson, H. (1996). *Expanding partnerships for vulnerable children, youth, and families.* Paper presented at the meeting of the Council on Social Work Education, Alexandria, VA.

Hoover, J. H., Oliver, R., & Hazler, R. L. (1992). Bullying: Perceptions of adolescent victims in the Midwestern USA. *Social Psychology International, 13,* 5–16.

Hoover, J. H., Oliver, R. L., & Thomson, K. A. (1993). Perceived victimization by school bullies: New research and future directions. *Journal of Humanistic Education and Development, 32,* 76–84.

Horn, L., & West, J. (1992). *A profile of parents of eighth graders. National Educational Longitudinal Study of 1988.* Washington, DC: National Center for Education Statistics. (ERIC Document Reproduction Service No. ED350341)

Horn, L. J., & Carroll, C. D. (1997). *Confronting the odds: Students at risk and the pipeline to higher education.* Statistical Analysis Report, National Center for Education Statistics (OERI Publication No. NCES 98-094). Washington, DC: Department of Education.

Housewright, E. (1999, October 17). Troubled children: Intervention, therapy called key for youths with mental disorders. *The Dallas Morning News,* p. 1A.

Howard, K. A., Flora, J., & Griffen, M. (1999). Violence-prevention programs in schools: State of the science and implications for future research. *Applied and Preventive Psychology, 8,* 197–215.

Hoyert, D. L., Kochanek, K. D., & Murphy, S. L. (1999). *Deaths: Final data for 1997. National vital statistics reports, 47,* 1–108. Hyattsville, MD: National Center for Health Statistics.

Hudson, W. W., & Faul, A. C. (1988). *The clinical measurement package: A field manual* (2nd ed.). Tallahassee, FL: WALMYR.

Hughes, J. N. (2000). The essential role of theory in the science of treating children: Beyond empirically supported treatments. *Journal of School Psychology, 38,* 301–330.

Hyman, I. A. (1990). *Reading, writing, and the hickory stick: The appalling story of physical and psychological abuse in American schools.* Lexington, MA: Lexington Books.

Hyman, I. A. (1997). *The case against spanking: How to discipline your child without hitting.* New York: Jossey-Bass.

Improving America's Schools Act, 1994, Pub. L. No. 103-382.

Individuals with Disabilities Education Act Amendments of 1997, Pub. L. 105-17, 111 Stat. 37-157.

Individuals with Disabilities Education Act of 1990, Pub. L. No. 101-476.

Ingersoll, S., & LeBoeuf, D. (1997, February). *Reaching out to youth out of the educational mainstream.* Washington, DC: U.S. Department of Justice, Office of Juvenile Justice and Delinquency Prevention.

Ingraham v. Wright, 430 U.S. 651, 97 S. Ct. 1401 (1977).

Institute for Health Policy Studies. (1995). *Street youth at risk for AIDS.* San Francisco: University of California.

Jacobson, L. (2000, September 13). Academic fate of foster children gaining more attention. *Education Week.* Retrieved from www.edweek.org

James, D. W. (Ed.). (1999). *More things that do make a difference for youth.* Washington, DC: American Youth Policy Forum.

James, M., & Jongeward, D. (1977). *Born to win: Transactional analysis with Gestalt experiments.* Reading, MA: Addison-Wesley.

Jayson, D., Wood, A., Kroll, L., Fraser, J., & Harrington, R. (1998). Which depressed patients respond to cognitive-behavioral treatment? *Journal of the American Academy of Child and Adolescent Psychiatry, 37,* 35–39.

Jenson, J. M., & Howard, M. O. (1999). *Youth violence: Current research and recent practice innovations.* Washington, DC: NASW Press.

Jones, E. M., Gottfredson, G. D., & Gottfredson, D. C. (1997). Success for some: An evaluation of a Success for All Program. *Evaluation Review, 21*, 643–670.

Juhnke, G. A., Charkow, W. B., Jordan, J., Curtis, R. C., Liles, R. G., Gmutza, B. M., et al. (1999). *Assessing potentially violent students.* Greensboro, NC: ERIC Clearinghouse on Counseling and Student Services. (ERIC Document Reproduction Service No. ED435894)

Juvenile Justice and Delinquency Prevention Act, 1974, Pub. L. No. 93-415.

Kahn, J. G., Brindis, C. D., & Glei, D. A. (1999). Pregnancies averted among U.S. teenagers by the use of contraceptives. *Family Planning Perspectives, 31*, 29–34.

Kann, L., Kinchen, S. A., Williams, B. I., Ross, J. G., Lowry, R., Hill, C. V., et al. (1998). Youth risk behavior surveillance–United States, 1997. *Morbidity and Mortality Weekly Report, 47*(SS-3), 1–89.

Kaufman, P., Kwon, J. Y., Klein, S., & Chapman, C. D. (2000). *Dropout rates in the United States: 1999* (NCES 2001-022). Washington, DC: National Center for Education Statistics.

Kendall, P. C. (1993). Cognitive-behavioral therapies with youth: Guiding theory, current status, and emerging developments. *Journal of Consulting and Clinical Psychology, 61*, 235–247.

Kerns, K. A., Eso, K., & Thomson, J. (1999). Investigation of a direct intervention for improving attention in young children with ADHD. *Developmental Neuropsychology, 16*, 273–295.

Khayatt, D. (1994). Surviving school as a lesbian student. *Gender and Education, 6*, 47–61.

King, K. A., Price, J. H., Telljohann, S. K., & Wahl, J. (1999). High school health teachers' knowledge of adolescent suicide. *American Journal of Health Studies, 15*, 156–163.

King, N., & Ollendick, T. H. (1989). Children's anxiety and phobic disorders in school settings: Classification, assessment, and intervention issues. *Review of Educational Research, 59*, 431–470.

Kirby, D., Barth, R. P., Leland, N., & Fetro, J. V. (1991). Reducing the risk: Impact of a new curriculum on sexual risk-taking. *Family Planning Perspectives, 23*, 253–262.

Kirby, D. J. (1994). Sex education in the schools. In J. A. Garrison, M. D. Smith, & D. J. Besharov (Eds.), *Sexuality and American social policy.* Menlo Park, CA: Henry J. Kaiser Family Foundation.

Kirby, D. J. (1997). *No easy answers: Research findings on programs to reduce teen pregnancy.* Scotts Valley, CA: ETR Associates.

Klerman, G. L., & Weissman, M. M. (1989). Increasing rates of depression. *Journal of the American Medical Association, 261*, 2229–2235.

Klingman, A., & Hochdorf, Z. (1993). Coping with distress and self harm: The impact of a primary prevention program among adolescents. *Journal of Adolescence, 16*, 121–140.

Knoblauch, B., & Sorenson, B. (1998). *IDEA's definition of disabilities.* Reston, VA: ERIC Clearinghouse on Disabilities and Gifted Education. (ERIC Document Reproduction Service No. ED429396)

Kochenderfer, B. J., & Ladd, G. W. (1996). Peer victimization: Manifestations and relations to school adjustment in kindergarten. *Journal of School Psychology, 34*, 267–283.

Kopels, S. (1993). Response to "Confidentiality: A different perspective" [As readers see it]. *Social Work in Education, 15*, 250-252.

Kopels, S. (2000). Securing equal educational opportunity: Language, race and sex. In P. Allen-Meares, R. O. Washington, & B. L. Welsh (Eds.), *Social work services in schools* (pp. 215–242). Needham Heights, MA: Allyn & Bacon.

Kopels, S., & Dupper, D. R. (1999). School-based peer sexual harassment. *Child Welfare, 78,* 435–460.

Kovacs, M. (1997). Psychiatric disorders in youths with IDDM: Rates and risk factors. *Diabetes Care, 20,* 36–44.

Kozol, J. (1989). *Rachel and her children.* New York: Crown.

Kumpfer, K. L. (1999). *Strengthening America's families: Exemplary parenting and family strategies for delinquency prevention.* Washington, DC: U.S. Department of Justice, Office of Juvenile Justice and Delinquency Prevention.

Lam, J. (1989). *The impact of conflict resolution programs on schools: A review and synthesis of the evidence* (2nd ed.). Amherst, MA: National Association for Mediation in Education.

Larson, J. (1994). Violence prevention in the schools: A review of selected programs and procedures. *School Psychology Review, 23,* 151–164.

LeCompte, M. D. (2000). Standing for just and right decisions: The long, slow path to school safety. *Education and Urban Society, 32,* 413–429.

Lee, L. J. (1983). The social worker in the political environment of a school system. *Social Work, 28,* 302–307.

Lewin, T. (2001). *Program finds success in reducing teenage pregnancy. New York Times on the Web.* Retrieved from www.nytimes.com /2001/0530/national/30TEEN.html

Lim, C., & Adelman, H. S. (1999). Establishing school-based, collaborative teams to coordinate resources: A case study. *Social Work in Education, 19,* 266–278.

Limber, S. P., & Nation, M. M. (1998). Bullying among children and youth. In J. L.

Arnette & M. C. Walsleben (Eds.), *Combating fear and restoring safety in schools* [Bulletin] (pp. 4–5). Washington, DC: U.S. Department of Justice, Office of Juvenile Justice and Delinquency Prevention.

Linsley, J. (2001). Working with gay and lesbian youth. *New Social Worker, 8,* 8–11.

Loewenberg, F. M., Dolgoff, R., & Harrington, D. (2000). *Ethical decisions for social work practice.* Itasca, IL: Peacock.

Lokerson, J. (1992). *Learning disabilities.* Reston, VA: ERIC Clearinghouse on Handicapped and Gifted Children. (ERIC Document Reproduction Service No. ED352779)

Lumsden, L. S. (1991). *The role of schools in sexual abuse prevention and intervention.* Eugene, OR: ERIC Clearinghouse on Educational Management. (ERIC Document Reproduction Service No. ED331152)

Mark, R. (1996). *Research made simple: A handbook for social workers.* Thousand Oaks, CA: Sage.

Massachusetts Advocacy Center. (1986). *The way out: Student exclusion practices in Boston middle schools.* Boston: Author.

Massachusetts Governor's Commission on Gay and Lesbian Youth. (1993). *Making schools safe for gay and lesbian youth.* Boston: Author.

Massey, M. S. (1998). *Promoting stress management: The role of comprehensive school health programs.* Washington, DC: ERIC Clearinghouse on Teaching and Teacher Education. (ERIC Document Reproduction Service No. ED421480)

Mayer, G. R., Butterworth, T., Nafpaktitus, M., & Sulzer-Azaroff, B. (1983). Preventing school vandalism and improving discipline: A three-year study. *Journal of Applied Behavior Analysis, 16,* 355–369.

Mayer, O. (1999). *Substance abuse prevention takes to the classroom* (No. 25, p. 24). Denver, CO: State Legislature.

McCullagh, J. G. (1982). Survival strategies for school social workers. *Social Work in Education, 4,* 5–15.

McDonald, L., & Billingham, S. (1998). *FAST orientation manual and elementary school FAST program workbook.* Madison, WI: FAST International.

McDonald, L., & Frey, H. E. (1999). *Families and schools together: Building relationships* [Bulletin]. Washington, DC: U.S. Department of Justice, Office of Juvenile Justice and Delinquency Prevention.

McDonald, L., & Sayger, T. (1998). Impact of a family and school based prevention program on protective factors for high risk youth. *Drugs and Society, 12,* 61–86.

McEvoy, A. (1990). Child abuse law and school policy. *Education and Urban Society, 22,* 247–257.

McGlauflin, H. (1998). Helping children grieve at school. *Professional School Counseling, 1,* 46–49.

McIntyre, T. (1987). Teacher awareness of child abuse and neglect. *Child Abuse and Neglect, 11,* 33–35.

McIntyre, T. (1989). *A resource book for remediating common behavior and learning problems.* Boston: Allyn & Bacon.

McKay, M., Tolan, P., Kohner, K., & Montaini, L. (1994). *Engagement of families in prevention/intervention child mental health research.* Manuscript submitted for publication.

McKethan, J. F. (2001). *Section 504 of the 1973 Rehabilitation Act: What all school personnel should know.* Research Triangle Park, NC: MicroScribe Publishing.

McPartland, J. M., & Slavin, R. E. (1990). *Increasing achievement of at-risk students at each grade level.* Washington, DC: U.S. Department of Education, Office of Educational Research and Improvement.

Menacker, J., Weldon, W., & Hurwitz, E. (1990). Community influences on school crime and violence. *Urban Education, 25,* 68–80.

Menke, E. M. (1998). The mental health of homeless school-age children. *Journal of Child and Adolescent Psychiatric Nursing, 11,* 87–98.

Mental health: A report of the Surgeon General. (1999). Washington, DC: Department of Health and Human Services. Retrieved from www.surgeongeneral.gov

Merritt, R. (1983). The effect of enrollment and school organization on the dropout rate. *Phi Delta Kappan, 65,* 224.

Metis Associates, Inc. (1990). *The Resolving Conflict Creatively Program: 1988–1989 summary of significant findings.* New York: Author.

Millennium hangover: Keeping score on alcohol. (1999). Drug strategies. Retrieved April 28, 2000, from www.drugstrategies.org /keepingscore1999/teen.html

Monitoring the future: National results on adolescent drug use, overview of key findings, 1999. (2000, April). (NIH Publication No. 00-4690). Bethesda, MD: National Institute on Drug Abuse.

Montague, M., McKinney, J., & Hocutt, A. (1996, April). *Project SUCCESS: A report on year one.* Paper presented at the annual meeting of the American Educational Research Association, New York.

Morey, C. K. (1999). Children of alcoholics: A school-based comparative study. *Journal of Drug Education, 29,* 63–75.

Morris, R., & Kratochwill, T. (1985). Behavioral treatment of children's fears and phobias: A review. *School Psychology Review, 14,* 84–93.

Moskowitz, J. M., Malvin, J. H., Schaeffer, G. A., & Schaps, E. (1984). Evaluation of an affective development teacher training program. *Journal of Primary Prevention, 4,* 150–162.

National Association of Social Workers. (1996). *Code of ethics.* Retrieved April 10,

2000, from www.naswdc.org/pubs/code/default.htm

National Association of Social Workers. (1997). *Individuals with Disabilities Education Act Amendments of 1997 (IDEA): Implications for Social Workers*. Washington, DC: Author.

National Association of Social Workers. (2001). *Confidentiality and school social work: A practice perspective, practice update from the National Association of Social Workers* (Vol. 2, No. 2). Retrieved January 18, 2002, from http://socialworkers.org/practice/pdae/dfs0202.html

National Coalition for the Homeless. (1999, June). *Education of homeless children and youth* (NCH Fact Sheet No. 10). Washington, DC: Author.

National Education Goals Panel. (1997). *The national education goals report: Building a nation of learners, 1997*. Washington, DC: U.S. Government Printing Office.

National Institute of Mental Health. (1993). *Learning disabilities* [Brochure]. Bethesda, MD: Author.

National Institute of Mental Health. (1996). *Attention deficit hyperactivity disorder* [Brochure]. Bethesda, MD: Author.

National Institute of Mental Health. (1997). *Autism* [Brochure]. Bethesda, MD: Author.

National Institute of Mental Health. (2000). *Depression in children and adolescents: A fact sheet for physicians*. Bethesda, MD: Author. Retrieved from www.nimh.nih.gov/publicat/depchildresfact.cfm

National School Safety Center. (1994). *Increasing student attendance*. Malibu, CA: Author.

New Jersey v. T.L.O., 469 U.S. 325, 105 S. Ct. 733 (1985).

Noble, L. S. (1997). The face of foster care. *Educational Leadership, 54*, 26–28.

Nord, M., & Luloff, A. E. (1995). Homeless children and their families in New Hampshire: A rural perspective. *Social Service Review, 69*, 461–478.

Office of Special Education and Rehabilitative Services. (2000). *A guide to the individualized education program*. Washington, DC: U.S. Department of Education.

Ohio Commission on Dispute Resolution and Conflict Management. (1994). *Conflict management in schools: Sowing seeds for a safer society*. Columbus, OH: Author.

Oliver, J. P., & Howley, C. (1992). *Charting new maps: Multicultural education in rural schools*. Charleston, WV: ERIC Clearinghouse on Rural Education ands Small Schools. (ERIC Document Reproduction Service No. ED348196)

Ollendick, T. H. (1983). Reliability and validity of the revised Fear Survey Schedule for Children (FSSC-R). *Behaviour Research and Therapy, 21*, 685–692.

Olson, L. (2000, September 27). Mixed needs of immigrants pose challenges for schools. Retrieved February 3, 2001, from http://www.edweek.org

Olsen, L., & Moore, M. (1984). *Voices from the classroom: Students and teachers speak out on the quality of teaching in our schools*. Oakland, CA: Citizens Policy Center. (ERIC Document Reproduction Service No. ED252497)

Olweus, D. (1991). Bully/victim problems among schoolchildren: Basic facts and effects of a school based intervention program. In D. J. Pepler & K. H. Rubin (Eds.), *The development and treatment of childhood aggression* (pp. 411–448). Hillsdale, NJ: Erlbaum.

Olweus, D. (1993). *Bullying at school: What we know and what we can do*. Oxford, England: Blackwell.

Olweus, D., Limber, S. P., & Mihalic, S. F. (1999). *Bullying Prevention Program*. In D. S. Elliott (Series Ed.), *Blueprints for violence prevention* (Book 9). Boulder: University of Colorado, Institute of Behavioral Science, Center for the Study and Prevention of Violence.

Osborne, J. W. (1997). Race and academic disidentification. *Journal of Educational Psychology, 89,* 728–735.

Osher, D., Osher, T., & Smith, C. (1994). Toward a national perspective in emotional and behavioral disorders: A developmental agenda. *Beyond Behavior, 6,* 6–17.

Ozonoff, S., & Cathcart, K. (1998). Effectiveness of a home program intervention for young children with autism. *Journal of Autism and Developmental Disorders, 28,* 25–32.

Pawlak, E. J., & Cousins, L. (1999). School social work: Organizational perspectives. In R. Constable, S. McDonald, & J. P. Flynn (Eds.), *School social work: Practice, policy, and research perspectives* (4th ed., pp. 150–165). Chicago: Lyceum Books.

Pilkington, N. W., & D'Augelli, A. R. (1995). Victimization of lesbian, gay, and bisexual youth in community settings. *Journal of Community Psychology, 23,* 34–56.

Pine, G. J., & Hilliard, A. G. (1990). Rx for racism: Imperatives for America's schools. *Phi Delta Kappan, 71,* 593–600.

Pitcher, G. D., & Poland, S. (1992). *Crisis intervention in the schools.* New York: Guilford Press.

Pollard, D. S. (1989). Reducing the impact of racism on students. *Educational Leadership, 47,* 73–75.

Portner, J. (1997, June 25). Gore claims expulsions prove weapons policies working. *Education Week,* p. 20.

Portner, J. (2000a). Complex set of ills spurs rising teen suicide rate. *Education Week, 19,* pp. 1, 22–25.

Portner, J. (2000b). Suicide: Many schools fall short on prevention. *Education Week, 19,* pp. 1, 20–22.

Potts, M. (1990). Adolescence and puberty: An overview. In J. Bancroft & J. M. Reinisch (Eds.), *Adolescence and puberty* (pp. 269–279). New York: Oxford University Press.

Pransky, J. (1991). *Prevention: The critical need.* Springfield, MO: Burrell Foundation & Paradigm Press.

Project 10. (1993). *Project 10 handbook: Addressing lesbian and gay issues in our schools.* Los Angeles: Friends of Project 10.

Quay, H. C., & Peterson, D. R. (1983). *Manual for the Revised Behavioral Problem Checklist.* Unpublished manuscript.

Quindlen, A. (1999, November 11). Mentally ill kids exist on margins. *Denver Rocky Mountain News,* p. 35A.

Radin, N. (1988). Assessing the effectiveness of school social workers: An update focused on simulations, graphics, and peers. In J. G. McCullagh & P. Allen-Meares (Eds.), *Conducting research: A handbook for school social workers.* Des Moines: Iowa Department of Education.

Radin, N. (1989). School social work practice: Past, present, and future trends. *Social Work in Education, 11,* 213–225.

Rathvon, N. (1999). *Effective school interventions: Strategies for enhancing academic achievement and social competence.* New York: Guilford Press.

Reid, J. B., Eddy, J. M., & Fetrow, R. A. (1999). Description and immediate impacts of a preventive intervention for conduct problems. *American Journal of Community Psychology, 27,* 483–517.

Reinecke, M. A., Ryan, N. E., & DuBois, D. L. (1998). Cognitive-behavioral therapy of depression and depressive symptoms during adolescence: A review and meta-analysis. *Journal of the American Academy of Child and Adolescent Psychiatry, 37,* 26–34.

Reyes, O., & Jason, L. A. (1993). Pilot study examining factors associated with academic success for Hispanic high school students. *Journal of Youth and Adolescence, 22,* 57–71.

Reynolds, C. R., & Richmond, B. O. (1978). "What I think and feel": A revised measure of children's manifest anxiety. *Journal of Abnormal Child Psychology, 6,* 271–280.

Rohrman, D. (1993). Combating truancy in our schools: A community effort. *NASSP Bulletin, 77,* 40–45.

Rothenberg, D. (1996). *Grandparents as parents: A primer for schools.* Urbana, IL: ERIC Clearinghouse on Elementary and Early Childhood Education. (ERIC Document Reproduction Service No. ED401044)

Ryan, N. D., Puig-Antich, J., & Ambrosini, P. (1987). The clinical picture of major depression in children and adolescents. *Archives of General Psychiatry, 44,* 854–861.

Safe Schools Act of 1994, Part of Pub. L. No. 103-227.

Safran, S., & Safran, J. (1985). Classroom context and teachers' perceptions of problem behaviors. *Journal of Educational Psychology, 77,* 20–28.

Sarason, S. B. (1971). *The culture of the school and the problem of change.* Boston: Allyn & Bacon.

Sarason, S. B., Davidson, K., Lighthall, F., & Waite, R. R. (1958). A test anxiety scale for children. *Child Development, 29,* 105–113.

Schinke, S. P., & Gilchrist, L. D. (1984). *Life skills counseling with adolescents.* Baltimore: University Park Press.

School Safety Update. (1997). *Truancy: An early indicator of future criminality.* Malibu, CA: Pepperdine University, National School Safety Center News Service.

School Social Work Association of America. (2001). School social workers and confidentiality: Position statement. Adopted March 15, 2001. Washington, DC: School Social Work Association of America.

Schroeder, C. S., & Gordon, B. N. (1991). *Assessment and treatment of childhood problems: A clinician's guide.* New York: Guilford Press.

Schumm, J. S., & Vaughn, S. (1992). Planning for mainstreamed special education students: Perceptions of general classroom teachers. *Exceptionality, 3,* 81–98.

Schwartz, W. (1994). *Improving the school experience for gay, lesbian, and bisexual students.* New York: ERIC Clearinghouse on Urban Education. (ERIC Document Reproduction Service No. ED377257)

Schwartz, W. (1995a). *School dropouts: New information about an old problem.* New York: ERIC Clearinghouse on Urban Education. (ERIC Document Reproduction Service No. ED386515)

Schwartz, W. (1995b). *School programs and practices for homeless students.* New York: ERIC Clearinghouse on Urban Education. (ERIC Document Reproduction Service No. ED383783)

Schwartz, W. (1999). *School support for foster families.* New York: ERIC Clearinghouse on Urban Education. (ERIC Document Reproduction Service No. ED434189)

Sears, J. T. (1987). Peering into the well of loneliness: The responsibility of educators to gay and lesbian youth. In A. Molnar (Ed.), *Social issues and education: Challenge and responsibility* (pp. 79–100). Alexandria, VA: Association for Supervision and Curriculum Development. (ERIC Document Reproduction Service No. ED280781).

Sears, J. T. (1992). Educators, homosexuality, and homosexual students: Are personal feelings related to professional beliefs (pp. 29–79). In K. Harbeck (Ed.), *Coming out of the classroom closet* (ED397002). New York: Harrington Park Press.

Sessions, P., Fanolis, V., Corwin, M., & Miller, J. (2001). Partners for success: A collaborative program between the Smith College School for Social Work and the Springfield Massachusetts public schools. *Smith College Studies in Social Work, 71,* 227–242.

Shaffer, D., Gould, M. S., Fisher, P., Trautment, P., Moreau, D., Kleinman, M., et al. (1996). Psychiatric diagnosis in child and adolescent suicide. *Archives of General Psychiatry, 53,* 339–348.

Shakeshift, C., Barber, E., Hergenrother, M., Johnson, Y. M., Mandel, L. S., & Sawyer, J. (1995). Peer harassment in schools. *Journal for a Just and Caring Education, 1,* 30–44.

Shapiro, E. S., & Kratochwill, T. R. (2000). *Conducting school-based assessments of child and adolescent behavior.* New York: Guilford Press.

Shinn, M., & Weitzman, B. (1996). Homeless families are different. In *Homelessness in America.* Washington, DC: National Coalition for the Homeless.

Short, P. M., & Short, R. J. (1987). Beyond technique: Personal and organizational influences on school discipline. *High School Journal, 71,* 31–36.

Shure, M. B. (1997). Interpersonal cognitive problem-solving: Primary prevention of early high risk behaviors in preschool and primary years. In G. W. Albee & T. P. Gullota (Eds.), *Primary prevention works* (pp. 167–190). Thousand Oaks, CA: Sage.

Skiba, R., & Peterson, R. (1999). The dark side of zero tolerance: Can punishment lead to safe schools? *Phi Delta Kappan, 80,* 381–382.

Slavin, R. E. (1991). *Student team learning: A practical guide to cooperative learning* (3rd ed.). Washington, DC: National Education Association.

Slavin, R. E., Madden, N. A., Donal, L. J., Wasik, B., Ross, S., Smith, L., et al. (1996). Success for all: A summary of research. *Journal of Education for Students Placed At Risk, 1,* 41–76.

Sloboda, Z., & David, S. L. (1997). *Preventing drug use among children and adolescents: A research-based guide.* Washington, DC: National Institute on Drug Abuse, National Institutes of Health.

Smith, P. K., & Sharp, S. (1994). *School bullying: Insights and perspectives.* London: Routledge.

Sniffen, M. J. (2000). 1.5 million kids have parent in prison. *Parents and children together.* Retrieved May 19, 2001, from http://abcnews.go.com/sections/us/DailyNews/prisonorchildren000831.htm

Snyder, H. N., & Sickmund, M. (1995). *Juvenile offenders and victims: A national report.* Washington, DC: U.S. Department of Justice, Office of Juvenile Justice and Delinquency Prevention.

Snyder, T., & Hoffman, C. (2000). *Digest of education statistics, 1999.* (NCES Publication No. 2000031). Retrieved October, 28, 2000, from http://nces.ed.gov/pubsearch/pubsinfo/asppubid=2000031

Spears, J. D., Oliver, J. P., & Maes, S. C. (1990). *Accommodating change and diversity: Multicultural practices in rural schools.* Manhattan, KS: The Rural Clearinghouse for Lifelong Education and Development. (ED326362)

Stahl, P. M. (1990). *Children on consignment: A handbook for parenting foster children and their special needs.* Lexington, MA: Lexington Books.

Stein, N. (1995). Sexual harassment in school: The public performance of gendered violence. *Harvard Educational Review, 65,* 145–162.

Stewart B. McKinney Homeless Assistance Act, 1987, Pub. L. No. 100-77.

Stewart B. McKinney Homeless Assistance Amendments Act of 1990, Pub. L. No. 100-645.

Stolberg, A. L., & Mahler, J. (1994). Enhancing treatment gains in a school-based intervention for children of divorce through skill-training parental involvement and transfer procedures. *Journal of Consulting and Clinical Psychology, 62,* 147–156.

Strong families: Strong schools. (1994). Retrieved April 8, 2001, from eric-web .tc.columbia.edu/families/strong

Stufft, D. L. (1989). Kids in limbo: Dealing with foster care children. *Principal, 68,* 34–35, 38.

Surgeon General's call to action to prevent suicide. (1999). At a glance: Suicide among the young. Retrieved from www. surgeongeneral.gov/library/calltoaction /fact3.htm

Symonds, W. C. (2001, March 19). How to fix America's schools. *Business Week Online.* Retrieved from www.businessweek .com/magazine/content/01_12/b3724001 .htm

Terry, P. (1998). Do schools make children fearful and phobic? *Journal for a Just and Caring Education, 4,* 193–211.

Thompson, C., & Rudolph, L. (1992). *Counseling children* (3rd ed.). Pacific Grove, CA: Brooks/Cole.

Thornberry, T. P., Wei, E. H., Stouthamer-Loeber, M., & Van Dyke, J. (2000). *Teenage fatherhood and delinquent behavior* [Bulletin]. Washington, DC: U.S. Department of Justice, Office of Juvenile Justice and Delinquency Prevention.

Tiefenthal, M., & Charak, R. (1999). The social developmental study. In R. Constable,

S. McDonald, & J. P. Flynn (Eds.), *School social work: Practice, policy, and research perspectives* (4th ed., pp. 277–288). Chicago: Lyceum Books.

Tinker v. Des Moines Independent Community School District, 393 U.S. 503, 89 S. Ct. 733, 21. (1969).

Torres, S., Jr. (1996). The status of school social workers in America. *Social Work in Education, 18,* 8–18.

Tutty, L. M. (1995). The revised Children's Knowledge of Abuse Questionnaire: Development of a measure of children's understanding of sexual abuse prevention concepts. *Social Work Research, 19,* 112–120.

Tutty, L. M. (2000). What children learn from sexual abuse prevention programs: Difficult concepts and developmental issues. *Research on Social Work Practice, 10,* 275–300.

Twenge, J. M. (2000). The age of anxiety? Birth cohort change in anxiety and neuroticism, 1952–1993. *Journal of Personality and Social Psychology, 79,* 1007–1021.

U.S. Department of Education. (1998). *To assure the free, appropriate public education of all children with disabilities: Twentieth annual report to Congress on the implementation of the Individuals with Disabilities Education Act.* Washington, DC: Author.

U.S. Department of Education. (2001). *Prevention research and the IDEA discipline provisions: A guide for school administrators.* Retrieved December 5, 2001, from www. ed.gov/offices/OSERS/OSEP

U.S. Departments of Education and Justice. (1999). *1999 Annual Report on School Safety.* Retrieved June 22, 2001, from http:// www.ed.gov/PDFDocs/InterimAR.pdf

U.S. General Accounting Office. (2000, October). *At-risk youth: School-community collaborations focus on improving student outcomes*. Report to the Honorable Charles B. Rangel, House of Representatives (GAO-0-66). Washington, DC: Author.

Van Acker, R. (1999). Adaptive behavior assessments. In R. Constable, S. McDonald, & J. P. Flynn (Eds.), *School social work: Practice, policy, and research perspectives* (4th ed., pp. 258–276). Chicago: Lyceum Books.

Vinter, R. D., & Sarri, R. C. (1965). Malperformance in the public school. *Social Work, 10,* 3–13.

Wagner, M. W. (1995). Outcomes for youth with serious emotional disturbance in secondary school and early adulthood. *Critical Issues for Children and Youth, 5,* 90–110.

Walberg, H. J. (1991). Does homework help? *School Community Journal, 1,* 13–15.

Walter, H. J., & Vaughn, R. D. (1993). AIDS risk reduction among a multi-ethnic sample of urban high school students. *Journal of the American Medical Association, 270,* 725–730.

Walton, F. X. (1980). *Winning teenagers over in home and school: A manual for parents, teachers, counselors, and principals.* Chicago: Practical Psychology Associates.

Wandersman, A., Morrissey, E., Davino, K., Seybolt, D., Crusto, C., Nation, M., et al. (1998). Comprehensive quality programming and accountability: Eight essential strategies for implementing successful prevention programs. *Journal of Primary Prevention, 19,* 3–30.

Wang, M. C., Haertel, G. D., & Walberg, H. J. (1997). Learning influences. In H. J. Walberg & G. D. Haertel (Eds.), *Psychology and educational practice* (pp. 199–211). Berkeley, CA: McCuthan.

Wassenich, L. P. (1972). Systems analysis applied to school social work. In R. C. Sarri & F. F. Maple (Eds.), *The school in the community* (pp. 196–210). Washington, DC: NASW Press.

Webb, M. (1990). *Multicultural education in elementary and secondary schools.* New York: ERIC Clearinghouse on Urban Education. (ERIC Document Reproduction Service No. ED327613)

Webb, N. B. (1993). Assessment of the bereaved child. In N. B. Webb (Ed.), *Helping bereaved children: A handbook for practitioners* (pp. 19–42). New York: Guilford Press.

Weddle, K. D., & Williams, F. (1993). *Implementing and assessing the effectiveness of the Interpersonal Cognitive Problem-Solving (ICPS) Curriculum in four experimental and four control classrooms* (Report to the Faculty Small Research Grant Program). Memphis, TN: Memphis State University.

Wehlage, G. G., Lipman, P., & Smith, G. (1989). *Empowering communities for school reform: The Annie E. Casey Foundations's New Futures Initiative.* Madison: Wisconsin Center for Education Research.

Wehlage, G. G., & Rutter, R. A. (1986). Dropping out: How much do schools contribute to the problem? *Teachers College Record, 87,* 374–392.

Weissman, M. M., Wolk, S., & Goldstein, R. B. (1999). Depressed adolescents grown up. *Journal of the American Medical Association, 281,* 1701–1713.

Wheeler, S. R., & Austin, J. (2000). The loss response list: A tool for measuring adolescent grief responses. *Death Studies, 24,* 21–34.

Wheelock, A., & Dorman, G. (1988). *Before it's too late: Dropout prevention in the middle grades.* Boston: Massachusetts Advocacy Center. (ERIC Document Reproduction Service No. ED301355)

Whittaker, J. K., Schinke, S. P., & Gilchrist, L. D. (1986). The ecological paradigm in child, youth, and family services: Implications for policy and practice. *Social Service Review, 60,* 483–503.

Whitted, B. R., & Constable, R. (1999). Educational mandates for children with disabilities: School policies, case law, and the school social worker. In R. Constable, S. McDonald, & J. P. Flynn (Eds.), *School social work: Practice, research, and policy perspectives* (4th ed., pp. 166–183). Chicago: Lyceum Books.

Wilgoren, J. (2001, May 3). Lawsuits touch off debate over paddling in schools. *The New York Times,* A1, column 5.

Winters, W. G. (1993). *African American mothers and urban schools: The power of participation.* New York: Lexington Books.

Wood v. Strickland, 420 U.S. 308, 95 S. Ct. 992 (1975).

Woods, C. J. (1997). Pappas school: A response to homeless students. *Clearing House, 70,* 302–304.

Wright, A. (1996). Success guaranteed: The Pathfinder Project. *Preventing School Failure, 67,* 70–71.

Yale University Bush Center in Child Development and Social Policy. (n.d.). *Research.* Retrieved December 10, 2000, from www.yale.edu/21c/about/res/res.html

Young, B. A., & Smith, T. M. (1997). *The social context of education. The condition of education 1997.* National Center for Education Statistics. (OERI Publication No. NCES 97-091). Washington, DC: U.S. Department of Health and Human Services, Department of Education.

Yung, B., & Hammond, R. (1998). Breaking the cycle: A culturally sensitive violence prevention program for African-American children. In L. Lutzker (Ed.), *Handbook of child abuse research and treatments* (pp. 319–340). New York: Plenum Press.

Zabel, R. H. (1988). *Emotional disturbances.* Reston, VA: ERIC Clearinghouse on Handicapped and Gifted Children. (ERIC Document reproduction Service No. ED295398)

Zima, B. T., Bussing, R., Forness, S. R., & Benjamin, B. (1997). Sheltered homeless children: Their eligibility and unmet needs for special education evaluations. *American Journal of Public Health, 87,* 236–240.

Author Index

Subject Index